Made in China 2025 – The Grand Initiative

From the "Workbench of the World" to the Innovation Nation

Made in China 2025 – The Grand Initiative

From the "Workbench of the World" to the Innovation Nation

Table of contents

Introduction

Between 2015 and 2025, a technological dynamic unfolded in the People's Republic of China that is unparalleled anywhere in the world. The story of this decade is not only one of progress and innovative strength, but also of cultural change, geopolitical repositioning, and societal reorientation. It is the story of a country that was long considered the world's workshop but is now establishing itself as a leading innovator in an increasingly digital world.

China's technological revolution during this period is neither a coincidence nor the sole result of individual disruptive inventions. Rather, it is an expression of a targeted, strategic pursuit of autonomy, influence, and competitiveness in a world increasingly dependent on information technology, artificial intelligence, biotechnology, and sustainable energy. These developments cannot be viewed in isolation from the country's political and economic reality, but are deeply rooted in it.

China recognized early on that technological progress is not only an economic driver but also a tool of power politics. The government has invested enormous sums in research and development, created innovation zones, built a nationwide digital infrastructure, and consistently geared the education sector toward future technologies. This systematic approach has made it possible not only to catch up with, but in some cases to overtake entire industries.

But technological development in China is more than just a major government project. It has become part of everyday life. Those who travel through cities like Shenzhen, Hangzhou, or Shanghai see not just visions of the future on paper, but experience a real, functioning ecosystem that ranges from intelligent mobility and digital administration to automated logistics processes. This urban reality is as fascinating as it is ambivalent, for progress is often coupled with questions of data protection, social control, and social justice.

In this foreword, we do not intend to offer a conclusive assessment, but rather a contextual, sober, and at the same time in-depth examination. What drives China's innovative strength? What cultural, historical, and political factors underlie it? And what does this change mean for the rest of the world? It is helpful to break away from simplistic narratives. China is neither the dystopian surveillance regime threatening digital totality, nor is it the technological savior seeking to overtake and save the West. The truth lies – as so often – in the complexity of reality, in the contradictions of a system that relies as much on state control as on entrepreneurial freedom, that is simultaneously nationalistic and global in its orientation.

This technological revolution is not just a Chinese affair. It is transforming supply chains, market mechanisms, diplomatic relations, security strategies, and societal expectations worldwide. The way China develops, introduces, and regulates technologies has long since had an impact beyond its borders. It is therefore crucial not only to see the results but also to understand the processes behind them.

This foreword aims to do just that: to take the reader on a narrative journey that is scientifically sound but not dry; that remains analytical but not unfeeling; that describes without preaching. The goal is to convey a sense of the "why" and "how" of these developments—embedded in historical continuities, geopolitical realities, and cultural peculiarities.

A central aspect of the international perception of China that has changed only slowly in recent years is the Western-influenced image of China as a backward copy machine, an economic giant lacking creative depth, a country that produces with speed but not with spirit and originality. This image is long outdated—and yet it persists in many political, media, and even academic discourses. It is a convenient narrative because it explains China's technological rise as a purely economic consequence of its mass production and thus does not seriously question the possibility that innovation leadership could be permanently displaced from the West.

But reality has long since overtaken this worldview. The idea that innovation arises exclusively in the West and finds a home only there is an illusion that is increasingly faltering. China's innovative strength is not the result of coincidence, plagiarism, or labor cost advantages.

It is structured, planned, strategic, and long-term. While many Western countries plan with political cycles of four or five years and technological development often relies on private ventures, China pursues a national innovation strategy with planning horizons of decades. Projects such as "Made in China 2025" or the long-term vision "China Standards 2035" are not mere PR initiatives, but rather the expression of a systematic understanding of how technology secures power, prosperity, and geopolitical influence.

The Western view of China also often ignores cultural differences in innovation culture. In many Asian countries, especially in China, innovation is not necessarily associated with radical individualism, but rather with collective improvement, social benefit, and national responsibility.

Whereas in the West the "lone genius" is considered the ideal image of the innovator, in China the success of networks, platforms, and community structures is often emphasized. Innovation there is not only created in laboratories or garages, but also in marketplaces, in tech ecosystems, in government-sponsored testing zones – sometimes even through government-supported experiments in cities that function as "regulatory sandboxes."

The speed with which new technologies are adapted and scaled in China often overwhelms Western understandings of technological progress. While in Europe or North America, for example, pilot projects often undergo years of discussion and approval, in China – provided political and societal approval is given – entire regions are equipped with new infrastructure, new technologies are rolled out within months, and feedback cycles are utilized in real time. This pragmatism is not only an expression of a different political system, but also of a different understanding of innovation, in which iteration, efficiency, and feasibility take precedence over ideological purity.

Furthermore, the long-outdated Western view of China is often coupled with a subliminal sense of moral superiority. The belief that true creativity and innovation are only possible in liberal democratic systems is increasingly being refuted by reality. Of course, the Chinese system brings with it its own ethical challenges—particularly in the areas of data protection, surveillance, and individual freedoms—but these issues cannot be equated with technological backwardness. Rather, China is demonstrating that authoritarian systems are very capable of fostering and structurally anchoring innovation—albeit with different motivations and consequences.

The West also often underestimates the depth and independence of Chinese innovation cultures. While the first smartphone models from China may have seemed like Western products with a different logo, today it is platforms such as WeChat, TikTok (Douyin), and Alipay that have created entirely new ecosystems that have no direct counterparts in the West. These are systems that combine services, communication, administration, finance, and social interaction in a digital space, thus enabling new forms of everyday life and society. This independence, this culturally influenced form of innovation, is often not recognized in the West – either out of ignorance, mistrust or fear of one's own superfluity.

In recent years, the West has finally begun to gradually acknowledge this reality – often hesitantly, sometimes alarmed, rarely with sober openness. The debates surrounding Huawei, TikTok, AI competition, and quantum communication are merely the visible symptoms of a deeper process: the realization that technological progress is no longer exclusively at home in the West. Rather, there is a global competition for standards, norms, ethics, and areas of application – and that China is engaging in this competition with determination, resources, and a clear compass.

This realization is painful because it touches on self-images. It demands a new way of thinking, a new self-understanding, and above all, the ability to understand global innovation dynamics not only as a threat, but also as a challenge for our own further development. China's technological rise is not a zero-sum game. It is a global phenomenon that creates new spaces for exchange, but also for confrontation. How the West responds to this—with openness, with competitiveness, with strategic intelligence—will help determine what the technological world order will look like in the coming decades.

The Western view of China is not only characterized by cognitive dissonance and cultural distortions, but often also by institutional inertia and political wishful thinking. A particularly illustrative example of this is the fact that countries like Germany—despite China's undeniable role as a technological superpower and the world's second-largest economy—still provide development aid. This practice not only raises economic policy questions but also reveals a deep-seated misunderstanding of reality.

The reasons for this paradoxical situation are complex. On the one hand, it results from outdated classification systems of international institutions. The OECD, for example, still lists China as an emerging economy in some contexts, a status derived from indicators such as per capita income or rural poverty, but largely ignores China's innovative strength, industrial performance, and geopolitical importance. This systemic inertia leads to development cooperation mechanisms continuing to operate even when they have long since failed to achieve their original purpose.

Secondly, German development cooperation with China is a relic of an era when China was still considered a traditional recipient country - particularly in the 1980s and 1990s. Back then, programs for rural healthcare, poverty reduction, or environmental protection were initiated, often with quite positive effects. But while China developed rapidly, cooperation at the institutional level did not adapt at the same pace. In some cases, it was even politically glorified: as a means of "rapprochement through cooperation," as an attempt to integrate China into international norms and to establish a form of political partnership through technical cooperation.

Another motivation lies in the internal logic of German development institutions themselves. Organizations such as the GIZ (German Society for International Cooperation) and the KfW Development Bank operate not only as aid providers but also as project management agencies with their own interests. The continuation of programs in China – often under the heading of "tackling global challenges together" – offers experience, symbolic partnerships, and access to a significant innovation hub. This leads to projects on sustainable urban development or energy efficiency, for example, in which German expertise is brought in as "help for self-help" – even though China is already a global leader in many of these areas.

The continuation of development aid to China ultimately exposes a Western bias in thinking: an insistence on old categories, a clinging to routines, a hesitancy to clearly identify geopolitical shifts. Those who still treat China as a recipient of development not only misjudge reality but are acting negligently – politically, economically, and ethically. It is time for institutional practice to recognize what has long been obvious: China is no longer a country that needs help. It is a country that has long been helping itself – and in doing so, is redefining the rules of the game in a globalized world.

Given the complexity and multifaceted nature of China's innovation dynamics, it is time to look at the concrete developments of the last decade.

This book is not intended to paint a complete picture in the sense of an all-encompassing encyclopedia – such an undertaking would be presumptuous given the speed at which technological developments are taking place in China. Instead, it aims to provide exemplary insights into the key areas of this transformation in order to develop a well-founded overall understanding.

The following chapters guide you through the key innovation fields in which China made significant progress between 2015 and 2025 – starting with the digital infrastructure, which forms the foundation for almost all technological developments. This demonstrates how consistently and forward-looking China has been in its commitment to widespread 5G expansion, smart city technologies, and digital administrative structures – with effects reaching into the deepest corners of everyday life.

This is followed by in-depth analyses of artificial intelligence, autonomous driving, robotics, aerospace, biotechnology, energy innovation, and the redesign of industrial production processes under the banner of Industry 4.0 with a Chinese character. Each chapter not only illuminates technological breakthroughs, but also their social, economic, and political implications – always with the goal of painting a balanced picture that allows for both fascination and criticism.

We will also not ignore where innovation reaches its limits: technical, ethical, ecological, or social. The dark sides of progress – such as widespread data collection, the merging of technology and social control, or the risks of dependence on digital platforms – are addressed, as are the achievements of Chinese startups, research institutions, and established corporations.

Finally, we offer a look ahead: Where might China's technological path lead? What international dynamics can be expected? And what answers – political, economic, and civil society – could or should the West find?

This book does not invite you to succumb to fear or freeze in admiration. It invites you to understand – and, on that basis, to act more wisely. China's technological revolution is no longer a distant phenomenon. It has long been part of our shared present and will help shape our future. Those who want to understand it must be willing to leave old images behind and embrace new perspectives.

With this in mind, let us embark on this journey.

China's transformation from the "workbench of the world" to an innovation nation

When Zhang Wei opened his small electronics store in Shenzhen in 2015, he still thought in terms of the tried-and-true Chinese economy: cheap production, fast delivery, low margins. Ten years later, the now 45-year-old stands in a state-of-the-art laboratory at his company, which develops artificial intelligence for autonomous vehicles. His story reflects what China has experienced in the past decade: one of the most dramatic economic transformations in modern history.

China's transformation from the so-called "workshop of the world" to a leading innovation nation between 2015 and 2025 represents not just an economic shift, but a fundamental realignment of an entire social system. This transformation touches every aspect of Chinese life, from the way people work and learn to the geopolitical power structures of our time. To understand this development, we must first consider the starting point China found itself in around 2015.

Since Deng Xiaoping's economic reforms in the late 1970s, the People's Republic of China had developed into a global manufacturing center. Millions of jobs were created in factories producing for Western brands. The country became synonymous with low-cost mass production, a reputation that was both a blessing and a curse. While the Chinese economy grew rapidly and lifted hundreds of millions of people out of poverty, the country often remained trapped at the bottom of the global value chain. Profits largely flowed to brand owners and designers in developed countries, while China primarily benefited from low labor costs.

However, this situation was already unsustainable by 2015. Labor costs continued to rise, other countries in Southeast Asia and Africa began to compete with China as the cheapest manufacturing base, and the Chinese leadership realized that a continuation of the previous model could lead the country into a middle-income trap. At the same time, a new generation of Chinese entrepreneurs and engineers was emerging who no longer wanted to simply copy but wanted to innovate themselves.

The Chinese government had recognized this challenge early on. As early as 2006, President Hu Jintao set the goal of making China an "innovation-oriented society" by 2020. But it wasn't until Xi Jinping took power in 2012 that this vision took concrete shape. In 2015, the "Made in China 2025" plan was published, setting out the strategic roadmap for the transition to a high-tech economy. This plan was more than just an economic program; it was a blueprint for reinventing a nation.

The timing was opportune. The global financial crisis of 2008 had shown how vulnerable export-dependent economies could be. At the same time, the fourth industrial revolution was beginning to gain momentum, driven by technologies such as artificial intelligence, the Internet of Things, robotics, and advanced data analytics. China realized that it needed to not just play a role in these areas, but become a leader to maintain and expand its position in the global economy.

The transformation began in the metropolises on the east coast, particularly Shenzhen, Shanghai, and Beijing. Shenzhen, once a sleepy fishing town bordering Hong Kong, had already developed into a center of electronics production in the 1980s. But starting in 2015, the city underwent another metamorphosis. Factories that once assembled iPhone components became research and development centers. Companies like Huawei, Tencent, and BYD invested billions in innovation and attracted talent from all over the world.

The change was physically palpable. Anyone who visited Shenzhen in 2015 and returned ten years later found a completely transformed city. Where factories once stood, glass and steel skyscrapers now housed the headquarters of tech giants and startups. The air had become cleaner, as many polluting industries had either closed or relocated to other regions. Electric buses and autonomous test vehicles plied the streets. The city hummed with digital energy.

But the transformation wasn't limited to the big cities. A crucial factor in China's success was the realization that innovation could not take place in a few centers, but had to be promoted nationwide. The concept of "innovation clusters" was rolled out nationwide. Smaller cities specialized in specific technologies or industries. Hangzhou became a center for e-commerce and fintech, led by Alibaba. Wuhan developed into a hub for optics and laser technology.

Even smaller cities in inland provinces received subsidies and incentives to build their own innovation ecosystems. Government support was crucial. Unlike in purely market-oriented systems, the Chinese government was able to mobilize massive resources and pursue long-term strategies without having to worry about short-term profitability. Between 2015 and 2020 alone, an estimated 1.4 trillion yuan was invested in research and development, both directly through government investment and indirectly through tax incentives, subsidies, and cheap loans.

These investments were concentrated in ten key areas defined in "Made in China 2025": new information technologies, computer-controlled machine tools and robotics, aerospace equipment, marine technology and high-tech shipbuilding, modern railway technology, new energy vehicles, energy equipment, agricultural technology, new materials, and biopharmaceuticals and medical devices. These areas were not chosen at random but represented both China's existing strengths and the industries that would shape the future of the global economy.

The development in the field of electric mobility was particularly impressive. In 2015, China was still a laggard in this sector, dominated by a few Western pioneers like Tesla. Ten years later, the tide had completely turned. Chinese companies such as BYD, NIO, XPeng, and Li Auto were among the world's leading manufacturers of electric vehicles. BYD even temporarily surpassed Tesla as the world's largest producer of electric cars. This success story was the result of a coordinated strategy that skillfully combined government support, private innovation, and market incentives.

The Chinese government recognized early on that the transition to electric mobility represented a historic opportunity. While Western automakers struggled with the burden of their existing combustion engine technology, Chinese companies were able to start from scratch and focus entirely on electric drivetrains. Massive investments in battery technology, especially lithium-ion batteries, paid off. Companies such as CATL (Contemporary Amperex Technology) became global market leaders in battery production, supplying not only Chinese but also international automakers.

At the same time, China built the world's largest electric vehicle charging infrastructure. By 2025, the country had more than 2.6 million public charging stations, more than the rest of the world combined. This infrastructure was not only a technical feat but also a strategic tool for promoting electromobility. Consumers who had previously been hesitant to switch to electric vehicles were encouraged by the widespread availability of charging stations.

The success story of China's electromobility illustrates a key principle of China's innovation strategy: the integration of technology development, infrastructure construction, and market creation. While Western approaches often rely on technologies to emerge organically in the market, China pursued a more holistic approach. The government created not only the technical prerequisites but also the market conditions necessary for the success of new technologies.

Another area in which China made dramatic progress was artificial intelligence. In 2015, the country was still a laggard in this field, significantly behind the United States. The major breakthroughs in AI came from Silicon Valley, from companies like Google, Facebook, and OpenAI. But China had one crucial advantage: data. With over 1.4 billion citizens and an increasingly digitalized society, the country generated enormous amounts of data every day, which is essential for training AI algorithms.

Chinese companies such as Baidu, Alibaba, and Tencent began investing heavily in AI research. They recruited talent from all over the world, often with salaries that exceeded even Silicon Valley standards. At the same time, specialized AI companies such as SenseTime, Face++, and iFlytek emerged, focusing on specific applications. SenseTime became one of the world's most valuable AI startups, specializing in computer vision and facial recognition. iFlytek dominated the field of speech recognition and synthesis.

From the beginning, Chinese AI development was strongly application-oriented. While Western researchers often worked on theoretical breakthroughs, Chinese companies focused on integrating AI technologies into real-world products and services. This led to rapid and visible successes. Chinese smartphones received AI-based camera features that automatically recognized scenes and optimized photos. Chinese e-commerce platforms used AI for personalized recommenddations and fraud detection. Chinese cities implemented comprehensive AI-based surveillance and traffic management systems.

Developments in the field of autonomous driving were particularly notable. Companies like Baidu with its Apollo platform, WeRide, Pony.ai, and AutoX made rapid progress in developing self-driving vehicles. Chinese cities like Beijing, Shanghai, and Shenzhen became test laboratories for autonomous vehicles, with dedicated test tracks and regulatory frameworks that enabled innovation.

The Chinese approach to autonomous driving differed from the Western philosophy. While companies like Tesla and Waymo focused on fully autonomous systems that would work in any situation, Chinese companies pursued a more incremental approach. They focused on specific use cases and environments where autonomous systems could already operate safely. This led to faster commercial implementations, for example, in autonomous delivery services on university campuses or in enclosed industrial parks.

The pandemic, which began in late 2019 and spread globally in 2020, initially posed a massive challenge to China's transformation plans. The economy temporarily came to a standstill, supply chains collapsed, and many companies struggled to survive. Yet, paradoxically, the pandemic ultimately accelerated many of the trends China was already pursuing.

The enforced lockdown led to the rapid digitalization of many areas of life. Home office, online education, telemedicine, and digital payment systems experienced an unprecedented boom. Chinese companies already active in these areas were able to strengthen their market position. Tencent's WeChat became an indispensable platform for communication, work, and commerce. Alibaba's DingTalk dominated the corporate communications market. Pinduoduo, a social commerce platform, benefited from the increased demand for online shopping.

At the same time, the pandemic demonstrated the importance of technology in addressing global challenges. China's use of AI and big data for contact tracing and epidemic control, although controversial, demonstrated the practical applications of advanced technologies. The rapid development and production of COVID-19 vaccines by Chinese companies such as Sinovac and Sinopharm underscored the growing capabilities of the Chinese biotechnology industry.

The pandemic also highlighted the importance of supply chain security and technological independence. Western countries that had been dependent on Chinese imports for decades began to diversify their supply chains and repatriate critical production. For China, this represented both a challenge and an opportunity. On the one hand, it threatened to lose traditional export markets, while on the other, it intensified the pressure to achieve technological independence.

This development was particularly evident in the semiconductor sector. Chips are the "oil of the 21st century," essential for all modern technologies from smartphones to electric cars. However, China was heavily dependent on imports, especially for advanced processors. Increasing trade tensions with the United States and restrictions on access to advanced semiconductor technologies made this dependence a strategic risk.

The Chinese response was characteristic of the country's new approach to innovation: massive investment in the domestic semiconductor industry. The National IC Industry Investment Fund, also known as the "Big Fund," was expanded and invested tens of billions of dollars in Chinese chip manufacturers. Companies such as SMIC (Semiconductor Manufacturing International Corporation), Yangtze Memory Technologies, and Cambricon Technologies received enormous support.

The progress was impressive, even though China had not yet caught up with the technological lead of Taiwan, South Korea, and the USA. SMIC began mass production of 14-nanometer chips and worked on even more advanced technologies. Yangtze Memory established itself as a major memory chip manufacturer. Cambricon developed specialized AI chips that were used in various applications.

In parallel with its chip production efforts, China invested heavily in the research and development of alternative technologies. Quantum computing, an area with the potential to revolutionize traditional chip architecture, became a particular focus. Chinese researchers achieved several breakthroughs in quantum technology, including the development of quantum computers with over 100 qubits.

The Hefei University of Science and Technology, led by Professor Pan Jianwei, became a global center for quantum research. The team developed "Jiuzhang," a quantum computer that demonstrated quantum superiority over classical computers for specific tasks. These successes positioned China as one of the leading players in quantum technology, alongside the US and Europe.

The significance of these developments went far beyond pure technology. They signaled that China was no longer a mere follower in technological development, but was beginning to take the lead in certain areas. This shift had profound implications for the global technology landscape and geopolitical power relations.

Another area in which China made dramatic progress was space. Chinese space exploration had already attracted attention in the 2000s with manned missions and moon landings. But between 2015 and 2025, the Chinese space program reached a new dimension. In 2021, the Chinese rover "Zhurong" successfully landed on Mars, making China the second nation after the United States to operate a functional rover on the Red Planet.

Even more impressive was the construction of the Chinese space station "Tiangong" (Sky Palace). After the planned decommissioning of the International Space Station (ISS) around 2030, Tiangong could be the only permanently manned space station in Earth's orbit. The station serves not only as a symbol of China's technological capabilities but also as a platform for scientific research and international cooperation.

Chinese space travel benefited from the same coordinated approach that characterized other areas of Chinese innovation. State investment, long-term planning, and the integration of diverse technologies enabled advances achieved in a shorter time than many experts had thought possible.

At the same time, a vibrant commercial space industry emerged in China. Companies such as iSpace, Landspace, and Galactic Energy developed low-cost rockets for transporting small satellites. These companies operated similarly to SpaceX in the United States, with the goal of drastically reducing the cost of accessing space.

The development of Chinese space travel also had practical implications for other technological fields. Satellite technology was used to improve navigation systems, telecommunications, and Earth observation. The Chinese BeiDou satellite navigation system became a viable alternative to the American GPS, offering even better accuracy in some regions.

However, China's transformation was not limited to high-tech sectors. Traditional industries also experienced remarkable modernization. The steel industry, once a symbol of China's polluting heavy industry, was revolutionized by the use of AI, robotics, and cleaner production processes. Baosteel, one of the world's largest steelmakers, implemented "smart factories" where algorithms optimized production and reduced energy consumption.

Similar transformations took place in the chemical, textile, and machinery industries. The concept of "smart manufacturing" became a central theme of Chinese industrial policy.

Factories were equipped with sensors, data analytics, and automated systems to increase efficiency and improve quality.

This modernization of traditional industries was particularly important because it affected millions of jobs. China had to strike a balance between promoting new technologies and preserving employment in existing sectors. The solution lay in gradual transformation, introducing new technologies to increase productivity without destroying large numbers of jobs.

At the same time, China invested heavily in retraining and upskilling its workforce. Vocational training programs were expanded to provide workers from traditional industries with the skills needed in the new economy. Universities and vocational schools adapted their curricula to produce more graduates in STEM (science, technology, engineering, and mathematics) subjects.

The education reforms were a crucial component of China's innovation strategy. The country recognized that the transition to a knowledge-based economy required a fundamentally different type of human capital. Instead of workers performing simple, repetitive tasks, China needed creative problem solvers, critical thinkers, and innovators.

This realization led to a fundamental reorientation of the Chinese education system. While the system had traditionally focused on memorization and test performance, schools and universities began to place greater emphasis on creativity, critical thinking, and practical application. STEM education was promoted, but fields such as design, crafts, and entrepreneurship also received increased attention.

Chinese universities began to aggressively recruit international talent. Programs such as the Thousand Talents Initiative attracted top researchers from around the world to China. At the same time, Chinese students were encouraged to study abroad and then return to China with their knowledge. This "return migration" brought valuable experience and networks to China.

The efforts paid off. Chinese universities climbed international rankings. Tsinghua University and Peking University established themselves as world-class institutions, rivaling Harvard and MIT. Chinese researchers began publishing more scientific papers and being cited more frequently.

Developments in biotechnology and medicine were particularly notable. China had traditionally lagged behind in these fields, but the combination of government support, private investment, and international cooperation led to rapid progress. Chinese companies such as BGI Genomics became global leaders in genome sequencing. WuXi AppTec established itself as a leading drug development service provider.

The COVID-19 pandemic provided Chinese biotech companies with an opportunity to demonstrate their capabilities. The rapid development and production of vaccines, testing procedures, and treatments demonstrated China's capacity to respond to global health crises. Chinese vaccines were deployed in dozens of countries, strengthening China's role as a global health partner.

Parallel to its technological development, China also experienced a remarkable cultural renaissance. The growing importance of innovation and creativity led to a revaluation of design, art, and entertainment. Chinese video games, films, and music productions gained international recognition. Companies like miHoYo with its game "Genshin Impact" demonstrated that Chinese creativity could conquer global markets.

This cultural dimension of China's transformation was important because it strengthened the country's soft power. While in the past, China was primarily perceived for its economic power and, increasingly, its military strength, the country now also began to shine culturally. Chinese technology brands such as Xiaomi, OnePlus, and DJI gained loyal followers worldwide, not only for their prices, but also for their design and innovation.

The role of the Chinese diaspora in this process could not be underestimated. Millions of Chinese living and working around the world served as bridges between China and other countries. They not only brought knowledge and experience back to China, but also helped establish Chinese products and services in their host countries.

At the same time, a new generation of Chinese entrepreneurs emerged who thought and acted globally. These entrepreneurs were no longer solely focused on producing for the Chinese market but wanted to build global companies from the outset. They understood both Chinese and Western business culture and were able to navigate between both worlds.

One example of this new generation was Zhang Yiming, the founder of ByteDance, the company behind TikTok. Zhang recognized early on the potential of AI-powered algorithms for personalized content and built a platform that was successful not only in China but worldwide. TikTok became one of the fastest-growing social media platforms in history and demonstrated that Chinese companies were capable of creating global internet services.

However, TikTok's success story also served as an example of the growing geopolitical tensions that accompanied China's rise. The platform faced security concerns and regulatory pressure in various countries, highlighting the complexity of Chinese technology companies' global expansion.

These tensions reflected a broader concern: China's rise as a technological superpower. While many welcomed the benefits of Chinese innovation—cheaper products, faster development, more competition—concerns grew at the same time about its impact on the global balance of power, data security, and the economic security of other countries.

The China-US trade war that began in 2018 was a manifestation of these tensions. Tariffs, sanctions, and technology embargoes became weapons in a larger struggle for technological dominance. For China, these conflicts increased the urgency of achieving technological independence. For other countries, they raised questions about dependence on Chinese technologies.

Paradoxically, these tensions, in some ways, accelerated China's innovation efforts. The pressure to become independent led to even greater investments in domestic technologies. At the same time, the trade restrictions forced Chinese companies to become more creative and efficient. Huawei, for example, responded to the US sanctions by developing its own operating system, HarmonyOS, and intensified its efforts to develop its own chip designs.

However, China's rapid technological development also brought with it fundamental ethical questions that profoundly changed the country's social fabric. The implementtation of new technologies often occurred at a pace and scale that would have been unthinkable in Western democracies, raising both benefits and serious concerns.

The city of Shenzhen became a testing ground for these technologies. By 2022, an estimated 2.6 million surveillance cameras were installed in the city, supported by AI systems that scanned and analyzed millions of faces around the clock. Authorities argued that these systems had drastically reduced crime rates and improved public safety. Indeed, Shenzhen experienced a significant decline in crimes such as theft and violent offenses.

But these technological capabilities raised fundamental questions about privacy, human rights, and social control. Surveillance technologies were used not only to combat crime but also to monitor political dissidents, religious minorities, and social activists. The situation in Xinjiang, where surveillance technologies were used to comprehensively control the Uyghur population, was widely criticized internationally and led to sanctions against Chinese technology companies.

The ethical dilemmas were further complexed by the introduction of the social credit system, an ambitious attempt to control the behavior of citizens and businesses through a comprehensive rating system. The system, which combined various data sources—from creditworthiness and debt levels to traffic violations and social media activity—promised to promote trust in society and reduce antisocial behavior.

For many Chinese, the social credit system did bring benefits. Individuals with high scores received access to better loans, preferential treatment in government transactions, and other perks. The system also helped combat fraudulent business practices, excessive indebtedness, and corruption, and strengthen trust between companies. In a society that historically struggled with trust issues in business, the system offered a technological solution to a real societal problem.

At the same time, however, the system also created new forms of social control and exclusion. People with low scores could be barred from purchasing airline tickets or high-speed train tickets, their children could have difficulty accessing certain schools, and they themselves could be disadvantaged professionally. The arbitrary nature of some evaluation criteria and the difficulty of regaining lost points created a system that could restrict social mobility.

Technological innovation in China thus developed in a tension between efficiency and control, between societal benefit and individual freedom. This tension was particularly visible in the way China dealt with data protection and privacy. While Western countries passed increasingly strict data protection laws, China pursued a more pragmatic approach that prioritized the societal benefits of data analysis over individual privacy rights.

These different approaches led to different innovation paths. Chinese companies were able to access vast amounts of data and use it to develop and improve their algorithms. This accelerated the development of AI applications and enabled innovations that would have been more difficult to realize in more privacy-restrictive environments.

At the same time, however, discussions also emerged within China about the appropriate limits of technological surveillance. Intellectuals, lawyers, and even some government officials began to ask questions about the right balance between security and freedom. These discussions often took place in academic circles or subtly on social media, as direct opposition to government policy remained risky.

The growing power of technology companies led to an interesting development in Chinese politics. While the government initially encouraged the growth of these companies, starting in 2020, it began to intervene through regulation. The antitrust proceedings against Alibaba, the data protection requirements for TikTok, and the education reforms that affected ed-tech companies signaled a new phase in the relationship between the state and technology companies.

This wave of regulation reflected the recognition that unchecked technological growth could lead to societal problems. The government was concerned about the emergence of monopolies, the exploitation of workers in the gig economy, and the impact of social media on mental health, especially among young people.

However, regulating the technology industry was a balancing act. On the one hand, the government wanted to control harmful excesses, but on the other, it did not want to stifle the industry's innovative power. The way this balancing act was handled had important implications for the future development of China's technology industry.

A particularly sensitive issue was the role of technology in education. Chinese ed-tech companies such as VIPKid, Yuanfudao, and Zuoyebang had experienced tremendous growth during the pandemic as millions of students relied on online learning. These companies developed advanced AI-powered learning systems that enabled personalized instruction and adaptive assessments.

But the government became increasingly concerned about the impact of these technologies on society. Intense competition in education, amplified by technological solutions, led to an "education race" that placed enormous financial and psychological pressure on families. Children increasingly spent time on additional online lessons, raising concerns about their physical and mental health.

In 2021, the government introduced drastic reforms in the edtech industry aimed at reducing pressure on families and promoting a more balanced development of children. These reforms demonstrated that China was willing to accept short-term economic losses in order to achieve long-term societal goals.

The ethical challenges of technological innovation were also evident in the field of biotechnology. China's rapid advances in genetic research and manipulation raised fundamental questions about the limits of scientific research. The case of He Jiankui, who announced in 2018 that he had created the world's first gene-edited babies, shocked the international scientific community and sparked intense discussions about the ethical limits of genetic engineering.

The Chinese government responded swiftly and sharply to He Jiankui's experiments. He was sentenced to three years in prison, and the government significantly tightened regulations on genetic research. This response demonstrated that, despite its drive for innovation, China did indeed set limits on acceptable scientific practices.

At the same time, China continued to invest heavily in biotechnology, albeit with greater ethical oversight. The development of gene therapies for serious diseases, stem cell research, and the development of personalized medicine were advanced, albeit under stricter ethical guidelines.

The issue of jobs and social justice was another important ethical aspect of technological transformation. While new technologies created millions of new jobs, they simultaneously threatened traditional forms of employment. Automation in factories, the use of AI in service sectors, and the digitalization of traditional industries led to significant shifts in the labor market.

China attempted to address these challenges through comprehensive retraining programs and the promotion of new forms of employment. The gig economy, driven by platforms such as Meituan for food delivery and Didi for ride-hailing, offered millions of people new income opportunities. At the same time, entirely new career fields emerged, from AI trainers to drone pilots.

But these new forms of work also brought new challenges. Gig workers often lacked traditional labor protection rights, health insurance, and job security. The platform economy created new forms of precariousness, where workers constantly competed for jobs and their incomes fluctuated sharply.

The Chinese government recognized these problems and began to develop new regulations for the platform economy. These efforts reflected a broader awareness that technological innovation should promote not only economic growth but also social cohesion.

Another important aspect was the environmental impact of technological transformation. While China made considerable progress in developing green technologies, rapid digitalization also brought with it new environmental challenges. The energy consumption of data centers, Bitcoin mining operations, and AI training was significant. The production of smartphones, laptops, and other electronic devices required rare minerals and generated electronic waste.

China responded to these challenges with a combination of technological solutions and regulatory measures. The country invested heavily in renewable energy to meet the growing energy demands of its digital infrastructure. At the same time, regulations for the recycling of electronic devices were tightened and incentives for the development of more energy-efficient technologies were created.

The emergence of "green innovation" became a key theme in China's technology strategy. Companies such as BYD in electric mobility, LONGi in solar technology, and CATL in battery technology positioned themselves as pioneers of sustainable technologies. These companies not only benefited from the growing domestic demand for green technologies but were also able to successfully expand into international markets.

The ethical dimensions of Chinese technology development also extended to international relations. China's technology exports, particularly in areas such as telecommunications infrastructure and surveillance technology, raised questions about the global spread of authoritarian technologies. The

Belt and Road Initiative, China's ambitious infrastructure project, increasingly included digital infrastructure, leading to concerns about "digital authoritarianism."

At the same time, Chinese representatives argued that their technologies could help developing countries leapfrog development and modernize more quickly. Chinese fintech solutions enabled the unbanked to use digital payments. Chinese e-commerce platforms helped small businesses reach global markets. Chinese surveillance technologies could be used to combat crime and provide disaster relief.

This dual nature of Chinese technology—simultaneously liberating and control-oriented—reflected the more complex ethical realities of modern technological development. Technologies were neither inherently good nor bad; rather, their effects depended on how they were implemented and regulated.

Chinese society itself underwent profound changes during this transformation. A new generation of Chinese, raised with smartphones and social media, had different expectations of technology and privacy than their parents. These younger Chinese were often more tech-savvy, more globally minded, and more critical of authority.

At the same time, rapid technological development led to a widening of the digital divide. While urban, educated Chinese benefited from the latest technologies, rural and older populations often lagged behind. The government recognized this challenge and implemented digital inclusion programs, but the gap remained a significant societal issue.

The role of women in China's technology industry was another important societal issue. While China had more female leaders in the technology industry than many Western countries, women remained underrepresented in technical roles. However, companies like Alibaba, led by strong female leaders like Lucy Peng, demonstrated that women could play important roles in China's technology development.

The cultural impact of technological transformation was also profound. Traditional Chinese values such as respect for age and authority sometimes clashed with the more egalitarian, meritocratic culture of the technology industry. Young entrepreneurs earning millions challenged traditional hierarchies. The "996 work culture" (9 a.m. to 9 p.m., six days a week) prevalent in many technology companies led to discussions about work-life balance and workers' rights.

These cultural tensions were also reflected in the way Chinese technology companies shaped their corporate cultures. Many attempted to adopt Western management practices while retaining Chinese cultural elements. The result was often a hybrid culture that was both innovative and respectful of traditions.

The emergence of a Chinese "technology philosophy" was another interesting aspect of the transformation. Chinese technology leaders began to articulate their own visions for the role of technology in society. These visions often differed from Western concepts, emphasizing collective benefits over individual rights and long-term societal stability over short-term disruption.

Jack Ma of Alibaba often spoke about the role of technology in creating a more inclusive economy. Pony Ma of Tencent emphasized the importance of technology in connecting people and communities. These philosophies influenced not only product development but also the way Chinese companies understood their social responsibility.

The ethical challenges of Chinese technology development were not limited to China, however. As Chinese technology companies expanded globally, they carried their values and practices to other countries. This raised important questions about technological sovereignty and the global governance of technology.

The debate over TikTok in the US and Europe exemplified these challenges. While TikTok began as an entertainment platform, critics raised questions about privacy, censorship, and the potential to influence young users. These debates reflected broader concerns about the power of Chinese technology companies and their relationship with the Chinese government.

Chinese companies responded to these concerns by adjusting their governance structures, establishing local data centers, and implementing more transparent policies. These adjustments demonstrated Chinese companies' willingness to respect international norms but also raised questions about the universality of technological values.

The development of international standards for emerging technologies became an important area of cooperation and competition between China and other countries. China actively participated in international standardization organizations, putting forward its own proposals for standards in areas such as 5G, AI, and IoT.

This participation in global standard-setting was both a recognition of China's technological capabilities and a source of geopolitical tension. Standards are not just technical specifications but can also reflect values and priorities. The question of whose standards would prevail had important implications for the future of global technology development.

The role of intellectual property (IP) was another key ethical and legal aspect of China's transformation. Historically, China had often been criticized as a "copymaster" that imitated Western technologies without paying appropriate royalties. But as Chinese companies became innovators themselves, their attitude toward intellectual property protection changed dramatically.

China significantly tightened its IP laws and increased penalties for patent infringement. Chinese companies began aggressively protecting their own patents and demanding royalties from others. Huawei, for example, became one of the largest patent holders in the world, with thousands of patents in areas such as 5G and AI.

This shift had important implications for the global innovation landscape. It signaled that China had become a technology provider rather than a technology taker. At the same time, it led to new forms of competition and collaboration, as companies from different countries had to negotiate licensing agreements and enter into cross-licensing deals.

China's transformation also had important implications for the global supply chain for technology products. While China remained a major manufacturing hub, its role shifted from pure assembly to higher-value activities such as design, research, and development. This shift forced other countries to rethink their own strategies and decide where they wanted to compete in the global technology value chain.

The impact of China's technological transformation on the global labor market was complex and multifaceted. On the one hand, Chinese innovation led to new products and services that created jobs in other countries. On the other hand, it increased competitive pressures on companies and workers worldwide.

The development of China's AI industry, for example, had both positive and negative effects on other countries. Chinese AI advances drove global innovation and lowered the cost of AI technologies. At the same time, they forced companies in other countries to innovate and invest more quickly to remain competitive.

This dynamic led to more intensive global collaboration in technology research. Chinese and foreign researchers increasingly collaborated, shared knowledge, and jointly developed new technologies. At the same time, however, new forms of competition and isolation emerged as countries sought to protect their technological advantages.

The role of the Chinese diaspora in this global technological development was particularly important. Millions of Chinese working in Silicon Valley, London, Toronto, and other technology centers served as bridges between different innovation ecosystems. They transferred knowledge and experience between countries and contributed to the global spread of technological innovations.

At the same time, these connections became increasingly politicized. Programs such as the US "China Initiative" aimed to combat Chinese espionage and technology theft, but also led to suspicion and discrimination against Chinese-American researchers. These developments threatened to undermine scientific collaboration and fragment the global innovation landscape.

The ethical challenges of Chinese technology development reflected broader questions about the role of technology in modern society. What should be the balance between innovation and regulation? How could technological progress be used to solve societal problems without creating new ones? How could the benefits of technology be distributed fairly?

These questions had no easy answers, and different countries and cultures developed different approaches. China's model, which combined state leadership with private entrepreneurship, offered an alternative to purely market-oriented or purely state-controlled approaches. Whether this model was sustainable and transferable remained an open question.

However, China's experience offered important lessons for other countries undergoing their own technological transformations. It demonstrated the importance of long-term planning, massive investments in education and infrastructure, and a willingness to address difficult ethical issues. It also demonstrated the need to understand technological development as part of a broader societal project, not just as an economic activity.

The story of China's transformation is far from over. While the country has achieved considerable successes, it still faces significant challenges. An aging population, environmental pollution, social inequalities, and geopolitical tensions all require innovative solutions. Whether China will be able to harness its technological capabilities to address these challenges will shape its future and the future of the world.

The ethical dimensions of these challenges will be crucial. How China addresses issues of social justice, environmental responsibility, and international cooperation will not only determine its own development but also set important precedents for other countries.

In this context, the story of Zhang Wei, an electronics store owner from Shenzhen, is exemplary of the broader transformations China has undergone. His journey from traditional manufacturing to AI development reflects the journey of an entire nation. Yet his story is also a reminder that technological transformation is ultimately a human affair, shaped by the choices and values of the people who drive it.

When Zhang stands in his lab, gazing at the blinking servers training his AI algorithms, he thinks not only about the technical challenges ahead, but also about the societal impact of his work. Like many of his contemporaries, he recognized that with great technological power comes great responsibility. How he and millions of other Chinese handle that responsibility will determine where humanity goes.

"Belt & Road" - The Impact on the Economy and Geopolitics

The "Belt and Road Initiative" (BRI), often referred to as the "New Silk Road," is one of the most ambitious infrastructure and economic projects of the 21st century. Launched by the People's Republic of China in 2013 under the leadership of President Xi Jinping, it links Asia, Europe, Africa, and beyond through a network of trade routes, infrastructure projects, and economic cooperation.

The BRI plays a central role in the context of "Made in China 2025," a strategic plan aimed at transforming China into a world-leading high-tech industrial nation. It is not just an infrastructure project, but a geopolitical and economic undertaking that is redefining global power relations. The BRI's economic and geopolitical impacts are profound, multifaceted, and often controversial. They range from economic growth and trade promotion to issues of dependency, environmental impact, and strategic influence. This text explores the complex dynamics of the BRI, its intertwining with "Made in China 2025," and its far-reaching consequences for the global order—told with a touch of narrative vibrancy to bring the scope of this historic project to life.

Imagine a caravan crossing the vast steppe of Central Asia. Not with camels and spice sacks, as it did a thousand years ago along the historic Silk Road, but with high-speed trains, container ships, and digital data streams. This modern caravan is the backbone of the BRI, connecting countries and continents, from the bustling ports of Shanghai to the industrial centers of Europe. But behind the shiny images of bridges, rails, and ports lies a story that goes far beyond concrete and steel. It is a story of economic transformation, geopolitical strategy, and the quest for global influence. To understand the significance of the BRI, we must first consider its origins and its connection to "Made in China 2025."

The BRI was announced in 2013, at a time when China was seeking ways to maintain its economic momentum while expanding its global influence. The initiative comprises two main strands: the "Silk Road Economic Belt," a network of land routes through Central Asia, Russia, and Europe, and the "21st Century Maritime Silk Road," connecting sea routes through the Indian Ocean, the Red Sea, and into Europe. Since its announcement, the BRI has drawn more than 140 countries into its orbit, from small states like Laos to economic heavyweights like Italy, which became the first G7 country to sign a BRI memorandum in 2019. The initiative is not a single program, but rather a loose web of bilateral agreements, investments, and projects financed and implemented by Chinese state-owned banks and companies.

"Made in China 2025," on the other hand, is a strategic plan unveiled in 2015 that aims to transform China from a "factory of the world" to a global innovation leader. The plan focuses on ten key industries, including artificial intelligence, robotics, biotechnology, and renewable energy. Its goal is to reduce dependence on foreign technologies, promote domestic innovation, and integrate Chinese companies into global value chains. The BRI and "Made in China 2025" are closely linked: While the BRI opens up markets and resources, "Made in China 2025" creates the technological and industrial capabilities China needs to dominate those markets. Together, they form a dual strategy that places China's economic and geopolitical ambitions at the center of the global order.

The economic impact of the BRI is enormous and multifaceted. For many developing countries, particularly in Asia and Africa, the initiative has provided much-needed infrastructure. In Ethiopia, for example, the Chinese-funded railway between Addis Ababa and Djibouti has facilitated trade and reduced transportation costs. In Pakistan, the China-Pakistan Economic Corridor (CPEC), a flagship project of the BRI, has brought over $60 billion in investments in roads, power plants, and ports. These projects have created jobs, boosted local economies, and improved access to global markets.

For China itself, the BRI offers a solution to the overcapacity in industries such as steel and construction that arose from the construction boom of the 2000s. By contributing their expertise and resources to BRI projects, Chinese companies can tap into new markets while simultaneously stabilizing the domestic economy.

But the economic benefits do not come without challenges. Many BRI projects are associated with high costs, often financed through loans from Chinese banks. Countries like Sri Lanka, which had to cede the Hambantota port to a Chinese company after defaulting on its debt, have highlighted the risks of so-called "debt-trap diplomacy." Critics argue that China deliberately grants loans to countries with little ability to repay them in order to acquire strategic assets or secure political influence. Supporters, however, emphasize that many BRI countries previously had little access to international loans and that Chinese investments represent a welcome alternative to Western institutions like the IMF, which often impose strict conditions.

Another aspect is the role of Chinese companies. Many BRI projects are implemented by Chinese state-owned enterprises or private companies, which often bring their own labor and materials. While this leads to efficient project implementation, it limits the economic benefits for the local population. In countries like Zambia and Kenya, there have been protests against the limited involvement of local workers and the environmental impact of large-scale projects. At the same time, Chinese companies have expanded their global presence through the BRI, which in turn is linked to "Made in China 2025." Companies like Huawei and CRRC (China Railway Rolling Stock Corporation) are using BRI projects to establish their technologies – from 5G networks to high-speed trains – worldwide.

The geopolitical implications of the BRI are equally far-reaching. The initiative has enabled China to expand its sphere of influence far beyond Asia. In Europe, for example, the expansion of ports such as Piraeus in Greece and Trieste in Italy have made China a key player in European infrastructure. However, these investments have also raised concerns, particularly in the EU, where some member states fear that the BRI undermines European unity. Countries like Hungary and Serbia, which maintain close ties with China, have partially distanced themselves from EU policies, making the geopolitical landscape more complex.

In Africa, the BRI has made China one of the most important partners for many countries. Countries such as Nigeria and Kenya benefit from Chinese investments in infrastructure, but at the same time, concerns about a new form of economic dependence are growing. Through the BRI, China has secured access to important resources such as rare earths and oil, which are crucial for the implementation of "Made in China 2025." At the same time, China is using its economic power to gain political influence, for example by supporting African countries in international forums such as the UN.

The BRI has also intensified rivalry with other major powers, particularly the United States. The United States sees the initiative as part of a Chinese quest for global dominance. Projects such as the expansion of the Gwadar port in Pakistan, which gives China access to the Indian Ocean, or the presence in strategic ports such as Djibouti, where China maintains a military base, have raised security concerns. In response, the US and its allies have launched alternatives such as the "Build Back Better World" (B3W) initiative and the EU Global Gateway Strategy to counter the BRI. These counter-initiatives demonstrate that the BRI is not only an economic but also a geopolitical chess game, centered around control of trade routes, resources, and influence.

An often overlooked aspect of the BRI is its cultural and digital dimension. China is using the initiative to strengthen its soft power. Scholarship programs, Confucius Institutes, and media collaborations accompany the infrastructure projects and promote a positive image of China. At the same time, the Digital Silk Road, a sub-segment of the BRI, plays a key role in the spread of Chinese technologies. Companies such as Huawei and ZTE are building 5G networks in BRI countries, while the "Made in China 2025" strategy is driving the development of these technologies. However, this digital expansion raises questions about data security and sovereignty, especially in countries that become heavily dependent on Chinese technology.

The environmental impact of the BRI is another controversial issue. Many projects, particularly coal-fired power plants and hydroelectric dams, have significant ecological consequences. In Indonesia, for example, BRI-funded power plants have exacerbated air pollution, while in Southeast Asia, hydroelectric dams threaten the livelihoods of fishermen. China has responded to this criticism by promoting "green" BRI projects, such as investments in solar and wind energy. However, these efforts conflict with the short-term economic goals of many projects.

The connection with "Made in China 2025" is also evident in the technological dimension of the BRI. The initiative serves as a testing ground for Chinese innovations. High-speed trains, drone technology, and AI-supported logistics systems are being tested and established in BRI projects. This not only strengthens the global competitiveness of Chinese companies but also supports the goal of positioning China as a technology leader. At the same time, the export of these technologies is causing tensions, particularly with Western countries that fear that Chinese standards could dominate global technology markets.

However, the BRI is not without its internal challenges. Within China itself, there are debates about the financial risks of the initiative. The estimated cost of the BRI is in the trillions of US dollars, and not all projects are commercially viable. Some experts warn that the high investments could burden the Chinese economy, especially in times of global economic uncertainty. Furthermore, there is growing skepticism about China's motives in BRI countries, leading to political tensions. In Malaysia, for example, BRI projects were renegotiated after changes in government to improve conditions.

The story of the BRI is a project that evokes both admiration and skepticism. It is a symbol of China's rise and the challenges it presents. For many countries, the BRI represents an opportunity to modernize their infrastructure and promote economic growth. For others, it represents a risk associated with dependency and geopolitical tensions. In the context of "Made in China 2025," the BRI is emerging as a catalyst for China's quest for technological and economic dominance. But like any great caravan that travels through history, it leaves its mark—some leading to prosperity, others to conflict. The coming decades will show whether the BRI brings the world closer together or creates new dividing lines.

The BRI narrative is also a human one. It's the story of construction workers in Pakistan pushing roads through the mountains, of traders in Kyrgyzstan getting their goods to Europe faster, and of politicians in Europe balancing economic opportunities with strategic concerns. It's a story of progress and risk, of cooperation and competition. The "New Silk Road" may no longer have camels, but its routes are just as vibrant, just as complex, and just as consequential as the paths of its historic predecessor.

From cheap copier to brand manufacturer

In the summer of 2015, the global economy was faced with a conundrum. The stock exchanges in Shanghai and Shenzhen, China's financial centers, were reeling. Within a few weeks, the country's stock markets lost almost a third of their value. International investors withdrew billions, and headlines about an impending economic crisis in China circulated. But amidst this chaos, something remarkable happened: In the factories of Shenzhen, in the Pearl River Delta, the production lines continued to run.

Smartphones, clothing, toys—the goods bearing the "Made in China" label flowed continuously into the world. China, often referred to as the "workshop of the world," seemed unshakenable. But behind the scenes, a transformation was brewing that would transform the country from a mere low-cost producer to a serious brand-name manufacturer in just a decade. This story tells how China underwent this transformation between 2015 and 2025—a story of ambition, innovation, challenges, and global influence.

The term "workshop of the world" has long been a double-edged sword. On the one hand, it represented China's unrivaled ability to produce goods in gigantic quantities and at low cost. By the early 2000s, the country had become the preferred location for the manufacture of consumer goods. From T-shirts to sneakers to electronic components, Western corporations such as Apple, Nike, and Walmart outsourced their production to China, lured by low wages, a well-developed infrastructure, and a government that welcomed foreign investment. On the other hand, the term implied a certain disdain: China was the place where Western ideas were put into practice, but hardly the source of its own innovations. Products "Made in China" were considered cheap but often inferior. This perception was deeply rooted in the years before 2015, but it was precisely at this time that the image began to change.

In 2015, China stood at a turning point. The country's economy had entered a slowdown after decades of rapid growth. GDP growth, which had regularly reached double-digit percentages in the 1990s and 2000s, fell to around 6.9 percent—the lowest rate in a quarter of a century. For a country that had lifted hundreds of millions of people out of poverty, this was a warning sign. China's reliance on exports and foreign investment made it vulnerable, particularly in the face of global uncertainties such as weakening demand in Europe and the United States. At the same time, domestic wages were rising, threatening the country's competitiveness as a low-cost producer. Countries such as Vietnam and Bangladesh began to take market share in certain sectors, such as textiles. The Chinese leadership realized that a new model was needed to maintain economic momentum.

A vivid example of this shift is the story of Huawei. By 2015, Huawei was already a major player in the telecommunications sector, known for its network equipment used in mobile networks around the world. But in the smartphone market, the company was still considered an outsider, sandwiched between Apple and Samsung. Huawei smartphones of the early 2010s were often perceived as affordable alternatives that were solid but not outstanding. Yet Huawei invested heavily in research and development—nearly $9.2 billion in 2015, more than many Western competitors. These investments led to breakthroughs, particularly in camera technology. Through a partnership with German optics specialist Leica, Huawei launched smartphones that set new standards in photography. By 2018, Huawei had not only surpassed Apple in many markets but also gained a global following that associated the brand with quality and innovation. Despite geopolitical tensions, particularly the trade dispute with the US, Huawei demonstrated how a Chinese company could overcome the "workbench" mentality.

Another example is BYD, a company that manufactured mobile phone batteries in the early 2000s but became a pioneer in electric mobility starting in 2015. Supported by government subsidies and a growing domestic electric vehicle market, BYD began producing vehicles that could compete with Western brands not only in terms of price but also in terms of technology. In 2023, BYD temporarily surpassed Tesla as the world's largest electric vehicle manufacturer, a milestone that caught the attention of the global automotive industry.

BYD's success story demonstrates how China was able to take the lead in a strategically important sector through targeted industrial policy and corporate initiative.But the path to becoming a brand manufacturer was not without obstacles. One of the biggest criticisms of China's economic strategy was the accusation of technology transfer and a lack of intellectual property protection. Western companies complained that they were forced to disclose their technologies to gain access to the Chinese market. These practices led to tensions, particularly with the United States, which imposed punitive tariffs on Chinese goods in 2018 under President Trump.

The trade war forced China to reduce its dependence on foreign technologies, which further accelerated the development of domestic innovations. Companies like SMIC, a Chinese chip manufacturer, received massive government support to close the gap with Western corporations like TSMC and Intel. By 2025, China had made progress in semiconductor production but was not yet completely independent of foreign technology.

Another obstacle was the international perception of Chinese brands. While companies like Xiaomi, Oppo, and Vivo gained large market shares in Asia and Africa, they struggled to gain a foothold in Western and European markets. Consumers in these regions often still associated Chinese products with low quality. To change this image, Chinese companies relied on targeted campaigns and partnerships with Western brands. Xiaomi, for example, sponsored Formula 1 races, while Huawei collaborated with renowned European designers. At the same time, these companies invested in building global sales and service networks to gain consumer trust.

The role of Chinese consumers themselves in this transformation should not be underestimated. By 2015, China's middle class had grown to over 500 million people—a gigantic consumer base that was increasingly developing brand awareness. These consumers increasingly preferred domestic products, not only for patriotic reasons, but because they valued the quality of these products. Brands like Li-Ning, a sporting goods manufacturer, and Haier, a home appliance company, became iconic brands in China before venturing into the international market. This domestic backing gave Chinese companies the stability they needed to compete globally.

By 2025, China had not only consolidated but also redefined its position as the "workshop of the world." The country continued to produce goods in gigantic quantities, but increasingly under its own brands and using its own technology. The "Made in China 2025" strategy had borne fruit, even if not all of its goals were met. China was no longer just the place where the world manufactured its products—it was a country that shaped the world with its own ideas and brands. The story of this transformation is one of ambition, innovation, and perseverance, but also of conflict and challenges. It shows how a country once known for cheap imitations reshaped the global economic order—and how it changed the world in the process.

China's transformation from a low-cost producer to a brand-name manufacturer between 2015 and 2025 is particularly striking in consumer goods production, a sector that shapes the daily lives of billions of people. During this period, the country underwent a remarkable transformation: It evolved from a mere imitator of Western products to a player that not only created its own global brands but also acquired Western trademarks and patents to strengthen its position in the global value chain. This process was characterized by economic foresight, strategic acquisitions, and a new self-confidence that led China to rewrite the rules of the global consumer goods industry.

At the beginning of the decade, around 2015, China was primarily known in consumer goods production for its role as a contract manufacturer. Factories in cities like Dongguan and Suzhou produced massive quantities of electronics, clothing, household goods, and toys for Western brands. These products often bore the logos of companies like Apple,

Adidas, or Mattel, while the Chinese manufacturers remained in the background. China's strength lay in its ability to produce quickly, efficiently, and cost-effectively. But this role had its limitations. Margins for contract manufacturers were slim, and dependence on foreign clients made companies vulnerable to fluctuations in global demand. At the same time, the perception of "Made in China" was negative in many markets. Consumer goods from China were often viewed as cheap copies of Western originals, lacking in quality and originality.

A central aspect of this image was the practice of counterfeiting. In the early 2010s, Chinese companies were notorious for copying Western designs—from handbags that looked like Gucci models to smartphones that resembled Apple's iPhone. Markets like the Huaqiangbei Electronics Market in Shenzhen were emblematic of this era. They sold so-called "Shanzhai" products—cheap imitations that often came to market with astonishing speed but rarely matched the quality or durability of the originals. This practice, however, was not only a sign of a lack of innovation, but also an expression of the adaptability and speed of Chinese industry. Companies learned to analyze, reproduce, and adapt complex products to local needs, often at a fraction of the cost.

But starting in 2015, this approach began to change. The Chinese government and companies realized that the image of a cheap copycat was neither economically nor strategically viable in the long term. The "Made in China 2025" plan provided a decisive impetus here as well. It not only promoted technological innovation but also the building of strong, independent brands in the consumer goods industry. Companies like Xiaomi, Oppo, and Vivo, originally known for their low-cost smartphones, began investing in design, quality, and marketing to break away from the perception of low-cost manufacturers. Xiaomi, for example, developed an ecosystem of smartphones, smart home devices, and wearables that stood out with a modern, minimalist design and competitive pricing. These products were no longer mere copies, but often offered features that Western competitors only later adopted, such as larger battery capacities or innovative fast-charging technologies.

A key moment in this transformation was the realization that brand building requires more than just product quality. Chinese companies began investing in marketing and global presence. They sponsored major sporting events, collaborated with international designers, and opened flagship stores in major cities such as London, Paris, and New York. DJI, the world's leading drone manufacturer, is a prime example. Originally a small company from Shenzhen, DJI developed drones that were not only technically superior but also conveyed an image of professionalism and innovation. By 2020, DJI dominated the global drone market with a share of over 70 percent, not least through clever branding and high-quality products that appealed to both hobbyists and professionals.

Parallel to this internal brand building, China began to strengthen its position by acquiring Western trademarks and patents. This move marked a turning point: Instead of copying Western products, China increasingly purchased the originals. A prominent example is the Midea Group's acquisition of the German household appliance manufacturer Miele in 2016.

Midea, a Chinese company that previously operated primarily as a supplier to Western brands, recognized the value of Miele's brand, technology, and distribution network. The acquisition not only allowed Midea to gain access to European markets but also strengthened consumer trust through the established Miele brand. A similar story followed Geely's acquisition of the Swedish automaker Volvo in 2010, the effects of which continued to unfold until 2025. Geely leveraged Volvo's engineering expertise and brand image to establish its own vehicles, such as the Lynk & Co. electric cars, which were well received in Europe and Asia.

These acquisitions were part of a larger strategy. Chinese companies invested billions in foreign firms between 2015 and 2025 to acquire technologies, patents, and trademarks. According to a study by the Rhodium Group, Chinese direct investment in Europe amounted to over €150 billion between 2015 and 2020, a significant portion of which went into consumer goods and technology companies. These investments enabled Chinese companies to expand not only their production capacities but also their innovation capabilities. Instead of imitations, they could now rely on patented technologies, which they either used directly or further developed. One example is Huawei's acquisition of patents in the field of 5G technology, which helped the company maintain a leading role in the global telecommunications market despite Western sanctions.

However, this transformation from copycat to owner also had dark sides. The aggressive takeover policies of Chinese companies led to mistrust in Western countries. Concerns grew in Europe and the US that strategically important technologies were falling into the hands of Chinese corporations.

This led to stricter investment controls, for example by the Committee on Foreign Investment in the United States (CFIUS), and new EU directives that made foreign takeovers in sensitive sectors more difficult. Nevertheless, China continued its strategy, often through indirect investments or partnerships, to secure access to Western markets and technologies.

The Role of Chinese "Headhunters" and Investors

The role of specialized Chinese "headhunters" for corporate acquisitions is a rather controversial aspect of China's transformation into a global brand manufacturer. These "headhunters" – in the context of mergers and acquisitions (M&A) more likely to be understood as strategic advisors or acquisition agents – were tasked with identifying innovative and technologically valuable European companies that might be of interest to Chinese investors. Their work was a central component of the Chinese strategy of gaining access to know-how, patents, and established brands through targeted acquisitions in order to realize the ambitions of the "Made in China 2025" program.

From 2015 onwards, China intensified its efforts to acquire European companies in key industries such as robotics, mechanical engineering, automotive supplies, and biotechnology. These acquisitions were not spontaneous decisions, but the result of carefully orchestrated processes in which specialized consulting firms and networks played a key role. These "headhunters" – often in the form of China-based investment firms, consultancies, or state-backed agencies – specialized in systematically scouring European markets for potential takeover candidates. They focused on companies that were either technological leaders, held valuable patents, or were in financial difficulty and therefore vulnerable to takeovers.

A prominent example is the acquisition of the German robot manufacturer Kuka by the Chinese Midea Group in 2016 for around €4.5 billion. This transaction was not initiated by chance, but was the result of targeted research by consultants who identified Kuka as strategically valuable for China's ambitions in robotics – a core area of "Made in China 2025." A similar process followed ChemChina's acquisition of the mechanical engineering company Krauss-Maffei for €925 million that same year. These "headhunters" used detailed market analyses, industry contacts, and sometimes local partners in Europe to prepare such deals. Their expertise lay in not only assessing a company's technological relevance but also navigating the political and legal frameworks in the target countries.

The methods used by these acquisition agents were diverse. They scoured publicly available data, such as annual reports and patent applications, participated in industry trade fairs, and established relationships with European trade associations. In some cases, they worked with European investment banks or consulting firms that had access to confidential information about companies in financial distress. Medium-sized companies in Germany, often known as "hidden champions," were particularly attractive targets because, despite their technological strength, they were often undercapitalized or had succession problems. The "headhunters" presented Chinese investors with detailed dossiers that described not only a company's economic situation but also its potential benefits for China's industrial policy.

The accusation against the "headhunters" was that, through these targeted purchases, China was "absorbing" strategically important technologies in order to integrate them into its own industry.

A 2016 report by the Berlin research institute Merics pointed out that government agencies in China actively supported many of these acquisitions, fueling suspicions that the "headhunters" often acted on behalf of or with the backing of the government. This led to tightening investment controls in Europe, for example through the EU regulation on foreign direct investment, which came into force in 2019. In Germany, acquisitions such as that of semiconductor manufacturer Aixtron were blocked by the government in 2016 after security concerns were raised.

Despite these hurdles, the "headhunters" remained active, albeit with an adjusted strategy. After the peak of Chinese acquisitions in Europe in 2016 – when, according to the consulting firm EY, around €72.9 billion flowed into European companies – the number of transactions declined, partly due to stricter regulations and geopolitical tensions. Nevertheless, the "headhunters" found ways to continue their work, for example through indirect investments or collaborations. One example is the takeover of the German audio specialist Beyerdynamic in 2025 by a Chinese competitor for €122 million, which was successfully completed despite public skepticism.

The work of these "headhunters" was a crucial catalyst for China's rise to brand status. They enabled Chinese companies to acquire not only production capacity but also innovative strength and brand value within a very short period of time and with little effort, thus reducing their dependence on

Western technologies. At the same time, their role highlights the complexity of global economic relations, in which economic ambitions, technological competition, and geopolitical tensions are inextricably linked. By 2025, these strategic acquisition agents had helped transform China from being perceived as the world's workshop to being a country actively shaping the global innovation landscape.

Another aspect of the change was the role of Chinese consumers. With the growth of the middle class—estimated to number over 600 million by 2025—a strong awareness of quality and brands developed. Chinese consumers began to prefer domestic brands such as Anta (sports goods) and Haier (home appliances), which were characterized by high quality and modern design. This demand strengthened the position of Chinese companies domestically and gave them the capital they needed to expand globally. At the same time, companies such as Alibaba, TEMU, and Nihaojewelry used digital platforms to market their products worldwide, often bypassing traditional Western distribution channels.

The Chinese auto industry, which experienced unprecedented growth between 2015 and 2025, also impressively illustrates the country's transformation from a low-cost producer to a brand-name manufacturer. Companies like BYD, Geely, and NIO no longer just produced low-cost vehicles, but electric cars that not only competed with global market leaders like Tesla or BMW in terms of quality, technology, and design, but were often far superior. BYD, for example, set new standards in safety and range with its Blade batteries, while Geely, through its acquisition of Volvo, gained access to world-class engineering expertise, which was channeled into its own brands like Lynk & Co. These vehicles not only impress in the domestic market but also gain a reputation in Europe and Asia, supported by modern designs, top-notch comfort, advanced driver assistance systems, and competitive pricing. By 2025, the Chinese auto industry had proven that "Made in China" stood for innovation and reliability in this sector.

By 2025, the consumer goods industry in China had undergone fundamental changes. Companies like Lenovo, which had acquired IBM's PC division in 2005, and TCL, which had established itself in the consumer electronics sector, were no longer mere manufacturers, but global brands with their own innovative strength. They not only competed with Western giants but also set new standards in many areas. The acquisition of Western trademarks and patents had enabled China to reduce its dependence on foreign technology while simultaneously expanding its global presence. This transformation was not only an economic but also a cultural achievement: China had proven that it could not only be the world's workshop, but also a creator of brands that enjoyed respect and recognition around the world.

This concludes the story of China's transformation from the world's workshop to a global brand manufacturer. In just a decade, the country has revolutionized not only its production capacity but also its innovative strength and brand presence. From smartphones to drones to electric cars, China has left a lasting mark on the global economic landscape by blurring the lines between imitator and pioneer. This development demonstrates how a country can redefine the global economy through strategic vision, economic discipline, and cultural self-confidence – a legacy that extends far beyond the workbenches of Shenzhen.

Artificial Intelligence: The Silent Revolution in China

In the early hours of March 12, 2016, Lee Sedol, one of the world's best Go players, sat in front of a computer terminal in Seoul, staring in disbelief at the board. AlphaGo, an artificial intelligence system developed by Google DeepMind, had just made a move that defied all expectations. Not only the spectators in the room, but also experts around the world were stunned. This moment marked not only a turning point in the history of artificial intelligence, but also the beginning of a quiet revolution that would spread across the entire Asian continent, with China as its undisputed epicenter.

What happened that spring in Seoul was more than just a victory of machine over man. It was the starting signal for a race that would fundamentally change the geopolitical balance of power in the 21st century. While the Western world was still debating the philosophical implications of artificial intelligence, China had already understood that what was emerging was not just a new technology, but a tool for reshaping the global order.

The story of China's AI revolution, however, doesn't begin with spectacular breakthroughs in research labs or with visionary entrepreneurs in gleaming office towers. It begins with a quiet but all the more impactful transformation that took place in China's megacities long before the world took notice. On the streets of Shenzhen, where millions of people pulled out their smartphones every day to pay bills, order food, or navigate traffic, the largest data repository in human history emerged.

Li Wei, a 34-year-old software engineer from Hangzhou, still remembers the day he realized how profoundly his everyday life had changed. It was an ordinary Tuesday in the fall of 2018 when he left his apartment in the morning and only realized in the evening that he hadn't used cash or a credit card once all day. His smartphone had accompanied his every step: buying breakfast from a street vendor, taking the subway to work, having lunch with colleagues, and shopping at the supermarket on the way home. What Li Wei didn't fully grasp at the time was that each of these seemingly mundane transactions represented a data point in a gigantic network that was revolutionizing the way machines learn about human behavior.

These everyday scenes were repeated millions of times across China. In Guangzhou, street vendors paid for their wares with QR codes hanging from makeshift stalls. In Beijing, tourists navigated the Forbidden City with the help of AI-powered translation apps that translated Mandarin into dozens of languages in real time. In Shanghai, intelligent transportation systems analyzed the movement patterns of millions of commuters and optimized traffic light cycles in real time. What appeared from the outside to be a technological modernization was in fact the construction of the world's largest AI training infrastructure.

The key to China's quiet lead lay not in a single groundbreaking invention, but in the unique combination of societal acceptance, government support, and sheer scale. While Europe and the US were engaged in years of debate about data protection and privacy, Chinese society adopted new technologies at a speed that repeatedly astonished Western observers. This willingness to embrace technology was not merely a cultural phenomenon, but the result of a specific historical development that made China an ideal testing ground for AI applications.

The transformation began in the early 2000s, when China evolved from a predominantly cash-based society to one of the most digitalized economies in the world. This leap was made possible because large segments of the population bypassed traditional financial services and switched directly to mobile payment systems. What economists call "leapfrogging" laid the foundation for something even more signifycant: the emergence of data streams with a granularity and completeness that would have been unthinkable in other countries.

Dr. Chen Xiaoli, a data analyst at one of China's leading tech companies, retrospectively describes the situation at the time as a "perfect storm for machine learning." In her office on the 47th floor of a high-rise in Shenzhen, she explains how the conditions for AI development in China differ fundamentally from those in the West: "We not only had more data, we had better data.

While American companies had to laboriously piece together information from different sources, we obtained a complete picture of user behavior from a single platform." This comprehensiveness of data collection was the result of a unique ecosystem structure that had developed in China. Unlike in the West, where various services were offered by specialized companies, so-called "super apps" emerged in China that combined a variety of functions into a single application. WeChat, originally launched as a messaging app, evolved into a platform through which users communicated, paid, shopped, booked appointments, read news, and even accessed government services.

The implications of this development for AI research were revolutionary. While Western researchers worked with fragmented datasets that often only depicted individual aspects of human behavior, Chinese developers had access to holistic profiles that encompassed virtually all areas of their users' lives. An algorithm could learn not only how people shop, but also how they communicate, get around, work, and spend their free time. This data integration enabled the development of AI systems that predict human behavior with a precision previously thought impossible.

The breakthrough came gradually, without major announcements or media attention. Patterns began to emerge in the recommendation algorithms of e-commerce platforms that went beyond simple product suggestions. The systems developed an intuitive understanding of their users' needs that often exceeded their own awareness. Zhang Ming, a 28-year-old marketing manager from Chengdu, recounts an experience that left a lasting impression on him: "I had spent days looking for a gift for my mother, not knowing what to give her. Then the app suddenly suggested an antique tea caddy that perfectly matched her collection. I had never looked for anything like this, never talked about it, but the algorithm had deduced from my other activities what the right gift might be."

Such anecdotes abounded throughout China. The AI systems began to recognize connections that weren't obvious to human observers. They predicted when people would get sick, even before symptoms appeared, based on subtle changes in their movement patterns and purchasing habits.

They identified potential loan defaults with an accuracy that far surpassed traditional banking methods. They optimized supply chains so efficiently that goods often arrived before customers had consciously decided to buy.

These developments did not go unnoticed. In the upper echelons of the Communist Party and in the government's planning departments, people began to understand that more than just a new industry was emerging. AI was establishing itself as an enabling technology with the potential to transform every aspect of society. This realization led to a strategic realignment unprecedented in its clarity and decisiveness.

In July 2017, the Chinese State Council published a development plan for artificial intelligence that clearly stated the country's ambitions: China was to become the world's leading AI nation by 2030. What at first glance appeared to be typical government rhetoric turned out to be a detailed roadmap for a technological revolution. The plan envisioned the Chinese AI industry reaching a value equivalent to $150 billion by 2030 and set specific milestones for various application areas.

But behind the sober numbers and targets lay a far-sighted vision that went far beyond economic considerations. The Chinese leadership had recognized that AI was not just a technology, but a new paradigm for organizing society and the economy. In the party's internal discussions, AI was referred to as the "electricity of the 21st century"—a foundational technology that would permeate and transform all other fields.

The implementation of this vision began with unprecedented speed. Cities competed to become AI centers and offered companies generous incentives to establish research and development activities. A 30-square-kilometer AI park was created in Tianjin, reserved exclusively for AI companies. Hangzhou invested billions in the development of a "City Brain" – an AI system designed to optimize all city traffic in real time. Shenzhen was declared a test zone for autonomous vehicles, with special road sections reserved exclusively for self-driving cars.

These initiatives were more than just industrial policy measures. They represented a systematic approach to creating optimal conditions for AI development. While other countries were still debating regulatory frameworks, China created space for experimentation. While ethical concerns elsewhere slowed development, China relied on practical testing under real-world conditions.

The results were not long in coming. In the following years, the number of Chinese AI startups exploded. Companies like SenseTime, Face++, and ByteDance emerged seemingly overnight and achieved valuations in the billions. What distinguished these companies was not only their technological innovation, but their ability to quickly and scalably implement AI solutions in real-world applications.

SenseTime, founded in 2014 by a group of scientists from the Chinese University of Hong Kong, is a prime example of the Chinese approach to AI development. The company began by developing facial recognition technology, but instead of focusing on theoretical perfection, the founders immediately sought practical applications. Within a few years, SenseTime had implemented its technology in hundreds of Chinese cities, from airport security systems to supermarket payment systems.

The speed of this implementation was only possible due to the unique combination of technological innovation and social acceptance that characterized China. While years of debate about the ethical implications of facial recognition raged in Europe, Chinese consumers readily adopted the technology as part of their everyday lives. In Kaifeng, a medium-sized city in Henan Province, tourists were able to visit historical sites without ever purchasing an entrance ticket as early as 2018. The facial recognition system automatically identified them, charged the entrance fee to their mobile payment account, and sent personalized information about the attractions directly to their smartphones.

Such seamless integrations of AI into everyday life became commonplace in China long before similar systems were even conceived in other countries. Practical testing under real-world conditions not only accelerated technological development but also created a tremendous competitive advantage for Chinese companies. They gained experience with AI implementations at a scale unavailable elsewhere.

This experience flowed directly into the next generation of AI systems. Machine learning algorithms trained with real-world user data from millions of interactions developed a robustness and reliability that lab-based systems could not match. An autonomous vehicle tested on Chinese roads learned to cope not only with ideal traffic situations, but also with the chaotic realities of Chinese traffic—with cyclists changing lanes abruptly, pedestrians crossing the street on red lights, and delivery vehicles double-parked.

Dr. Wang Jianning, a researcher at the Institute of Automation of the Chinese Academy of Sciences, describes this advantage as a "reality premium": "Our algorithms had to deal with the full complexity of the real world from the very beginning. This made them more resilient and versatile than systems developed in controlled environments."

This resilience proved to be a decisive factor when Chinese AI companies began to enter international markets. Their systems, hardened by years of testing under the most challenging conditions, often exceeded expectations in less complex environments. A facial recognition system that worked in Shanghai's crowded subways had no trouble coping with the more orderly conditions of European transportation systems.

But the true breakthrough of the Chinese AI revolution lay not in individual technological successes, but in the systematic integration of various AI technologies into coherent ecosystems. While Western companies often focused on specialized applications, Chinese firms developed comprehensive platforms that combined various AI functions.

At the same time, a discussion about the societal impact of the AI revolution developed in China. While the technology clearly brought many benefits, its downsides also became apparent. Jobs were lost as AI systems replaced human workers. Alibaba's "City Brain" project in Hangzhou exemplifies this holistic approach. What began as a traffic optimization system evolved into a comprehensive AI platform for city management. The system integrates data from traffic cameras, weather sensors, social media, e-commerce platforms, and government databases to create a real-time picture of the city. It not only optimizes traffic light timing but also predicts traffic congestion, identifies environmental problems, detects safety risks, and coordinates emergency response.

Liu Xiaoming, the technical director of the City Brain project, explains the philosophy behind this approach: "We realized that true AI is not made up of isolated algorithms, but of the intelligent interconnection of different systems. A city is a complex ecosystem, and it needs an AI that is just as complex and interconnected."

This interconnectedness extended beyond individual applications to entire industries. In the financial industry, Chinese companies developed AI systems that not only assessed credit risks but also optimized investment strategies, performed fraud detection, and offered personalized financial advice. Ant Financial, Alibaba's fintech arm, processed over a billion transactions daily using AI systems that performed real-time risk assessments and identified suspicious activity.

The speed and efficiency of these systems surpassed anything traditional banks could achieve. Yu Shengfa, a small business owner from Anhui Province, recounts his experience with AI-based lending: "I urgently needed a loan for my business, but the bank wanted to conduct weeks of checks. Then I tried using an app on my phone. Within three minutes, I had an approval, and the money was in my account. The system analyzed my payment history, my business data, and even my supplier ratings and decided I was creditworthy."

Such stories were repeated millions of times across China. AI systems democratized access to financial services, enabling even small business owners and individuals without traditional credit histories to access capital. This inclusion had far-reaching socioeconomic impacts and contributed to the economic development of entire regions.

However, the impact went far beyond the financial sector. In agriculture, AI systems revolutionized crop management practices. Drones equipped with computer vision analyzed crops for diseases and pests, enabling precise, localized treatments. Predictive analytics optimized irrigation times and fertilizer application based on weather data, soil conditions, and plant growth models.

Wang Desheng, a rice farmer from Jiangsu Province, describes the transformation of his work: "Before, I had to walk my fields every day, looking for problems. Now, I get a notification on my phone whenever a problem arises. The AI tells me exactly which field is affected, what the problem is, and how to solve it. My yields have increased by 30 percent, while I use fewer pesticides."

These practical successes led to a self-reinforcing dynamic. The more people had positive experiences with AI systems, the greater their willingness to adopt new AI applications. China developed a culture of technological openness that stood in sharp contrast to the skepticism prevailing in many Western countries.

This cultural acceptance was not only the result of successful implementations, but also of a conscious strategy by the Chinese government to promote AI awareness. Educational programs in schools and universities integrated AI topics into the curriculum. Public information campaigns explained the benefits of AI technologies for everyday life. Media reports focused on success stories and positive impacts.

At the same time, China invested heavily in AI research and education. New university programs in artificial intelligence emerged, and existing computer science and engineering programs were expanded to include AI components. The government funded research projects worth billions of dollars and created incentives for international talent to come to China. These investments in human capital began to pay off. Chinese researchers increasingly published in leading AI journals and won prizes at international conferences. What's more, they began to define new research directions and set standards that were adopted by the international community.

Dr. Li Feifei, a Chinese-born AI researcher who teaches at Stanford, observed this development with fascination: "What happened in China was not just a quantitative increase in AI research, but a qualitative change. Researchers developed new approaches specifically tailored to the needs of large-scale, real-world applications. This was a paradigm shift from theoretical to applied AI research."

This paradigm shift manifested itself in a new generation of AI algorithms specifically designed to address the challenges posed by scaling to hundreds of millions of users. Traditional machine learning approaches, which worked well with smaller datasets, reached their limits with the gigantic amounts of data processed by Chinese companies. Chinese researchers developed new architectures for deep learning networks that could handle large amounts of data more efficiently.

These technological innovations were incorporated into commercial products that set new standards for performance and efficiency. ByteDance's algorithm for the video platform TikTok revolutionized the way content was curated and personalized. The system analyzed not only what users watched, but also how long they watched, at which moments they paused, what content they shared, and how they interacted with other users. This multimodal analysis enabled personalization so precise it was sometimes uncanny.

Lisa Chen, a 22-year-old student from Shanghai, describes her experience with the app: "Sometimes I feel like TikTok knows me better than I know myself. It shows me videos I didn't even know I'd be interested in, but then I can't stop watching. It's like it has direct access to my subconscious."

This intuitive understanding of human preferences was the result of years of data collection and algorithm optimization. The AI systems learned not only individual preferences, but also cultural patterns, generational differences, and even local trends. They were able to predict what type of content would be popular in certain regions or at certain times.

TikTok's success in international markets demonstrated the global competitiveness of Chinese AI technology. The app became the most downloaded app in over 150 countries and reached over a billion active users within a few years. Its success was based not only on entertaining content, but on an AI system that could overcome cultural and linguistic barriers.

But the international success of Chinese AI companies also brought with it new challenges. In the US and Europe, concerns grew about Chinese technology companies and their ties to the Chinese government. Security experts warned of potential data breaches and espionage. Politicians called for regulations and, in extreme cases, bans on Chinese apps and services.

These geopolitical tensions shed new light on the AI revolution in China. What initially appeared to be a purely technological and economic development was increasingly perceived as a strategic power shift. AI was not just a tool for increasing efficiency or maximizing profits, but an instrument of soft power and geopolitical influence.

The Chinese government reinforced this perception by explicitly integrating AI into its foreign policy strategy. The "Digital Silk Road" initiative, part of the larger Belt and Road Initiative, envisioned exporting Chinese AI technologies to dozens of countries. Smart city projects in Africa, Southeast Asia, and Latin America were to be realized using Chinese AI technology.

These projects were more than just business opportunities. They established technological standards and created dependencies that could have long-term strategic implications. A country that built its transportation infrastructure with Chinese AI systems would continue to rely on Chinese technology and expertise in the future.

Dr. Sarah Johnson, a technology policy expert at Georgetown University, analyzes this development: "China is using AI as a tool for exporting its technological norms and standards. This is a form of digital colonialism that is more subtle but potentially more effective than traditional power projections."

This geopolitical dimension of the AI revolution did not go unnoticed in China. The strategic implications of AI leadership were intensely discussed in academic circles and government think tanks. The realization took hold that AI was not just a technology, but a new medium for exercising power.

Data privacy concerns grew, although they were discussed less prominently than in the West. The growing reliance on

AI systems raised questions about human autonomy and agency.

These concerns led to a more nuanced view of AI development. Chinese researchers began to think more deeply about the ethical implications of their work. Companies developed guidelines for responsible AI development. The government issued the first regulations for specific AI applications.

Professor Zhang Wei of Tsinghua University, one of China's leading AI ethicists, explains this development: "We have learned that technological progress alone is not enough. We must ensure that AI serves society as a whole, not just the interests of a few."

This reflection led to a new phase of Chinese AI development, characterized less by pure speed and more by sustainability and social responsibility. Companies began to develop AI systems explicitly geared toward social welfare.

Another example of the transformative power of these technologies is the story of Zhang Mei, a teacher in a rural area of Guizhou Province. Her school, which previously struggled with outdated teaching materials and overcrowded classes, now uses an AI-powered education system. This system, developed by a Hangzhou-based startup, analyzes students' learning progress in real time and adapts lessons to their individual needs. For Zhang Mei, this not only provides relief but also the opportunity to offer her students an education that was previously only available in affluent cities. Such applications demonstrate how AI is being used in China not only in high-tech centers but also in remote regions to reduce social and economic inequalities.

Another area where China is pioneering work is medicine. In a hospital in Beijing, Dr. Wang, a radiologist, is assisted by an AI system that analyzes X-ray images in seconds. The system, developed by a company called Infervision, detects abnormalities such as tumors or pneumonia with an accuracy that often surpasses human diagnosis. For Dr. Wang, this technology is a tool that allows him to focus on more complex cases while AI takes over routine tasks. Such systems are particularly valuable in rural areas where there is a shortage of qualified specialists. Through telemedicine and AI-assisted diagnoses, patients in remote villages can gain access to cutting-edge medical care.

China's innovation in AI is also driven by close collaboration between government, academia, and industry. In contrast to Western models, where innovation is often dominated by the private sector, China is pursuing a hybrid approach. Companies like Baidu, Alibaba, and Tencent, known collectively as "BAT," play a central role, but they work closely with state institutions. Baidu, for example, has opened a research center for autonomous vehicles, supported by the government with data and infrastructure. This collaboration makes it possible to harness large amounts of data, which are uniquely available in China due to its huge population and widespread digitalization.

However, not everything about China's AI revolution is uncontroversial. The country not only has the ability to rapidly scale technologies but also the willingness to apply them to virtually all areas of life. In agriculture, for example, farmers in Shandong Province use drones equipped with AI to monitor fields and optimize pesticide use. In logistics, JD.com, an e-commerce giant, has developed warehouses operated entirely by AI-controlled robots. These applications are not futuristic, but reality and show how deeply AI has already penetrated everyday life.

The international dimension of China's AI revolution cannot be overlooked. Chinese companies such as Huawei and ByteDance, the company behind TikTok, export their technologies and influence global markets. At the same time, China is a magnet for international talent. Engineers and researchers from all over the world now work in Shenzhen and Beijing, attracted by the opportunities the country offers. However, this globalization of AI development has also triggered geopolitical tensions, particularly with the US, where competition for technological supremacy is intense. Nevertheless, China remains committed to cooperation, for example through partnerships with European universities or participation in international AI conferences.

A look to the future shows that China's AI revolution is far from complete. In cities such as Xiong'an, a newly built "smart city" near Beijing, AI is being integrated into every aspect of urban life, from energy supply to waste management. At the same time, the country is working on the next generation of AI technologies, such as quantum computing and neuromorphic chips, which could further increase computing power. For people like Li Wei, Zhang Mei, and Dr. Wang, this future is already within reach. They live in a world where AI is no longer science fiction, but a tool that shapes their everyday lives.

What makes China's AI revolution so special? It's the combination of vision, pragmatism, and the ability to put technology at the service of society. While the world often views China through the lens of competition or controversy, a closer look reveals a country that is shaping a new era with quiet determination. This revolution isn't loud, but it is profound, and its effects will be felt for a long time to come—not just in China, but worldwide..

5G and communication technologies: China's claim to global leadership

In 2019, engineers, politicians, and business leaders gathered in a glass-walled conference room in Shenzhen, the beating heart of China's technology industry. The air was filled with a mixture of tension and urgency. On the table was an ambitious goal: China would not just become a player in the global communications revolution, but lead it. 5G, the fifth generation of mobile technology, was the battleground on which this drama would unfold. For China, it was more than just technology—it was a question of national identity, economic power, and geopolitical influence.

In the years that followed, the world would witness an unprecedented race as China took the stage with companies like Huawei and ZTE to realize its vision of a connected future. But this rise was not without controversy, hurdles, and global tensions. How did China manage to position itself at the forefront of the 5G revolution, and what does this leadership mean for the world? The story of China's quest for communications technology dominance is one of innovation, strategy, and geopolitical chess. It doesn't begin with 5G, but rather stretches back to the dawn of Chinese modernization. In the 1980s, when Deng Xiaoping opened China's doors to the global economy, the country was a technological laggard.

Communications infrastructure was rudimentary, and most Chinese people didn't have access to landline telephones, let alone mobile networks. But the government recognized early on that technology was the key to economic and political strength. In the decades that followed, China invested heavily in education, research, and infrastructure to catch up. These efforts culminated in the development of 5G, a technology that promised not only faster internet but also a foundation for the next industrial revolution: the Internet of Things, autonomous vehicles, smart cities, and artificial intelligence.

5G is more than just an evolution of mobile communications. It is a paradigm shift. Compared to 4G, 5G not only offers higher speeds but also lower latency, allowing data to be transmitted in near real time. 5G can also connect a far greater number of devices simultaneously, making it the ideal platform for the Internet of Things. These characteristics make 5G a key technology for the future. But the development and global rollout of 5G poses more than just technical challenges—they are also a geopolitical minefield. Control over 5G networks means control over data, infrastructure, and, to some extent, a country's digital sovereignty. It's hardly surprising, then, that China, a country with a clear vision for its global role, set out to take the lead in this area.

The foundation for China's 5G ambitions was laid in the early 2000s when the country began building its own mobile communications industry. Companies like Huawei, originally a small startup from Shenzhen, grew into global giants during this period. Huawei invested heavily in research and development, often more than ten percent of its annual revenue. These investments paid off: Huawei developed not only cost-effective but also technologically advanced solutions that could compete with Western rivals such as Nokia and Ericsson. At the same time, the Chinese government relied on a combination of state support and strategic planning. The "Made in China 2025" program, launched in 2015, was a decisive step. It aimed to make China a global leader in key industries such as telecommunications, artificial intelligence, and robotics, with 5G identified as a central pillar.

A key moment in China's rise was the standardization of 5G technologies. The development of a global standard for mobile communications technologies is a complex process coordinated by international organizations such as the 3rd Generation Partnership Project (3GPP). China played an increasingly large role in this forum, which brings together engineers and experts from all over the world. Chinese companies like Huawei and ZTE contributed significantly to defining 5G standards by filing thousands of patents and submitting technical proposals. By 2020, Huawei held more 5G patents than any other company worldwide. These patents were not only a sign of technological expertise but also a strategic tool: They enabled Huawei to generate licensing revenue and play a central role in the global 5G supply chain.

But China's rise was not only a success story. It was also marked by mistrust and conflict. The United States, in particular, viewed China's 5G ambitions as a threat to its national security. Huawei was accused of having close ties to the Chinese government and potentially engaging in espionage. These allegations culminated in a series of sanctions in 2019 that restricted Huawei's access to American technologies, including semiconductors and software. The US also pressured its allies to exclude Huawei from their 5G networks, leading to bans in countries like Australia and the UK. These conflicts were more than just a trade dispute—they were an expression of a larger geopolitical competition for control over the digital infrastructure of the future.

Despite these challenges, China stayed the course. Domestically, 5G deployments advanced at an unprecedented pace. By 2020, China had already installed more 5G base stations than the rest of the world combined. Cities like Beijing, Shanghai, and Shenzhen became test laboratories for 5G applications, from autonomous buses to smart hospitals. These projects were not just technological experiments, but also demonstrations of strength. They were intended to show the world that China could not only keep up, but shape the future. At the same time, China exported its 5G technology to countries along the New Silk Road, particularly in Africa, Southeast Asia, and Latin America. These countries, often with limited resources, were receptive to China's offer: low-cost, turnkey 5G solutions, coupled with generous loans.

One example of China's global strategy is its cooperation with Ethiopia. In Addis Ababa, the country's capital, Huawei built a nationwide 5G network that not only improved communications but also laid the foundation for digital services such as mobile payment systems. Such projects were part of a larger vision: the Digital Silk Road, an ambitious plan to infuse the digital infrastructure of developing countries with Chinese technology. But this expansion also drew criticism. Some countries feared losing their digital sovereignty by becoming dependent on Chinese technology. Others pointed to data protection concerns, particularly in countries with authoritarian regimes, where 5G networks could potentially be used for surveillance.

The debate about 5G and China's role in it is complex and multifaceted. On the one hand, China has proven its technological and strategic ability to dominate a key industry. On the other hand, its rise has sparked suspicion and resistance, particularly in Western countries. For many observers, 5G symbolizes the larger competition between China and the West—a competition that is not just about technology, but also about values, influence, and power. In this context, it's important to take a sober view of China's success: It is the result of decades of investment, strategic planning, and a clear vision. At the same time, it raises questions that go far beyond technology: How can the world harness such a powerful technology without compromising its national security or autonomy? How can a global standard for communications be maintained when geopolitical tensions make cooperation difficult?

The story of China's 5G ambitions is far from over. As the country continues to invest in the next generation of communications technologies—6G is already on the horizon—time will tell whether it can maintain its leadership position. For the world, this means preparing for a future in which communications technologies not only create connections but also define power relations. In Shenzhen, where it all began, the lights of the skyscrapers continue to shine brightly. But behind the facades, a race rages whose outcome will shape the world for decades.

The development of 5G was not only a technological triumph for China, but also a cultural one. In the early days of mobile technology, the country was largely dependent on Western companies like Motorola and Nokia. For many Chinese, this dependence was a painful reminder of the country's technological backwardness. But with 5G, China has proven that it can not only catch up, but take the lead. This transformation has boosted the nation's self-confidence and inspired a new generation of engineers and entrepreneurs. At universities like Tsinghua University in Beijing and Zhejiang University in Hangzhou, young talent is flocking to electrical engineering and computer science programs, attracted by the prospect of being part of a global technological revolution.

A particularly fascinating aspect of China's 5G strategy is the role of public-private partnerships. While in Western countries, 5G development was largely driven by private companies such as Nokia, Ericsson, and Qualcomm, China pursued a hybrid approach. The government played a central role in coordination and financing, while companies such as Huawei and ZTE handled the technical implementation. This collaboration enabled China to efficiently pool resources and advance 5G deployment at a pace that often astounded Western countries. However, critics argue that this approach also carries risks. The close ties between government and companies have raised concerns, particularly regarding the independence of Chinese tech companies and their potential obligations to the government.

One example of this strategy is its cooperation with Pakistan. As part of the China-Pakistan Economic Corridor (CPEC), Huawei has initiated several 5G projects in cities such as Islamabad and Lahore. These projects have not only improved communications but also laid the foundation for digital services such as mobile payment systems and e-government platforms. Such projects are an example of China's ability to use technology as a tool for diplomatic influence. But they also raise questions. Critics point out that reliance on Chinese technology could endanger these countries' digital sovereignty. Others emphasize the advantages: For many developing countries, China's solutions are the only way to use modern technologies at affordable prices.

The global spread of China's 5G technology also has a cultural dimension. In many countries, especially in Africa and Asia, China's success is seen as an inspiration. For governments and companies in these regions, China is an example of how a country can catapult itself to the top of the technological world through its own efforts. This admiration has also created soft power: China is perceived not only as an economic power but also as a role model. But this perception is not without controversy. In Western countries, China's rise is often viewed with skepticism, particularly due to concerns about data protection, surveillance, and human rights.

The debate about 5G and China's role in it is a microcosm of the larger competition between China and the West. On the one hand, there is China, a country with a clear vision and a strategic approach that has enabled it to take the lead in a key industry. On the other side is the West, which is responding with a mixture of suspicion, innovation, and geopolitical strategy. For the world, this means preparing for a future in which communication technologies not only create connections but also define power relations. In this sense, China's 5G story is not only a technological one, but also a human one—a story of ambition, conflict, and the search for a place in a changing world.

Li-Fi: Data Transmission by Light—Technology, Potential, and Research in China

In a bustling research facility in Shanghai, where the hum of machines and the quiet murmurs of concentrated scientists fill the air, a simple LED lamp glows. But this lamp is more than just a light source—it transmits data at speeds that dwarf even the most modern cellular networks. This technology, known as Li-Fi, or Light Fidelity, uses visible light to send information wirelessly and promises a revolution in the way we connect to the digital world. While China has conquered the 5G world with companies like Huawei, the country is already turning its sights to the next frontier: communication via light. But what exactly makes Li-Fi so special, how could it complement or even replace our conventional internet, and how far has China progressed with this promising technology?

Imagine you're sitting in a café, and instead of searching for a Wi-Fi password, your smartphone automatically connects to the light from the ceiling lamp above you. In a fraction of a second, you can download a movie or stream a concert in the highest quality. Li-Fi works by switching light sources like LEDs on and off millions of times per second, so fast that the human eye doesn't notice them.

These light pulses encode data in binary form—an "on" for a one, an "off" for a zero. At the other end, a light sensor, such as a photodiode, captures these signals and converts them into electrical pulses that your device interprets as data. For the return channel, or upload, devices can send infrared light to communicate with the light source. The light spectrum used by Li-Fi is vast—about 10,000 times larger than the radio spectrum that powers Wi-Fi or 5G. In laboratories, researchers have already achieved speeds of over 200 gigabits per second, enough to transmit dozens of movies in one second.

The strengths of this technology are impressive. Because light doesn't penetrate walls, Li-Fi is inherently secure—a hacker would have to be physically in the same room to access the network. Unlike radio waves, which are often disrupted in densely populated cities or factories, Li-Fi remains free from electromagnetic interference. It is also energy-efficient because it can use existing lighting systems to illuminate and transmit data simultaneously. In hospitals, it could connect medical devices without affecting their sensitive electronics, while on airplanes, it enables high-speed internet without radio radiation. For some, Li-Fi is even an answer to health concerns because it doesn't generate electromagnetic waves like Wi-Fi or 5G. But despite these advantages, Li-Fi isn't perfect. It requires a direct line of sight between transmitter and receiver, meaning a book, hand, or wall can interrupt the connection. Its range is limited to a few meters, and in dark rooms it only works with additional infrared sources. Furthermore, devices like smartphones must be equipped with special sensors, which complicates costs and adoption.

Could Li-Fi one day replace the traditional internet as we know it? The answer is complex. In certain areas, Li-Fi has the potential to surpass Wi-Fi or cellular networks. In a factory, where robots need to exchange data in real time, Li-Fi could be the perfect solution because it is fast, secure, and interference-free. In military facilities, where security against eavesdropping is critical, it offers an alternative to vulnerable radio networks.

Imagine a smart city where streetlights not only illuminate but also send data to self-driving cars or pedestrians, such as traffic information or maps. But in private homes, where we want to move freely and stay connected across walls, Wi-Fi remains more flexible. Li-Fi is unlikely to replace the internet, but rather complement it, for example in hybrid networks where it is used for data-intensive tasks like 8K streaming, while Wi-Fi handles general connectivity.

The possibilities opened up by Li-Fi extend far beyond faster browsing. In a world where billions of devices—from refrigerators to traffic sensors—are interconnected, Li-Fi could form the foundation of the Internet of Things. It could power augmented reality headsets that deliver high-resolution images in real time or enable virtual surgeries where doctors work remotely with minimal delay.

Underwater, where radio waves are barely effective, diving robots or submarines could communicate using light. Cars could use their headlights to send crash warnings to other vehicles, while banks could use Li-Fi to secure sensitive transactions in shielded spaces. In poorer regions where building cell towers is expensive, simple LED bulbs could enable digital education or mobile payments. These visions demonstrate that Li-Fi isn't just a gadget, but a tool to change the world.

In China, a country that has already set global standards with 5G, research into Li-Fi is being pursued with great determination. In the laboratories of Fudan University in Shanghai, scientists have developed prototypes that enable internet access via simple light bulbs. Over a decade ago, these researchers began using light as a data carrier with the goal of making Li-Fi affordable and practical.

At the same time, China has made impressive progress in related fields such as laser-based communications. In early 2025, a Changchun-based company reported transmitting high-resolution satellite images at 100 gigabits per second via laser beams—a technology closely related to Li-Fi, demonstrating China's ability to precisely harness light for data transmission. This development even surpasses the performance of some Western satellite systems and hints at China's ambitions to dominate the next generation of communications.

Research in China is not only academic but also strongly focused on practical applications. In factories, companies are testing Li-Fi to control machines in real time, while the government is funding projects that incorporate optical communications into its vision of 6G networks. These future networks are expected to offer even faster and more reliable connections, and Li-Fi could play a key role. China is also involved in international bodies to set standards for Li-Fi, demonstrating that the country is committed not only to research but also to shaping the global market. These efforts are part of a larger strategy: Having proven its technological leadership with 5G, China aims to shape the digital future with technologies like Li-Fi.

But the road to widespread adoption of Li-Fi is still long. The technology needs to become more affordable, and everyday devices like laptops and smartphones need to be equipped with the necessary sensors. Furthermore, integration into existing infrastructure—for example, in offices or cities—requires significant investment. China, with its experience in rapidly expanding 5G networks, is well positioned to overcome these hurdles, but it will need international cooperation to establish Li-Fi worldwide. For the world, Li-Fi represents an opportunity to close the digital divide and create new forms of connectivity. In Shanghai, the LED lamp continues to shine, a silent symbol of a technology that could illuminate our future.

High-speed trains and infrastructure wonders

Over the past decade, China has undergone an unprecedented transformation in the world of infrastructure and mobility, one that has not only changed the face of the country but also set global standards for technological innovation and construction speed. We're talking about a network of high-speed trains that connects cities, crosses deserts, climbs mountains, and keeps millions of people moving—a system often described as the "modern marvel" of engineering. But behind the gleaming trains and futuristic stations lies a complex story of ambitious visions, economic challenges, technological breakthroughs, and societal change. This chapter tells the story of China's rise to high-speed infrastructure superpower, illuminating the mechanisms that enabled this transformation and examining the impact on its people, its economy, and global perception.

The story begins with a country determined, in the early 2000s, to modernize its infrastructure from the ground up. China, once known for its overcrowded, slow trains and bumpy roads, set out to revolutionize the mobility of its 1.4 billion people. By 2015, the country was already a leader in the length of its high-speed rail network, which at the time covered approximately 19,000 kilometers—more than the entire rest of the world combined.

But what happened in the following ten years was even more impressive: By 2025, the network grew to over 50,000 kilometers, a network that not only connected major metropolises like Beijing, Shanghai, and Guangzhou, but also catapulted remote regions like Xinjiang, Tibet, and Yunnan into the modern age of mobility. This development was no accident, but the result of a combination of government planning, technological innovation, and an unwavering will to shape the future of transportation.

Known in China as "Fuxing" (revival) and "Harmony," the high-speed trains are more than just a means of transportation. They are a symbol of China's ambitions, a feat of engineering capable of reaching speeds of up to 350 kilometers per hour while offering comfort, safety, and efficiency.

A traveler boarding one of these trains in Beijing in 2015 could reach Shanghai in just over four hours—a distance of over 1,200 kilometers that once took almost a full day. By 2025, this time had been further reduced by optimized routes and even faster trains, and new lines like the one between Beijing and Hong Kong made it possible to connect the two metropolises in under nine hours. But this speed and efficiency are just the tip of the iceberg. To understand the significance of this transformation, we need to delve deeper—into the technology, the politics, the economics, and the stories of the people experiencing this progress.

Building a Giant: Technology and Engineering

China's high-speed trains are the result of years of research, development, and a unique blend of domestic innovation and international expertise. When China began building its high-speed rail network in the 2000s, it initially imported technology from companies such as Siemens, Alstom, and Kawasaki. But instead of relying on foreign expertise, China pursued a strategy of "technology transfer." This policy required foreign companies to share their knowledge with Chinese partners to build local capacity. The result was the establishment of the China Railway Rolling Stock Corporation (CRRC), which is now the world's largest manufacturer of rolling stock. By 2015, CRRC had already developed its own models, such as the CRH380A, a train that not only competed with international standards but exceeded them in many ways.

The development of the Fuxing train, launched in 2017, marked a turning point. This train, entirely designed and produced in China, was a testament to the maturity of the Chinese railway industry. With a top speed of 350 kilometers per hour and advanced safety and comfort features such as low-vibration chassis and state-of-the-art onboard entertainment systems, the Fuxing set new standards. By 2025, Fuxing trains were in service on most major routes, and their reliability—with a punctuality rate of over 95 percent—made them a model for other countries.

But the true engineering feat lies not only in the trains themselves, but in the infrastructure that enables them. Over the past decade, China has built bridges, tunnels, and railway stations at a pace that astonishes even experts. One example is the Beijing-Zhangjiakou high-speed railway, built for the 2022 Winter Olympics. This line, which runs through mountainous terrain, includes the 12-kilometer-long Badaling Tunnel, which passes beneath the Great Wall of China—an engineering feat that combines precision and respect for cultural heritage. By 2025, China had built over 10,000 bridges and 15,000 tunnels, many in challenging terrain such as the karst mountains of Guizhou or the desert regions of Gansu. These structures are not only functional but also architecturally impressive, with stations such as the futuristic

Beijing South or Shanghai Hongqiao that resemble airports rather than traditional railway stations.

The challenge of building such a network in such a short time required innovative construction techniques. China relied on prefabricated components produced in factories and assembled on-site, which drastically reduced construction time. One example is the Danyang-Kunshan Bridge, which, at 164 kilometers, is the longest bridge in the world. It was completed in less than two years, a pace that would be unthinkable in other countries. This efficiency is the result of a combination of centralized planning, enormous financial resources, and a virtually inexhaustible pool of labor and engineers. But it did not come without costs—both financial and social.

But the story of China's high-speed rail network is not only one of economic ambition and societal change; it is, above all, one of technological and engineering feat that has redefined the boundaries of what is possible. The section on the construction of this behemoth deserves a deeper look, as the complexity and level of innovation of the technologies, as well as the engineering challenges overcome between 2015 and 2025, are central pillars of China's infrastructure miracle. The development of high-speed trains and their infrastructure is a fascinating interplay of precision, scale and an almost unprecedented ability to overcome seemingly insurmountable obstacles.

The technological evolution of Chinese high-speed trains began with a strategic decision that went far beyond simply importing technology. When China began building its network in the early 2000s, it relied heavily on foreign expertise. Trains like the CRH1, based on the technology of the

German ICE, or the CRH2, inspired by the Japanese Shinkansen, were the first steps into a new era of mobility. But China was not content to be a buyer. Through contracts requiring technology transfer, foreign companies committed to sharing their knowledge with Chinese partners. This led to the development of domestic capacity, which peaked between 2015 and 2025. The China Railway Rolling Stock Corporation (CRRC) played a key role in this. With over 200,000 employees and production facilities across China, CRRC became not only the backbone of the domestic railway industry but also a global player, controlling more than 50 percent of the global rail market by 2025.

A milestone in this development was the launch of the Fuxing train in 2017, hailed as "fully Chinese." The Fuxing, meaning "revival" in Chinese, was not only a symbol of national pride but also a technological statement. Its design addressed the unique challenges of the Chinese network, such as extreme climatic conditions—from the freezing winters of Heilongjiang to the scorching summers of Xinjiang—and the need to maintain high speeds over long distances. The trains featured an aerodynamic design that minimized drag and an advanced propulsion system that enabled smooth acceleration and braking. By 2025, various versions of the Fuxing trains were in operation, including models with sleeping cars for overnight routes and even autonomous versions tested on the Beijing-Zhangjiakou line. These autonomous trains used artificial intelligence to optimize schedules, reduce energy consumption, and minimize safety risks.

Safety has been a central aspect of technological development, especially after the tragic Wenzhou accident in 2011, which killed 40 people. This incident led to a comprehensive overhaul of safety protocols and technologies. By 2015, China had implemented a state-of-the-art train control system called CTCS (Chinese Train Control System), based on the European ETCS but adapted to the specific requirements of the Chinese network. CTCS uses a combination of ground-based sensors, satellite navigation, and real-time data transmission to prevent collisions and control trains with the utmost precision. By 2025, the system was refined to the point where it ensured near-perfect operational reliability, with a failure rate of less than 0.01 percent. Complementing this, the trains were equipped with advanced diagnostic systems capable of detecting and reporting potential mechanical problems in real time, before they caused failures.

The speed with which these projects were implemented is another marvel. China relied on a combination of standardized building elements and highly organized construction processes to minimize construction times. A video that went viral in 2019 showed how a train station in Fujian was rebuilt in just nine hours, thanks to an army of workers and precisely choreographed procedures. This efficiency was only possible thanks to the Chinese government's centralized control of the project, which was able to mobilize resources and labor on a scale unimaginable in other countries. But this speed also had its downsides. Working conditions on construction sites were often harsh, and reports of accidents and inadequate safety measures regularly made headlines. Nevertheless, national pride and the prospect of economic benefits drove the projects forward.

Another aspect of engineering excellence is the integration of high-speed rail into existing transportation systems. Often referred to as "city gates," the stations are more than just stops—they are transportation hubs that seamlessly connect trains, subways, buses, and even air services. Beijing South Railway Station, which was expanded in 2018, is an example of this integration. With an area of over 320,000 square meters and a capacity of 30,000 passengers per hour, it is one of the largest railway stations in the world. Its architecture, reminiscent of traditional Chinese palaces, combines cultural aesthetics with modern functionality, including energy-efficient lighting and intelligent passenger guidance systems.

The future of technology and engineering in China's high-speed rail network lies in exploring new frontiers. Maglev trains, based on magnetic levitation, are a promising field. The Shanghai Maglev line, in operation since 2004, was a first step, but new lines have been planned for 2025, including a connection between Guangzhou and Shenzhen that is expected to reach speeds of over 600 kilometers per hour. These trains float above the rails, eliminating friction and increasing both speed and energy efficiency. At the same time, China is experimenting with hyperloop technologies, which could move trains in vacuum tubes at speeds of up to 1,000 kilometers per hour. While these projects are still in development, they demonstrate China's ambition to shape the next generation of transportation.

The engineering and technological achievements of China's high-speed rail network are a reflection of the country's ability to turn vision into reality. They are the result of decades of hard work, strategic planning, and a tireless pursuit of progress. But they are also a reminder that such massive projects always come with trade-offs—be it in the form of environmental costs, social challenges, or financial risks. The story of building this behemoth is far from over, but it has already shown what is possible when a country pools its resources and will to shape the future.

The Economic Dimension: Investments and Challenges

The construction of the high-speed rail network was a colossal economic undertaking. Between 2015 and 2025, China invested an estimated over $1.5 trillion in its railway infrastructure, an amount that exceeds the budgets of many countries. These investments were largely financed by the Chinese government and state-owned banks, often through loans extended to the China Railway Corporation. While these investments stimulated economic growth—by creating millions of jobs in the construction and manufacturing industries—they also resulted in a significant debt burden. By 2025, the China Railway Corporation had accumulated debts exceeding $800 billion, raising questions about the system's long-term viability.

Despite these challenges, the high-speed rail network has proven to be an economic engine. It has accelerated urbanization by connecting smaller cities with metropolitan areas, creating new economic centers. Cities like Zhengzhou, once a provincial backwater, developed into logistics and trade centers thanks to their connections to the network. The trains also boosted tourism, as remote regions like the historic city of Xi'an or the scenic landscapes of Yangshuo became more accessible. For companies, the network meant shorter delivery times and better access to markets, which was particularly crucial in an export-oriented economy like China's.

Another economic benefit was the creation of a global brand. CRRC began exporting high-speed trains and technology to countries like Indonesia, Thailand, and even Europe. The Jakarta-Bandung line, which opened in 2023, was the first major overseas project built entirely with Chinese technology. By 2025, China had signed contracts for similar projects in over 20 countries, bringing not only economic but also geopolitical benefits. However, the high costs and dependence on state financing remained a risk repeatedly raised by critics.

The economic dimension of China's high-speed rail network and the associated urban infrastructure expansion between 2015 and 2025 is a fascinating chapter, illuminating the immense financial power, strategic planning, and complex challenges of a country that emerged in record time as a global infrastructure superpower. At the same time, this period marks a remarkable reversal in environmental awareness, demonstrating how China attempted to reconcile economic progress with sustainable practices. This development is a story of gigantic investments, economic multiplier effects, structural risks, and a growing understanding of the ecological consequences of such an ambitious project. The economic multiplier effects of these projects were enormous. According to World Bank estimates, every yuan invested in infrastructure generated approximately 2.5 yuan of additionnal economic activity.

This was particularly important in the years following the 2008 global economic crisis, when China used its infrastructure investments to stabilize economic growth. Between 2015 and 2025, the high-speed rail network created millions of jobs, both directly and indirectly, from engineers and construction workers to service staff in stations and trains. The logistics industry also benefited, as the fast and reliable connection between production centers and ports made supply chains more efficient. High-speed rail played a key role, particularly in the e-commerce sector, which experienced explosive growth in China during this period, by shortening delivery times for goods and reducing costs.

In parallel with these economic developments, between 2015 and 2025, China underwent a remarkable reversal in its environmental awareness, which had a lasting impact on infrastructure policy. In the early years of high-speed rail expansion, the speed of projects often took precedence over ecological considerations. The construction of bridges, tunnels, and lines through fragile ecosystems, such as the wetlands of the Yangtze River Delta or the forests of Yunnan, caused significant environmental damage. The immense demand for concrete and steel—China consumed more cement during this period than the United States did in the entire 20th century—contributed significantly to CO2 emissions. By 2015, China was the world's largest emitter of greenhouse gases, and infrastructure projects were a key driver of this development.

But starting in the mid-2010s, a shift in thinking began. The deteriorating air quality in cities like Beijing and growing public concern about environmental problems forced the government to make sustainability a priority. In the context of the high-speed network, this was reflected in several initiatives. First, the energy consumption of the trains was optimized. New models like the Fuxing CR400 were approximately 20 percent more energy-efficient than their predecessors by 2025, thanks to lighter materials and improved propulsion systems. Second, China began to integrate renewable energy into the grid. On the Beijing-Shanghai line, solar panels were installed along the line, covering approximately 10 percent of the electricity demand. Third, "green stations" were developed, such as the Hangzhou East Railway Station, which was equipped with energy-efficient air conditioning, rainwater harvesting, and green roofs.

Another step was the renaturalization of areas affected by construction. In Sichuan Province, where the Chengdu-Chongqing railway line runs through forests and river landscapes, the government launched reforestation programs to restore lost vegetation. By 2025, China had renaturalized over 100,000 hectares of land related to infrastructure projects, a sign of its growing commitment to environmental protection. Environmental impact assessments for new projects were also tightened to ensure that sensitive eco-systems were protected. These measures were not only a response to public pressure but also part of a global strategy to strengthen China's image as a responsible superpower, particularly in the run-up to the climate conferences of the 2020s.

Despite this progress, the environmental record remained mixed. The savings from using high-speed trains instead of cars or planes were significant—it is estimated that the network avoided approximately 60 million tons of CO2 per year by 2025. But the construction phase itself left a massive ecological footprint that can only be offset over the long term. Critics argued that China should have invested more in electrifying existing conventional lines or expanding public transport instead of focusing on prestigious megaprojects. Supporters, however, saw the network as an essential component of a low-carbon mobility strategy that would help China achieve its climate goals by 2060.

The economic dimension of the high-speed rail network and the reversal in environmental awareness reflect the duality of China's infrastructure miracle: on the one hand, a testament to the country's ability to implement large-scale projects with unprecedented speed and scale, and on the other, a reminder of the complexity of making such projects financially viable and ecologically sustainable. The coming years will show whether China can further expand this balance, but the progress between 2015 and 2025 suggests that the country is willing to learn from both its successes and its mistakes.

Social Impact: Changes in Everyday Life

For the people of China, the high-speed rail network has fundamentally changed life. It has redefined the way people travel, work, and connect with each other. The network has also facilitated labor migration. Millions of migrant workers who previously traveled on crowded, slow trains to their jobs in coastal cities can now commute faster and more comfortably. This has not only improved their quality of life but also promoted social mobility, as people from rural areas gained easier access to better job opportunities. However, not all effects have been positive. The construction of the lines led to forced relocations in some regions, and many villagers lamented the loss of farmland or traditional ways of life. The government offered compensation, but these were often criticized as inadequate.

Another aspect is the cultural connection the network has created. China is a country of enormous cultural and linguistic diversity, and the high-speed rail network has made it easier to experience this diversity. Today, a student from Shanghai can travel to Xi'an on the weekend to see the Terracotta Army or to Chengdu to sample the famous Sichuan cuisine. This mobility has increased awareness of the country's cultural diversity while fostering a sense of national cohesion. But it has also brought with it challenges, such as the pressure on urban infrastructure from the influx of tourists and commuters.

The social impact of China's high-speed rail network between 2015 and 2025 goes far beyond simply improving mobility. It has transformed the daily lives of millions of people, created new social dynamics, and fundamentally changed the understanding of distance, time, and community in a country of over 1.4 billion inhabitants. The high-speed trains, with their gleaming carriages and futuristic stations, are not only a symbol of technological progress, but also a catalyst for profound changes in people's everyday lives—from the way they travel and work to their family ties, their access to education, and their perception of China's cultural diversity. This transformation is a story of connection, opportunity, and the challenges that come with such rapid change.

A key aspect of this change has been the facilitation of labor migration. China is a country with one of the largest labor migration flows in the world, as millions of people move from rural areas to coastal cities to find work. Before the expansion of the high-speed rail network, these journeys were often arduous and time-consuming, particularly during the annual Chunyun period, the Chinese New Year, when hundreds of millions of people visit their home villages. High-speed rail has dramatically simplified this process. In 2025, a worker like Liu Fang, who works in a factory in Shenzhen, could reach her family in Henan Province in less than six hours, instead of the previously typical 20 hours on overcrowded regional trains. This improved mobility has not only reduced physical strain but also strengthened emotional connections with families and communities, as regular visits have become more affordable and feasible.

Another significant impact of the network has been the strengthening of tourism and cultural connectivity. China is a country with enormous cultural diversity, from the Buddhist temples of Tibet to the historical sites in Xi'an. Before the high-speed rail network, many of these places were difficult to reach for the general public, especially those with limited income or time. With the opening of routes such as the Beijing-Xi'an Line or the Shanghai-Kunming Line, it became possible to reach such destinations in a few hours. In 2025, for example, a family from Guangzhou could travel to Huangshan on the weekend to see the famous Misty Mountains or to Lijiang to experience the culture of the Naxi minority.

This easier access not only boosted domestic tourism—in 2025, China recorded over 6 billion domestic trips per year—but also increased awareness of the country's cultural diversity. For many Chinese, it was the first time they explored regions beyond their home province, contributing to a renewed sense of national solidarity.

But the social impact was not entirely positive. The construction of the high-speed rail lines led to significant social tensions in many regions, particularly through forced relocations. In provinces such as Zhejiang and Anhui, entire villages were relocated to make way for new lines or train stations. Those affected, such as the Wang family from a village near Hangzhou, reported inadequate compensation and the loss of their traditional way of life. "We lost the land our family had farmed for generations," said Ms. Wang. "The money we received wasn't enough to start a new life somewhere else." Such stories were not isolated incidents, and local protests against relocations regularly made headlines. The government responded with improved compensation programs, but tensions persisted in many regions.

Another problem was the growing gap between those who benefited from the network and those who could not. While wealthier urban residents used the trains to enrich their leisure time or careers, the system remained unaffordable for many poorer citizens. Although ticket prices were relatively moderate compared to airplanes, they often still represented a financial hurdle for people in rural areas. This led to criticism that the network primarily served the needs of the urban middle class, while marginalized groups benefited only to a limited extent. To address this problem, the government introduced subsidies for certain routes in 2025 to make the trains more accessible to low-income citizens, but the implementation of these measures was uneven.

The high-speed trains also spawned new social behaviors. A distinct culture of travel developed on the trains themselves, characterized by cutting-edge technology and a focus on efficiency. Passengers could use free Wi-Fi, watch movies on screens, or work in quiet zones on the Fuxing trains. At the same time, the high punctuality rate—over 97 percent in 2025—led to a new sense of time. Delays, often accepted in other countries, became rare in China, shaping people's expectations of efficiency and reliability. But this culture of speed also brought pressure: Many commuters reported a sense of their lives accelerating, as the ability to travel long distances quickly often came with higher expectations of productivity and flexibility.

The changes to everyday life brought about by the high-speed rail network reflect the dynamics that shaped China between 2015 and 2025: a country that was modernizing at breathtaking speed but also faced the challenges of inequality, displacement, and social change. For millions of people, the trains represented freedom, opportunity, and a new way of experiencing the world. For others, they symbolized the sacrifices that progress demanded. This ambivalence is what makes the network's social impact so fascinating – it's a testament to the transformative power of infrastructure, but also a reminder that progress always comes at a price.

Environment and Sustainability: A Double-Edged Sword

The environmental and sustainability dimension of China's high-speed rail network between 2015 and 2025 is a complex and multifaceted issue that highlights the tension between technological progress and ecological responsibility. While high-speed trains are celebrated as an environmentally friendly alternative to cars and airplanes, the construction and operation of the network, as well as the associated major infrastructure projects, raise significant questions about sustainability. This ambivalence reflects China's efforts to reconcile its ambitious development goals with growing global and domestic pressure to reduce environmental impact and create a more sustainable future. The story of the network's environmental performance is marked by impressive progress, but also by challenges that demonstrate the difficulty of balancing progress and sustainability in a country of China's size and ambition.

One of the greatest advantages of high-speed trains from an environmental perspective is their efficiency compared to other modes of transport. A train like the Fuxing CR400, which is used on most major routes, consumes about one-third the energy of an airplane and less than half the energy of a car per passenger-kilometer. By 2025, the network had helped to significantly reduce the much-cited CO2 emissions in the transport sector, particularly on busy routes like Beijing-Shanghai, where hundreds of thousands of passengers used the trains every day. According to a study by the Chinese Ministry of Transport, high-speed trains prevented approximately 70 million tons of CO2 emissions annually between 2015 and 2025, compared to a scenario in which the same number of journeys would have been made by plane or car. This made the network a central component of China's strategy to achieve its climate goals.

Another positive aspect was the reduction in dependence on fossil fuels in the transport sector. High-speed trains are fully electrified, and China has significantly increased the share of renewable energy in its electricity mix over the past decade. By 2025, approximately 30 percent of the electricity for the railway network came from renewable sources, particularly wind and solar power.

One example is the Qinghai-Tibet railway, which is partially powered by solar energy generated by plants on the region's high plateaus. This integration of renewable energy has not only reduced the environmental impact of the trains themselves but has also served as a model for other sectors seeking ways to diversify their energy sources.

But the environmental impact of the high-speed rail network is by no means entirely positive. The construction of the infrastructure—including more than 50,000 kilometers of track, thousands of bridges and tunnels, and vast station complexes—was an enormous ecological stress test. Added to this was the ecological damage caused by construction in sensitive areas such as the wetlands of Lake Poyang and the forests of Guangxi Province. These projects led to the destruction of habitats, water pollution, and the disruption of migration routes for wildlife, with long-term impacts on biodiversity.

The social and environmental costs of construction were particularly felt in rural areas. In Yunnan Province, where the Kunming-Dali railway runs through tropical rainforests, large areas of deforestation were destabilized, destabilizing local ecosystems and threatening the livelihoods of indigenous communities. Environmental activists criticized the fact that environmental impact assessments in the early years of the expansion were often conducted hastily to meet the government's strict timelines. By 2018, public criticism of such practices had intensified, forcing the government to introduce stricter regulations. These new regulations requireed more detailed environmental studies and public consultations, but implementation was uneven, and in many cases, economic priorities continued to prevail.

Another aspect of the environmental debate was energy consumption during construction. The construction of tunnels such as the Gaoligong Tunnel in Yunnan, which is over 34 kilometers long, required the use of heavy machinery and explosives, which consumed enormous amounts of energy and caused local air and water pollution. At the same time, the displacement of millions of tons of earth and rock led to soil erosion and changes in local water systems. These problems were particularly noticeable in geologically unstable regions such as the Sichuan Basin, where landslides became more frequent after the construction of railway lines through mountainous terrain. The government responded with measures such as erosion control walls and renaturation projects, but these often only partially repaired the damage.

Despite these challenges, China made significant progress toward more sustainable infrastructure between 2015 and 2025. A key to this was the adoption of so-called "green construction technologies." Many new stations, such as Xi'an North Railway Station, were built with energy-efficient materials and equipped with technologies such as solar-powered air conditioning and rainwater collection systems. These stations served as models for sustainable architecture and were often promoted as "eco-hubs," reducing energy consumption by up to 40 percent. China also began incurporating recycled materials into the construction of new lines, for example, by using recycled concrete for foundations and embankments.

Further progress was the development of low-emission construction processes. In Jiangsu Province, the government experimented with modular construction techniques, in which track sections were prefabricated in factories and assembled on site, reducing energy consumption and waste. These techniques were applied to approximately 30 percent of new lines by 2025, marking an important step toward more sustainable construction practices. At the same time, China invested in research and development to further minimize the environmental impact of high-speed rail. One example is the low-energy train pilot project on the Beijing-Tianjin line, which tested hydrogen as an alternative energy source. Although this technology was not yet widely deployed in 2025, it demonstrated the potential for an even greener future for the network.

Public perception of environmental problems also played an important role. In the early 2010s, environmental issues in China were often secondary to economic growth. However, with the rise of air pollution in cities like Beijing and growing global attention to climate change, public opinion began to put more pressure on the government. Social media platforms like Weibo became a forum for environmental activists to point out the damage caused by infrastructure projects and demand transparency. This movement led to greater public involvement in the planning of new lines, especially after 2020, when the government began making public consultations mandatory for major projects.

Despite this progress, the environmental impact of the high-speed rail network remains mixed. The positive impacts—such as reducing emissions by shifting traffic from road and air to rail—are undeniable, but the environmental costs of construction and the challenges of restoring degraded ecosystems remain significant. China has shown that it is capable of responding to criticism and developing innovative solutions, but the question remains whether these measures are sufficient to address the long-term environmental impacts. The years 2015 to 2025 were a turning point in which China began to seriously integrate sustainability into its infrastructure policy, but the road to truly green mobility is still long.

Global Perspectives: China as a Role Model and Competitor

The high-speed rail network has put China in the spotlight not only domestically but also internationally. Countries like India, Brazil, and the United States have gazed with amazement at China's progress while struggling with their own infrastructure projects. China's ability to deliver complex projects in record time has inspired many, but also stoked fears. In Europe, where high-speed trains like the TGV and ICE have been in operation for decades, China is increasingly seen as a competitor, particularly due to its aggressive export strategies. Projects like the Belgrade-Budapest railway, built with Chinese financing and technology, demonstrate how China is expanding its influence in Europe.

But China's involvement is not viewed positively everywhere. In countries like Malaysia and Thailand, there has been controversy over the costs and terms of Chinese loans, often granted as part of the Belt and Road Initiative. Critics speak of a "debt trap" that could drive smaller countries into dependence on China. Nevertheless, interest in Chinese technology remains high, especially in developing countries impressed by the speed and efficiency of Chinese construction.

The global perspectives on China's high-speed rail network between 2015 and 2025 reveal a fascinating picture of a country that has established itself not only as a technological and economic leader, but also as an influential player on the international stage.

China's unprecedented success in building a high-speed rail network spanning over 50,000 kilometers has attracted worldwide attention, both as a source of inspiration for other nations and as a challenge to established industrialized countries. China's ability to implement complex infrastructure projects with breathtaking speed and precision has made it a role model for developing countries, while simultaneously being perceived as a competitor for Western nations grappling with their own infrastructure challenges. This dual role—role model and competitor—is closely intertwined with China's geopolitical ambitions, its economic expansion, and the controversies that surround its global presence.

China's high-speed rail network has inspired other countries to rethink their own infrastructure goals. In developing countries, which often struggle with outdated transportation systems and limited resources, the Chinese model is viewed as a blueprint. The speed with which China built lines like the Beijing-Guangzhou line—a 2,300-kilometer link completed in less than five years—has impressed governments in Asia, Africa, and Latin America.

A prominent example is Indonesia, where the Jakarta-Bandung high-speed rail line, which opened in 2023, was hailed as a milestone. This 142-kilometer project, realized entirely with Chinese technology and financing, reduced travel time between the two cities from over three hours to about 40 minutes. For Indonesia, it was not just an infrastructure project but a symbol of modernization and economic revival. Similar projects were initiated in countries such as Thailand, where the Bangkok-Nakhon Ratchasima line was under construction until 2025, and in Laos, where the Vientiane-Boten line connected the remote nation to the Chinese market.

These international projects are part of China's "Belt and Road Initiative" (BRI), a global infrastructure strategy aimed at strengthening trade routes and expanding China's influence. By 2025, China had signed contracts for railway projects in over 30 countries, from Pakistan to Ethiopia. The China Railway Rolling Stock Corporation (CRRC), the world's leading manufacturer of rolling stock, played a key role in this, not only supplying trains but also offering technical expertise and maintenance services. These exports were an economic boon to China, creating jobs and boosting demand for Chinese products such as steel and electronics. At the same time, they strengthened China's geopolitical influence, as countries dependent on Chinese loans and technology often developed a closer political alignment with Beijing.

But China's role as a role model is not without controversy. In many countries participating in the BRI, there are concerns about the financial sustainability of the projects. The loans China provides for infrastructure projects often come with high interest rates and strict repayment terms, leading to fears that smaller countries could fall into a "debt trap." One example is Sri Lanka, where the Hambantota port, built with Chinese loans, was leased to China after the country defaulted on its debt. Similar controversies arose in Malaysia, where the cost of the East Coast Rail Link sparked heated political debate. By 2025, China had responded to these criticisms by offering more flexible financing terms and adapting more to local needs, but mistrust remained in some regions.

In developed countries, China is perceived less as a role model than as a competitor. In Europe, where high-speed trains such as the French TGV and the German ICE have been in use for decades, China's rise has raised concerns. The efficiency and cost advantages of Chinese technology—a Fuxing train costs about half the price of a comparable European model—have made CRRC a serious competitor in the global market. Projects like the Belgrade-Budapest railway, built with Chinese financing and technology, demonstrate how China is expanding its influence in Europe. This has led to tensions, particularly in the European Union, where some member states fear that Chinese investments could undermine their economic and political independence. By 2025, countries like Germany and France had begun to introduce stricter requirements for foreign investment in critical infrastructure to protect themselves against Chinese competition.

Even in the United States, where the expansion of high-speed rail lags far behind China, China's success is viewed with a mixture of admiration and concern. Projects like the planned California High-Speed Rail, which has been in the planning stages for decades, stand in stark contrast to China's ability to build lines in a few years. This has led to discussions about the need to modernize American infrastructure, but also to warnings about overreliance on Chinese technology. An attempt to build a high-speed rail line in Texas with Chinese participation failed in 2020 due to political and security concerns. These reactions highlight how China's rise as an infrastructure superpower raises not only economic but also strategic questions.

Another aspect of the global perspective is the cultural and technological soft power that China exerts through its high-speed network. The futuristic stations, punctual and comfortable trains, and impressive engineering feats such as the

Nanpanjiang Bridge have reinforced China's image as a modern, innovative country. International media regularly reported on these achievements, and visitors from around the world who traveled on a Fuxing train were often impressed by the efficiency and comfort. This positive perception has helped China reinforce its narrative as a global leader, especially in contrast to countries whose infrastructure projects are often plagued by delays and cost overruns.

Nevertheless, there are also critical voices questioning China's approach. Environmental organizations around the world have pointed out that BRI projects often come with significant environmental costs, especially in countries with weak environmental regulations. In Pakistan, for example, the construction of the China-Pakistan Economic Corridor railway led to soil erosion and water pollution, burdening local communities. This criticism has prompted China to promote "green BRI" initiatives that incorporate more sustainable construction practices and renewable energy, but the implementation of these promises is still underway.

The global perspective on China's high-speed rail network reveals a country that has rewritten the rules of infrastructure policy. As a role model, it inspires nations striving for rapid modernization, while as a competitor, it challenges established powers to rethink their own standards. But with this role comes responsibilities – financial, environmental, and geopolitical. The years 2015 to 2025 have shown that China is ready to take on these challenges, but the long-term effects of its global ambitions will continue to concern the world for a long time to come.

The Future: Where Does the Road Lead?

In 2025, China is at a crossroads. The high-speed rail network is undoubtedly a triumph, but there is still much to do. The government has plans to expand the network to 70,000 kilometers by 2035, with a focus on connecting even more remote regions. At the same time, pressure is growing to make the system more sustainable and financially viable. New technologies such as Maglev trains, which can reach speeds of over 600 kilometers per hour, are already in the testing phase, and the first commercial Maglev line between Shanghai and Hangzhou is expected to open in 2027.

But the biggest challenge will be striking the balance between growth and sustainability. The coming years will show whether China can further refine its model and cement its position as a global leader in infrastructure. For the people who travel across the country every day on the gleaming Fuxing trains, one thing is clear: the mobility available to them today was unthinkable ten years ago. It is a story of progress, of challenges, and of a country that dared to redefine the future of mobility.

The future of China's high-speed rail network offers a fascinating glimpse into the continued development of a system already considered one of the modern world's greatest infrastructural wonders. In 2025, China stands at a pivotal point where the achievements of the past decade—a network of over 50,000 kilometers that has connected millions of people and revolutionized the economy—serve as a springboard for even more ambitious goals. The question "Where does the road lead?" is not only about the technical and economic development of the network, but also about how China shapes its role as a global leader in mobility, strikes the balance between growth and sustainability, and meets the needs of its population in a changing world. The coming years promise innovations that will further push the boundaries of what is possible, but also challenges that will force the country to carefully consider its priorities.

China is also researching futuristic technologies such as Hyperloop systems, which could move trains in vacuum tubes at speeds of up to 1,000 kilometers per hour. A pilot project in Zhejiang Province, which entered the testing phase in 2025, is investigating the feasibility of such systems for freight and passenger transport. Although Hyperloop is still in its early stages and faces technical and financial hurdles, China's willingness to invest in such technologies demonstrates its ambition to define the next generation of mobility. These innovations could not only revolutionize the domestic network but also strengthen China's position as an exporter of cutting-edge technology, as countries such as India and Brazil have already expressed interest in such solutions.

Another future focus is the digitalization and automation of the network. As early as 2025, autonomous trains were tested on some routes, such as the Beijing-Zhangjiakou line, which use artificial intelligence to optimize schedules, reduce energy consumption, and increase safety. These trains use advanced sensors and data analytics to consider weather conditions, track conditions, and passenger flows in real time. By 2030, China plans to have approximately 20 percent of its high-speed network fully autonomous, which should reduce operating costs and further increase efficiency. At the same time, the integration of 5G and, in the future, 6G technologies will improve connectivity on trains, allowing passengers to work, stream, or communicate seamlessly—an aspect that is particularly attractive to business travelers and the younger generation.

Sustainability will be another crucial factor for the future of the network. Given China's international commitments to achieve carbon neutrality by 2060, the country is under pressure to make its infrastructure projects more environmentally friendly. Future lines are expected to increasingly use renewable energy, and plans call for at least 50 percent of the network's electricity needs to be met by solar, wind, and hydropower by 2035. New construction projects are increasingly being planned according to strict environmental standards, with a focus on minimizing land use and using recycled materials. One example is the planned Shenzhen-Zhanjiang line, which runs along the coast and is specifically designed to protect fragile coastal ecosystems by using elevated tracks and environmentally friendly construction techniques. These efforts reflect a growing awareness that progress cannot come at the expense of the environment and could serve as a model for other countries.

However, the economic viability of the network remains one of the biggest challenges. The China Railway Corporation's enormous debt, which exceeded US$900 billion in 2025, requires innovative financing models to make the system viable in the long term. One strategy is to increase the involvement of private investors, who invest in new lines and stations through public-private partnerships (PPPs). One example is the Guangzhou-Shenzhen-Hong Kong corridor, where private companies received shares in the real estate revenues from the station sites. At the same time, the government plans to increase revenue by expanding premium services such as business-class carriages and tourist experience trains running on scenic routes like the Chengdu-Jiuzhaigou Line. These measures are intended to reduce the financial burden without limiting accessibility for the general public.

The social impact of future development will also be important. The network has the potential to further reduce regional inequalities by better connecting remote areas to economic centers. However, this will require targeted measures to ensure that low-income groups also reap the benefits. Plans for subsidized tickets and special fares for students and senior citizens are already under discussion to promote social inclusion. At the same time, the government will face the challenge of managing the social tensions that further expansion could create, especially in regions where land expropriation and relocation are necessary. Transparent communication and fair compensation will be crucial to maintaining public trust.

Globally, China will further expand its role as an infrastructure leader. Exports of high-speed trains and technologies to Belt and Road Initiative countries will increase, and China plans to implement railway projects in over 50 countries by 2035. At the same time, the country will seek to counter criticism of its "debt-trap" diplomacy by developing more sustainable and transparent financing models.

The future of the high-speed rail network is a story of vision, innovation, and responsibility. China has proven capable of achieving great things, but the coming years will show whether it can leverage this legacy to create mobility that is not only fast and efficient, but also sustainable and inclusive. The path leads in a direction the world will be watching closely, as China's decisions will shape not only its own country but the global mobility landscape.

E-mobility and the transport revolution

Li Wei, a taxi driver from Beijing, sat behind the wheel of an electric car for the first time in late 2015. The car, a BYD e6, hummed quietly as it glided through the bustling streets of the capital. For Li, it was more than just a new vehicle; it was a window into a future China was shaping at breathtaking speed. Little did he know at the time that within a decade, his country would revolutionize the world mobility stage, transforming from congested, smog-filled metropolises to a network of electric vehicles, high-speed trains, and smart infrastructure.

The story of electric mobility in China doesn't begin with a grand bang, but rather with a series of pragmatic decisions rooted in the country's challenges. At the beginning of the decade, China faced a double crisis: rampant air pollution in its cities, and a growing dependence on imported oil. In Beijing, Shanghai, and other megacities, clear-sky days had become rare. The smog that settled over the cities like a gray veil was not only a health hazard but also a political problem. The growing middle class began to demand clean air and a livable environment. At the same time, the geopolitical situation was tense: around 60 percent of the oil China needed came from abroad, making the country vulnerable. Electromobility offered a solution that made both ecological and strategic sense.

The Chinese government recognized early on that electric vehicles represented not only an environmental project but also an economic opportunity. As early as 2009, the country had launched an ambitious program called "Ten Cities, One Thousand Vehicles," which promoted the use of electric buses and taxis in selected cities. But 2015 marked a turning point. That year, the government set a clear roadmap: By 2020, there would be five million electric vehicles on China's roads, and by 2025, the country would be a world leader in the production and use of electric vehicles. Subsidies were introduced that provided financial relief to electric car buyers, while manufacturers such as BYD, NIO, and Xpeng invested in research and development with government support. At the same time, the expansion of a nationwide network of charging stations began, laying the foundation for the e-mobility revolution.

Li Wei, our taxi driver, was one of the first to benefit from these measures. His BYD e6 became affordable thanks to government subsidies, and the city of Beijing provided charging stations in his neighborhood. But the transition was not without hurdles. His car's range was about 300 kilometers—sufficient for a workday, but tight when customers drove long distances. Charging times of several hours meant he had to plan his trips carefully. Furthermore, the technology was still immature: batteries were expensive, and the infrastructure for fast charging was nonexistent in many parts of the city. Nevertheless, Li sensed a change. His customers, especially young professionals, began to prefer electric taxis. They were quieter, cleaner, and felt like a step into the future.

Parallel to the promotion of electric cars, China invested heavily in expanding its public transportation systems. High-speed trains, connecting cities like Beijing and Shanghai in a few hours, became the backbone of interurban mobility. By 2025, China had the world's largest network of high-speed rail lines, with over 50,000 kilometers of track, accounting for more than two-thirds of global capacity. These trains, traveling at speeds of up to 350 kilometers per hour, were not only a symbol of technological progress but also a catalyst for the country's economic integration. Cities that were once isolated suddenly became accessible, fueling trade, tourism, and the exchange of ideas.

In the cities themselves, metro systems grew at a pace that astonished even Western observers. Cities like Shenzhen, which already had a modern metro network in 2015, doubled their track length within a decade. New lines were built in record time, often with the help of tunnel boring machines operating around the clock. These systems were not only efficient but also increasingly electrified. In Guangzhou, for example, by 2025, almost all subways were powered by renewable energy, a move that drastically reduced the city's CO2 emissions. For commuters like Zhang Mei, a young engineer from Shenzhen, this meant not only shorter travel times but also a quality of life she could not have imagined ten years ago. "I used to spend an hour in traffic jams," she said. "Now I can get to the office in 20 minutes, and the air is so much cleaner."

But China's mobility revolution was more than just a story of cars and trains. It was also a digital transformation. With the rise of smartphone apps like Didi Chuxing, which were China's equivalent of Uber, access to mobility was democratized. Suddenly, people in remote suburbs could call an electric taxi or rent a car-sharing vehicle with just a few clicks. These platforms integrated various modes of transport—from e-bikes to buses to subways—into a unified system that worked seamlessly. For someone like Li Wei, this meant a new way of working. Instead of searching for customers on the street, he received orders through the Didi app, which helped him optimize his routes and minimize empty runs.

A crucial factor in the success of this transformation was China's ability to integrate technologies like artificial intelligence and the Internet of Things into mobility. Cities like Hangzhou introduced intelligent traffic management systems that controlled traffic lights in real time to avoid congestion. Sensors at intersections and highways collected data that was analyzed in central data centers to optimize traffic flows and prevent accidents. These systems were so effective that by 2025, Hangzhou was considered one of the first cities in the world where traffic flowed almost seamlessly. For drivers like Li Wei, this was a relief, but it also meant an adjustment: his job was increasingly shaped by algorithms that influenced his routes and income.

Another key element was the expansion of charging infrastructure. In 2015, the lack of charging stations was one of the biggest obstacles to the adoption of electric vehicles. But China tackled the problem with typical determination. State-owned energy companies like State Grid and private players like Teld built a network of fast-charging stations spanning highways, parking lots, and residential areas. By 2025, China had more than two million public charging points, more than the rest of the world combined. In Shanghai, for example, you could find a charging station on almost every major street, often with rapid charging options that charged a vehicle in less than 20 minutes. For Li Wei, this meant he could now use his breaks productively instead of waiting for hours for a free outlet.

The role of battery technology in this story cannot be underestimated. In early 2015, batteries were expensive and had limited energy density, limiting the range of electric vehicles. But through massive investments in research and development, Chinese companies like CATL and BYD managed to drastically reduce the cost of lithium-ion batteries. By 2025, prices had fallen to below $100 per kilowatt-hour, a turning point that made electric vehicles competitive with internal combustion engines. At the same time, new technologies like solid-state batteries improved safety and range. For consumers like Zhang Mei, this meant that electric cars were not only environmentally friendly, but also practical and affordable. Her NIO ES8, which she bought in 2023, could travel over 500 kilometers on a single charge—more than enough for her daily commutes and weekend getaways.

But the electric mobility revolution was not without controversy. Critics pointed out that battery production was environmentally damaging, especially in regions like Inner Mongolia, where coal-fired power plants provided a large portion of the electricity. The dependence on rare earth elements and metals like lithium and cobalt also raised ethical questions, as mining often took place under questionable conditions. The Chinese government responded by promoting recycling programs and investing in alternative technologies like sodium-ion batteries, which require fewer critical raw materials. Nevertheless, these challenges remained a shadow over the progress that had been made.

Another aspect that is often overlooked is the social dimension of the change. For people like Li Wei, the transition to electric mobility brought both opportunities and uncertainties. On the one hand, platforms like Didi offered new sources of income and flexibility. On the other hand, automation and the introduction of autonomous vehicles led to fears of job losses. In cities like Shanghai, the first pilot projects with self-driving taxis, operated by companies like AutoX, began in 2024. For Li, this was a wake-up call. He began training to pursue a new career in electric vehicle maintenance. His story reflects the experiences of many Chinese who have had to reinvent themselves in a rapidly changing world.

The international dimension of China's e-mobility revolution is also remarkable. Until 2025, China was still a laggard in the global automotive industry, dominated by brands like Toyota, Volkswagen, and Mercedes. But by focusing on electric vehicles, Chinese companies managed to change the rules of the game. Brands like NIO, XPeng, and BYD not only conquered the domestic market but also expanded into Europe, Southeast Asia, and even North America. Their vehicles combined affordable prices with cutting-edge technology and maximum convenience, such as over-the-air updates and integrated AI. By 2025, China was the world's largest exporter of electric vehicles, a testament to the competitiveness of its industry.

The impact of this transformation extended far beyond the automotive industry. The massive expansion of renewable energy—particularly solar and wind power—was fueled by demand for clean electricity for electric vehicles and trains. By 2025, China met over 40% of its electricity needs from renewable sources, an impressive leap compared to 2015. This not only reduced CO2 emissions but, more importantly, improved air quality in cities. For people like Zhang Mei, this was tangible: "I remember barely being able to see the stars as a child in Shenzhen," she said. "Today, clear nights are normal."

The cultural impact of e-mobility was also profound. Electric vehicles became a symbol of progress and prosperity, especially for the younger generation. In cities like Beijing and Shanghai, it was not uncommon to see young couples proudly displaying their new electric SUVs in front of their homes. At the same time, improved mobility fostered a new lifestyle. Weekend trips to the mountains or the seaside became more affordable and easier as charging infrastructure expanded even in rural areas. For many Chinese, the freedom offered by electric mobility was more than just practical—it was an expression of change and opportunity.

Nevertheless, challenges remained. Rapid urbanization and population growth put pressure on infrastructure, even in cities with advanced transportation systems. At the same time, dependence on critical raw materials and the social costs of transformation raised questions that had not yet been fully resolved. The introduction of autonomous vehicles and the automation of the transportation sector brought new uncertainties, especially for workers like Li Wei who were being displaced from traditional jobs. But China's ability to find pragmatic solutions—whether through government support, innovation, or international cooperation—gave hope that these challenges could be overcome.

At the end of 2025, Li Wei stood in front of his new job, an electric vehicle maintenance center in Shenzhen. His journey from taxi driver to technician had not been easy, but it was a reflection of the transformation China had undergone. From smog-choked streets to clean cities, from combustion engines to electric vehicles, from isolated villages to connected metropolises – China's mobility revolution has been a story of ambition, innovation and adaptability. For Li, it was a personal journey that not only secured his livelihood but also gave him a sense of pride in being part of a larger movement.

E-Mobility in the Commercial and Private Sector

What once began as an ambitious experiment is now a revolution that is transforming the global automotive market. China is not only the largest producer and consumer of electric vehicles, but also a center of innovation rewriting the rules of mobility. Electric mobility in China is more than just a technological development; it is a social, economic, and political phenomenon. In the streets of Beijing, where smog once obscured visibility, air quality has noticeably improved, a direct result of the government's aggressive promotion of electric vehicles. For over a decade, China has been paving the way for an electric future with a combination of subsidies, regulatory incentives, and infrastructure investments.

But what makes China's approach so unique? How did a country that was dominated by bicycles and simple combustion-engine vehicles just a few decades ago manage to overshadow the global automotive industry? To understand this, we need to look at the various facets of this transformation: the policy framework, the technological breakthroughs, the role of companies like BYD and NIO, the impact on the private and commercial sectors, and the challenges that still lie ahead.

Back in 2009, China launched the "Ten Cities, One Thousand Buses" program, which aimed to integrate electric buses into public transport on a large scale. Shenzhen, now a global symbol of sustainable mobility, was one of the first cities to be included in this program. By 2017, Shenzhen had converted its entire bus fleet of over 17,000 vehicles to electric buses—a milestone that garnered worldwide attention. However, this program was just the beginning. The government introduced generous subsidies for the purchase of electric vehicles, appealing to both private buyers and commercial fleet operators. These subsidies covered up to 50 percent of the purchase price, making electric cars affordable for many.

Another ingenious move was the introduction of a license plate system that favors electric vehicles. Obtaining a license plate is notoriously difficult in many Chinese cities. For conventional combustion-engine vehicles, which carry blue license plates, waiting times can be years, and the cost of a license plate often runs into the tens of thousands of euros. Green license plates for electric vehicles, on the other hand, are issued more quickly, and there are fewer restrictions on their use in cities with strict traffic regulations. This incentive has encouraged many to switch to electric cars, even if they also purchase a luxury combustion-engine vehicle to circumvent urban driving bans.

However, government support went far beyond subsidies. China invested heavily in infrastructure, particularly in a comprehensive network of charging stations. Today, the country has more than 1.8 million public charging points, more than the US and Europe combined. In cities like Shenzhen, charging stations are so ubiquitous that the fear of running out of battery—so-called range anxiety—is a thing of the past for many drivers. This infrastructure has boosted not only the private sector but also the commercial sector, particularly in areas such as logistics and public transportation.

Yet China's political strategy has been not only about incentives, but also about competition. While Western countries are often reluctant to increase government intervention in the economy, China has created a mix of planned economy and free-market competition. The government set clear goals, such as requiring the majority of vehicles sold to be electric by 2035, while leaving room for innovation and competition. This approach has led to the explosive growth of EV startups, which are vying for market share and innovating at a pace that often astounds Western manufacturers.

For the average Chinese, electric mobility is more than just an environmentally friendly alternative—it's a symbol of progress and modernity. On the busy streets of Shanghai or Hangzhou, you can see young professionals in gleaming electric cars from manufacturers like NIO or Xpeng, equipped with state-of-the-art touchscreens and voice control. These vehicles are not just a means of transportation, but also an expression of a lifestyle that combines technology, sustainability, and prestige.

The popularity of electric cars in the private sector is closely linked to government incentives, but also to a cultural shift. In China, where status symbols play a major role, electric cars have created a new form of prestige. Brands like NIO have recognized this trend and are focusing on a premium experience that goes far beyond the vehicle itself. NIO Houses, luxurious lounges where customers can drink coffee, work, or socialize with other EV enthusiasts, are one example of how manufacturers are linking the brand to a lifestyle. This strategy has particularly appealed to the young, tech-savvy middle class, who see electric cars not just as a means of transportation but as a statement.

Another factor is affordability. While electric cars in Europe and the US are often more expensive than their combustion-engine counterparts, intense competition in China has driven down prices. On average, an electric car in China costs about half of what it costs in Western markets. Manufacturers like BYD offer models available for less than €20,000 without compromising on quality or technology. This price war, which analysts like Paul Gong of UBS Bank cite as crucial to China's success, also has its downsides. Manufacturers' margins are shrinking, and some startups have already had to file for bankruptcy because they couldn't withstand the pressure.

The innovative strength of Chinese manufacturers is also evident in their software. While German manufacturers are often praised for their engineering and hardware quality, Chinese companies like NIO and Li Auto have focused on software. Their vehicles are equipped with sophisticated operating systems that receive regular over-the-air updates, similar to a smartphone. These updates not only improve vehicle performance but also introduce new features, such as improved voice assistants or autonomous driving. For many Chinese consumers, the seamless integration of vehicle and digital ecosystem is a key purchasing factor.

But it's not just the technology itself that has conquered the private market, but also the way it's presented. Chinese manufacturers have understood that electric cars must be not only environmentally friendly, but also "cool." Marketing campaigns that rely on social media and influencers specifically target young buyers. One example is Xpeng, which is capturing the attention of Generation Z with futuristic designs and clever commercials. This dynamic has led to electric cars in China not just being an alternative, but often the first choice.

While the private sector is embracing electromobility as a lifestyle, it has become an indispensable tool in the commercial sector. From logistics companies to public transport operators, electric vehicles have fundamentally changed the way business is conducted in China. One particularly impressive example is the electrification of public transport. In cities like Shenzhen, not only the buses but also a large portion of the taxi fleets are electric. This change has not only reduced operating costs but also improved air quality in cities, which is of enormous importance for China's densely populated urban centers.

Chinese manufacturers also have a lead in the area of software. While traditional automakers often struggle with complex legacy systems, companies like Xpeng and Li Auto have relied on digital platforms from the outset. Their vehicles are equipped with operating systems that are seamlessly connected to the internet and offer features such as voice control, real-time navigation, and personalized service. A key factor for success in the commercial sector is the availability of electric vehicles specifically designed for commercial purposes. Manufacturers like BYD, a global leader in electric bus production, have created customized solutions for mass transit.

These buses are not only emission-free but also cost-effective. Compared to diesel buses, electric buses have lower maintenance costs and benefit from China's low electricity prices. According to experts like Cui Dongshu of the China Auto Industry Association, the operating costs of electric buses are about one-third lower than those of diesel buses, making them attractive to cities and operators.

Electric mobility has also gained a foothold in the logistics sector. Companies like JD.com and Alibaba, the giants of Chinese e-commerce, are increasingly relying on electric delivery vehicles to distribute their goods in urban areas. These vehicles are not only environmentally friendly but also practical, as they are exempt from traffic restrictions for combustion vehicles in many cities. The electrification of logistics fleets has also helped reduce these companies' carbon footprints, which represents a competitive advantage at a time when sustainability is a key issue.

Another exciting example is the integration of electric vehicles into the sharing economy. Platforms like Didi Chuxing, China's equivalent of Uber, have begun converting their fleets to electric vehicles. In cities like Hangzhou, there are dedicated charging stations for Didi drivers, allowing them to quickly recharge their vehicles and get back on the road. This development has not only reduced costs for drivers but also increased the availability of electric vehicles for end customers, further boosting adoption.

The innovative power of the commercial sector is also evident in the development of new business models. One example is NIO's battery swap system, which is particularly attractive to commercial users. Instead of waiting hours to charge a battery, drivers can swap their empty battery for a full one in just a few minutes at dedicated swap stations. This system, which is already available at over 2,000 stations in China, has significantly increased the efficiency of electric vehicles in commercial use. It is no coincidence that NIO is also exporting this model to Europe, where it could be of particular interest to logistics companies.

Behind the success of electric mobility in China is a wave of technological innovations that has catapulted the country to the forefront of the global automotive industry. One of the biggest breakthroughs is battery technology. China is the world's largest producer of lithium-ion batteries, and companies like CATL (Contemporary Amperex Technology Co. Limited) dominate the market. CATL supplies batteries not only to Chinese manufacturers like BYD and NIO, but also to international giants like Tesla and Volkswagen. CATL's innovations, such as the development of sodium-ion batteries, which are more cost-effective and sustainable, demonstrate how China is revolutionizing battery technology.

Another field in which China is leading is autonomous driving. While Western countries are still debating the ethical and legal implications of self-driving cars, China has already launched pilot projects in cities like Shanghai and Beijing. Companies like Baidu, which has developed an open platform for autonomous driving with its Apollo program, and AutoX, a startup that operates robotaxis, are setting new standards. These vehicles use advanced sensors, artificial intelligence, and 5G connectivity to navigate safely through dense urban traffic. The Chinese government is supporting these developments by investing in 5G infrastructure, which is more advanced in China than in many Western countries.

Provide user experiences. This software-centric approach has led to Chinese electric cars often being referred to as "smartphones on wheels." Another example of China's innovative strength is the integration of electric vehicles into smart city concepts. In cities like Shenzhen, electric vehicles are being integrated into a larger digital ecosystem that links traffic management, energy supply, and urban planning. For example, electric cars can serve as energy storage devices, storing excess energy from renewable sources and feeding it back into the grid when needed. This vehicle-to-grid technology is further proof that China is not only thinking about the mobility of tomorrow, but also about the energy infrastructure of the future.

Despite the impressive progress, electric mobility in China is not without challenges. While intense competition has fueled innovation, it has also led to overcapacity and a price war that has driven many smaller manufacturers into insolvency. Companies like Byton, Weltmeister, and Human Horizons have had to close down, which not only cost jobs but also raises questions about the sustainability of their business model. Customers who have purchased vehicles from insolvent manufacturers often face the problem that spare parts or software updates are no longer available.

Another problem is the dependence on subsidies. Although the Chinese government has reduced subsidies in recent years, they were a key driver of the EV boom. With the expiration of these subsidies, manufacturers must now prove that they can compete even without government support. This is particularly important in an international context, as the EU and other regions are scrutinizing Chinese manufacturers for potentially unfair subsidies and are considering punitive tariffs.

The environmental impact of electric mobility is also controversial. While electric vehicles reduce emissions during operation, battery production is energy-intensive and generates significant CO2 emissions. In China, where a significant portion of electricity production is still based on coal, the environmental advantage of electric cars is limited. However, the government has ambitious plans to increase the share of renewable energy, which could improve the sustainability of electric mobility in the long term.

Geopolitical tensions pose a further challenge. Competition with Western manufacturers, particularly from Europe and the US, has led to tensions. The EU has launched investigations to examine whether Chinese manufacturers have an unfair advantage due to government subsidies. At the same time, Western manufacturers are trying to expand their presence in China, creating a complex dynamic. German companies such as BMW and Volkswagen have opened large research and development centers in China to benefit from the country's innovative power, but are also in competition with domestic manufacturers.

While China is promoting hydrogen technology as an additionnal pillar of electromobility, it continues to focus primarily on battery-electric vehicles. Hydrogen vehicles, which generate electricity using fuel cells and emit only water vapor, offer advantages such as fast refueling (around three minutes) and long ranges (up to 700 km), making them particularly suitable for commercial vehicles such as buses and trucks, especially in cold regions where batteries are less efficient.

At the end of 2020, around 7,300 fuel cell vehicles (FCEVs) were in use, primarily commercial vehicles. Manufacturers such as Changan began producing hydrogen passenger cars in 2022, while Great Wall Motor is developing cost-effective fuel cells. Innovative solutions such as Geely's methanol-hydrogen drive, which converts methanol into hydrogen in the vehicle, demonstrate China's creative approach. Despite these efforts, hydrogen remains marginal compared to battery-electric vehicles.

China is strategically promoting hydrogen mobility but remains open to new technologies and is clearly committed to electric vehicles. Hydrogen plays a key role in commercial vehicles and specialized applications, supported by government plans and innovative technologies. However, costs and infrastructure remain hurdles that currently limit the widespread use of hydrogen vehicles.

Electric mobility in China is at a turning point. With a market share of over 50 percent in new car sales in 2025 and an ambitious goal of selling almost exclusively electric vehicles by 2035, China has charted a clear course. However, the path forward is not without obstacles. Market consolidation will continue, and only the strongest and most innovative companies will survive. At the same time, the international expansion of Chinese manufacturers such as BYD, NIO, and Xpeng will play a crucial role. These companies have already begun to gain a foothold in Europe and other markets, which presents both opportunities and risks.

For the private sector, electric mobility will continue to symbolize progress and innovation. With increasing affordability and steady improvements in technology, electric cars will become the first choice for more and more Chinese. In the commercial sector, the integration of electric vehicles into logistics, mass transit, and the sharing economy will continue to advance, supported by technological innovations such as battery-swapping systems and autonomous driving.

The greatest challenge, however, will be striking the balance between economic growth, environmental sustainability, and geopolitical stability. China has shown that it is capable of not only following global trends, but also shaping them. Electromobility is proof that visionary policies, technological innovation, and societal change can go hand in hand. But the story is not over yet. While the streets of Shenzhen and Shanghai continue to be dominated by electric cars, the world will be watching closely how China further expands its role as a pioneer in electromobility—and what lessons the rest of the world can learn from it.

The world looked to China, which had established itself as a pioneer in electromobility. But the story was not over yet. With new technologies such as hydrogen propulsion, autonomous vehicles, and sustainable batteries, the country faced new opportunities and challenges. For people like Li Wei, Zhang Mei, and millions of other Chinese, the future was open—a future in which mobility was not just a means to an end, but an expression of progress, freedom, and sustainability. And as the streets of Beijing, Shanghai, and Guangzhou continued to hum, one thing was clear: China had rewritten the rules of transportation, and the world would follow.

Fintech and cashless payments

In the streets of Beijing, Shanghai, or Shenzhen, a sight is now as commonplace as morning traffic: people paying for a coffee, hailing a taxi, or even settling their electricity bill with a quick swipe of their smartphone. What still sounds like a futuristic scenario to many in the West has become reality in China since the mid-2010s. Between 2015 and 2025, the country evolved at a breathtaking pace from a cash-dependent society to a global pioneer of cashless payments. This transformation is not just a technological achievement, but a profound social, economic, and cultural shift led by fintech companies such as Alibaba and Tencent. The story of this transformation is a fascinating mix of innovation, government support, societal adaptation, and the challenges that accompany such rapid digitalization.

In 2015, China was still a country where cash was king. In rural areas, as well as in many cities, people carried bundles of yuan bills to make larger purchases. The highest denomination, 100 yuan, was equivalent to about 13 euros at the time, meaning that even medium-sized purchases were often paid for with thick stacks of paper money. While bank cards were widespread in major cities, the credit and debit card system was underdeveloped compared to Western standards. Long lines at bank counters were not uncommon, and withdrawing cash could be a time-consuming undertaking. At the same time, more and more Chinese owned smartphones, and mobile internet usage exploded. According to the China Internet Network Information Center (CNNIC), by 2015, over 90 percent of internet users in China were already using their mobile phones to go online. This technological foundation laid the foundation for a revolution that would change payment in China forever. The driving force behind this revolution were two giants of the Chinese tech world: Alibaba with its payment platform Alipay and Tencent with WeChat Pay. Both companies had already begun building digital ecosystems in the early 2010s that went far beyond simple payment services. Alipay, originally developed as a payment solution for Alibaba's e-commerce platform Taobao, was founded in 2004 to increase user confidence in online transactions. WeChat, on the other hand, launched as a messaging app in 2011 and quickly developed into a so-called super app, combining communication, social media, e-commerce, and financial services under one roof. Both platforms recognized the potential of mobile payments early on and relied on a technology that would become ubiquitous in China: the QR code.

The simplicity of the QR code was a crucial factor in the success of cashless payments. Unlike NFC (Near Field Communication) technologies, which were used in Western countries like Germany for contactless payments with credit cards or smartphones, QR codes did not require expensive infrastructure. A merchant, whether a large supermarket or a small street vendor, could receive payments by simply printing a QR code. Customers simply had to open the relevant app, scan the code, confirm the amount, and the transaction was complete. This low barrier to entry made it possible for even people in remote regions or with low incomes to access digital payment systems. A kiosk owner in a small town could accept cashless payments just as easily as a luxury store in Shanghai.

The speed with which this technology spread was breathtaking. 2015 was a pivotal year in setting the stage for change.

In a speech at the World Economic Forum in Davos, Premier Li Keqiang called for a wave of innovation that would propel China into a new era of economic development. That same year, he visited Zhongguancun, Beijing's answer to Silicon Valley, signaling government support for tech startups. This political backing triggered a wave of startups: In 2015 alone, four million new companies were registered in China, many of them in the fintech sector.

Alibaba and Tencent benefited from this climate, but smaller players like JD.com and ICBC e-wallet also sought to secure their place in the market. However, government support was not purely ideological. China invested heavily in digital infrastructure, particularly in the expansion of 4G and later 5G networks, which laid the foundation for the widespread use of mobile apps.

Another catalyst was the Chinese people's cultural openness to new technologies. In contrast to countries like Germany, where data protection concerns often slowed the adoption of new payment methods, the Chinese were willing to prioritize convenience over privacy. For many, the ability to pay with a smartphone was not only practical but also a status symbol. It demonstrated that they were part of modern, urban society.

This enthusiasm for experimentation was further fueled by the business models of Alipay and WeChat Pay. Both platforms not only offered payment services but also integrated them into a wide range of everyday functions. With WeChat, you could not only message friends, but also rent a bike, order food, or schedule a doctor's appointment – all with the same app. Alipay, on the other hand, developed into a lifestyle platform, ranging from wealth management and lending to health advice. This interconnectedness made the apps indispensable and tied users to the platforms.

By 2018, cashless payment had largely become established in Chinese cities. A report in the Welt newspaper this year described how even beggars in China were using QR codes to collect donations. Around 470 million Chinese people paid with their smartphones in 2017, and the numbers continued to rise. Alipay led the market with over 700 million active users, followed by WeChat Pay with around one billion user accounts. The two platforms dominated the market to such an extent that smaller providers had little chance. Alibaba and Tencent, each with a market capitalization of around $500 billion, were not only national champions but global fintech giants.

Ant Financial, Alipay's parent company, was ranked the most valuable fintech company in the world. But this success also had its downsides. The rapid spread of cashless payments brought with it new risks. One of the biggest was the dependence on two dominant platforms. Alibaba and Tencent not only controlled payment transactions but also collected vast amounts of data on users' consumption behavior, social contacts, and financial transactions. This data was a valuable commodity, used for both targeted advertising and lending.

Alipay, for example, used the collected information to provide microloans to users who would otherwise have had no access to bank loans. However, the comprehensive monitoring of transactions also raised concerns. The Chinese government had access to this data through its strict internet control, fueling fears that cashless payments could become a tool of state surveillance. For many Chinese, however, this was an acceptable price to pay for the convenience and security the system offered. Pickpocketing became less common, and the transparency of payments made illegal activities such as money laundering more difficult.

Another risk was financial stability. Alipay and WeChat Pay charged hardly any fees for transactions, which made them attractive to merchants, but they invested the money parked with them in risky financial products. Financial experts warned of a systemic risk: If these investments failed, the platforms could face a crisis that would destabilize the entire financial system. To address this risk, the Chinese central bank introduced a clearing house in 2016 to monitor transactions between the platforms and the banking system. By 2018, this house was capable of processing up to 180,000 transactions per second, underscoring the robustness of the system. However, the dependence on a few large players remained a challenge.

The 2020 coronavirus pandemic further accelerated the trend toward cashless payments. Hygiene concerns led more and more people to switch to mobile payments, even in traditionally cash-oriented regions. At the same time, China began preparing for the next stage of digitalization: the introduction of a state-run digital currency, the e-yuan. Unlike private platforms like Alipay or WeChat Pay, the e-yuan would be directly controlled by the central bank.

Pilot projects began in 2020 in cities like Shenzhen and Suzhou, and experts predicted that the e-yuan could be rolled out nationwide by 2022 at the latest. This development was not only a technological advancement, but also a geopolitical signal. China wanted to use the e-yuan to expand its influence in the global financial world and create an alternative to Western currencies like the US dollar.

Between 2020 and 2025, China's cashless society further consolidated. In cities, cash payments had almost completely disappeared, and even in rural areas, smartphones became the primary means of payment. The integration of fintech solutions into everyday life went far beyond payments. WeChat and Alipay now offered services ranging from tax returns and scheduling appointments with government agencies to managing pension funds.

At the same time, government regulation increased. The government tightened its control over fintech companies to prevent monopolies and ensure financial stability. Ant Financial was forced to undergo a comprehensive restructuring in 2021, and the listing of its subsidiary Ant Group was halted. These measures demonstrated that while the government encouraged innovation, it did not want to relinquish control over strategically important sectors.

The social impact of the change was equally profound. For many Chinese, cashless payments meant greater convenience and efficiency in everyday life. At the same time, it led to new forms of social inequality. Older people and those in remote areas who lacked access to smartphones or high-speed internet were at risk of being left behind. The government launched programs to integrate these groups into the digital economy, for example by setting up internet access points in rural areas and providing training for seniors. Nevertheless, the digital divide remained a challenge.

A particularly fascinating aspect of the transformation was the cultural shift that accompanied cashless payments. In China, where cash had long been not only a means of payment but also a symbol of wealth and social interaction, digitalization transformed the way people interacted with one another. Traditional gestures such as handing over red envelopes (hongbao) containing money on holidays were digitized: WeChat and Alipay made it possible to send digital hongbao, which was particularly popular with younger generations. At the same time, the transparency of digital payments led to a new awareness of financial responsibility. Many users used the apps' analytics tools to monitor their spending and set savings goals.

The international perspective on China's transformation was divided. For many Western observers, China was a model for the possibilities of digitalization. Countries such as India and Nigeria attempted to adopt similar models, for example by introducing QR code-based payment systems. At the same time, China's model raised concerns, particularly regarding data protection and government surveillance. In Europe, where the GDPR stipulates strict rules for handling personal data, the idea of such an interconnected digital economy was unimaginable for many. Nevertheless, it was clear that China, with its fintech revolution, had set a global standard that would have a lasting impact on the future of payments.

In 2025, China is a country where cash is nothing more than a nostalgic memory. Street stalls in metropolises, as well as luxury boutiques, only accept digital payments. The e-yuan has established itself as a complement to Alipay and WeChat Pay, and the integration of blockchain technologies has further increased the security and efficiency of transactions. At the same time, China faces new challenges: How can the digital divide be closed? How can dependence on a few tech giants be reduced? And how can the balance between innovation and regulation be struck? These questions will shape the coming years, but one thing is certain: The change that took place between 2015 and 2025 has transformed China not only economically, but also socially and culturally.

The story of China's fintech revolution is one of courage, innovation, and adaptation. It shows how a country that, just a decade ago, struggled with the limitations of an underdeveloped financial system harnessed the opportunities of digitalization to usher in a new era. For the Chinese, the smartphone has long been more than a communication device—it's a key to a world where everything, from daily shopping to life planning, is just a scan away. And while the world looks to China, the question remains whether other countries will follow this path—or whether they will find their own paths to a cashless future.

Chinese Super Apps: The Digital Ecosystem

In the streets of Shanghai, where the neon lights of skyscrapers illuminate the night and the scent of steamed baozi from small food stalls fills the air, a young woman named Li Mei reaches for her smartphone. It's an evening in 2025, and like millions of others in China, she doesn't start her day with a trip to the bank, a visit to the grocery store, or a call to a friend. Instead, she opens a single app on her phone: WeChat. With a few swipes, she pays her rent, orders dinner, books a taxi, and tells her friends in a group that she's joining her for a karaoke night later. This scene, which would have sounded like science fiction a decade ago, is now an everyday reality in China. Super apps like WeChat and Alipay have not only simplified the lives of people in the People's Republic, they have revolutionized them. They are more than just applications—they are digital ecosystems that integrate nearly every aspect of life, from communication to commerce to healthcare.

How did China create such a digital universe in just one decade, between 2015 and 2025? What forces drove this transformation, and what consequences does it have for society, the economy, and the global technology landscape? This chapter tells the story of China's super apps, a story of innovation, control, and a unique interplay of technology and culture.

The roots of super apps lie in a unique constellation of historical, economic, and technological factors that distinguish China from other countries. In the early 2010s, China faced a challenge that also represented an opportunity: While Western countries were already highly digitized, with established infrastructures for credit cards, online banking, and e-commerce platforms like Amazon, China was a country in transition. Many people, especially in rural areas, lacked access to traditional financial services. Bank accounts were not ubiquitous, and cash dominated everyday life. At the same time, smartphone penetration was growing rapidly. By 2015, over 500 million Chinese already owned a smartphone, and the availability of affordable devices made technology affordable for the middle class and beyond. This combination—an underdeveloped traditional infrastructure coupled with an explosive adoption of mobile technology—created fertile ground for innovations that would have been almost unimaginable elsewhere.

Companies like Tencent and Alibaba stepped into this gap, developing WeChat and Alipay, two of the world's most powerful super apps. WeChat began in 2011 as a simple messaging app, comparable to WhatsApp, but it soon evolved into a platform that went far beyond sending text messages. Tencent recognized early on that the future lay not in isolated applications, but in integrated platforms that simplify users' lives.

Alipay, originally a payments platform for Alibaba's e-commerce ecosystem, evolved in parallel into an all-in-one financial tool. Both apps leveraged their platforms' open architecture to integrate third-party services, from ride-hailing to food delivery to insurance. This integration was key: Instead of downloading multiple apps for different tasks, users could do everything within a single application. This concept, which was only replicated in the West years later with tentative attempts by companies like Meta and Google, was already a reality in China by 2015.

A key driver of this change was the role of so-called mini-programs, which WeChat, in particular, popularized starting in 2017. These small, lightweight applications, running within the WeChat platform, enabled businesses to offer their services without developing standalone apps. A cafe in Guangzhou was able to create a mini-program through which customers could reserve tables, order food, or collect loyalty points without ever leaving the WeChat app. For businesses, this was a boon: Development costs were minimal, and the reach enormous, as WeChat was expected to have over 1.3 billion monthly users by 2025. For users, this meant a seamless experience that saved time and effort. But the mini-applications were more than just a technical feature. They were a cultural turning point that redefined the way people interact with digital services.

The rapid proliferation of super apps, however, was not solely due to technological innovations. The Chinese government played a central role in this change. While the period from 2015 to 2025 was characterized by unprecedented economic growth, the government focused on promoting the digital economy. Programs such as "Internet Plus," introduced in 2015, aimed to connect traditional industries with digital technologies. At the same time, the government created a regulatory framework that made it easier for domestic companies like Tencent and Alibaba to dominate, while foreign competitors like Google and Facebook were excluded by the "Great Firewall."

This isolation, often criticized as a restriction of freedom of expression, allowed Chinese companies to experiment and grow without the pressure of global competition. But this control also had a downside. The close integration of super apps with state surveillance systems raised concerns about data privacy and individual freedom. Every transaction, every message, every interaction within these apps was potentially recorded, placing an unprecedented amount of data in the hands of companies and the state.

Another factor that fueled the development of super apps was Chinese society's cultural predisposition toward collective and networked solutions. In contrast to Western cultures, which often emphasize individualism and specialization, Chinese society favors holistic approaches. Super apps reflect this philosophy: They are not just tools, but digital habitats where people can fulfill their social, economic, and even personal needs. This cultural component explains why super apps have been so much more successful in China than elsewhere. While Western users are accustomed to using a specialized app for every task—Uber for transportation, PayPal for payments, Instagram for social media—Chinese users value the simplicity and integration offered by super apps.

The economic impact of super apps is hard to overestimate. Between 2015 and 2025, the mobile payments market in China grew from approximately 1 trillion yuan (approximately US$150 billion) to over 400 trillion yuan (approximately US$60 trillion). Alipay and WeChat Pay dominated this market, marginalizing traditional banks. Small street vendors who previously only accepted cash now scan QR codes linked directly to customers' accounts.

This development has had far-reaching consequences: It promoted financial inclusion by bringing millions of previously unbanked people into the digital economy. At the same time, it led to a concentration of economic power in the hands of a few technology companies. Tencent and Alibaba now control not only payments, but also large parts of e-commerce, cloud services, and even the entertainment industry.

The story of super apps is thus not only a success story. It also raises questions about dependency, monopolization, and data security. With the increasing integration of services into super apps, users have become increasingly tied to these platforms. Those who do not use WeChat or Alipay are virtually excluded from large parts of social and economic life in many parts of China. This dependency has led critics to speak of a "digital feudalism" in which technology companies assume the role of feudal lords. At the same time, the close cooperation between these companies and the government has heightened concerns about surveillance. The social credit system, which is partly based on data from super apps, evaluates citizens based on their financial and social behavior and can result in consequences such as the loss of privileges. This development demonstrates how closely innovation and control are intertwined in China.

From a certain perspective, however, the social credit system in China can also be viewed as entirely legitimate, as it is deeply connected to the cultural and moral values of Chinese society. China has a long tradition of collectivist values that place the common good above individual interests. Confucian principles such as harmony, social responsibility, and moral behavior shape societal thinking. In this context, the social credit system is viewed as a tool to promote trust, honesty, and social stability—values that are considered essential but also fragile in a densely populated, rapidly growing society.

The system aims to sanction misconduct such as fraud, corruption, or violations of social norms, while rewarding virtuous behavior, such as timely payments or charitable work. This reflects the Chinese notion that moral action is important not only for the individual but also for society as a whole. In a culture that relies heavily on mutual trust and collective responsibility, such a system appears to be a logical extension of traditional values to address modern challenges such as urbanization and digitalization.

Furthermore, stability has historically been viewed in China as a prerequisite for prosperity and progress. After centuries of unrest and economic uncertainty, the government views the social credit system as a means of establishing order and predictability. For many Chinese, the idea of individual behavior being monitored and regulated is less foreign, having grown up in a culture where community often takes precedence over privacy.

Nevertheless, it's worth noting that this legitimacy is often viewed critically from a Western perspective, as it clashes with concerns about surveillance and individual freedom. From the Chinese perspective, however, the system fits a cultural framework that views social control as necessary for the functioning of a harmonious society.

Another fascinating aspect of super apps is their role in the global technology landscape. While Western companies like Apple and Google have long dominated the global tech scene, Chinese super apps have proven that alternative models exist. Countries in Southeast Asia, Africa, and Latin America that face similar challenges to those of China a decade ago—low banking density but high smartphone penetration—are now looking to the Chinese model.

Apps like Gojek in Indonesia or Rappi in Colombia are directly inspired by WeChat and Alipay. Yet the global spread of Chinese super apps themselves remains limited, partly due to geopolitical tensions and partly due to cultural differences. While WeChat is ubiquitous in China, its use abroad remains confined to the Chinese diaspora.

The story of super apps is also a story of people like Li Mei, who benefit from the convenience of these platforms in their everyday lives but also face the challenges they pose. For Li Mei, WeChat is not just convenience but also a form of social connection. Her family, who live in a rural province, is connected to her through WeChat groups, and she can send them money or share photos with just a few clicks. At the same time, she is aware that her every interaction is potentially monitored. This duality—convenience paired with control—is at the heart of the super app revolution.

Between 2015 and 2025, China created a digital ecosystem that is unique in the world. Super apps have not only transformed the way people shop, communicate, and travel, but have also redefined the boundaries of what technology can achieve. They are a product of innovation, government guidance, and cultural nuances, but also a reflection of the challenges that come with an increasingly connected world. As the world looks to the future, the question remains whether the super app model will be adopted globally or whether it will remain a unique phenomenon that has only been able to thrive in this form in China. One thing is certain, however: the story of super apps is far from over, and their impact will continue to shape the world for many years to come.

Ultimately, the question is whether a digital ecosystem like the one super apps have created in China could take root in Western countries. The answer is complex, as it depends on technological, cultural, and legal differences that both enable and limit the success of such platforms.

In the West, the technological landscape is characterized by significant fragmentation. Users are accustomed to using specialized apps for different needs: PayPal or Venmo for payments, Uber or Lyft for transportation, Amazon for shopping, WhatsApp or iMessage for communication. This specialization has its advantages, as each app is optimized in its field, but it also leads to a fragmentation of the user experience.

An attempt to bundle all these functions into a single super-app would face significant hurdles. Large technology companies like Apple or Google have the resources to develop such platforms, but they are in direct competition with each other. Unlike China, where Tencent and Alibaba dominate the market, the Western market is characterized by a multitude of players who would be reluctant to integrate their data or services into a single platform. A company like Meta, which has introduced super-app-like features with its Facebook or WhatsApp platform, also struggles with user distrust, who reject such a concentration of power and data.

Culturally, super apps in the West face another challenge: the strong emphasis on individualism and data privacy. In Western societies, particularly in Europe, where the General Data Protection Regulation (GDPR) imposes strict rules, users are sensitive to the risks of data sharing. An app that integrates all aspects of life—from finances to health to social interactions—would immediately raise questions about data security and surveillance.

In China, where collectivist values and a higher acceptance of government control prevail, such concerns are often set aside in favor of convenience. In the West, however, the willingness to hand over personal data to a single platform is significantly lower. This is evident, for example, in the skepticism towards projects like Facebook's Libra (later Diem), a planned digital currency that failed due to regulatory and public concerns.

Regulatory hurdles are another crucial factor. In Western countries, particularly in the EU and the US, there are strict antitrust regulations that prevent a single company from dominating a market. In China, however, the government actively supported the expansion of Tencent and Alibaba as long as they were consistent with state objectives.

In the West, a super app combining payments, e-commerce, and social media would immediately attract the attention of competition authorities. The breakup of monopolies, such as those discussed at Microsoft in the 1990s or currently at Google and Amazon, demonstrates that Western governments would not tolerate such market concentration. Furthermore, differing national laws within the EU make it difficult to create a unified platform, whereas China operates as a unified market with centralized regulation. Despite these obstacles, there are signs that Western companies are inspired by the super app model.

Smart Cities and Urban Transformation

Dawn breaks over Shenzhen, a city that was once a sleepy fishing village and is now considered the beating heart of global technology. In 2015, Shenzhen was already a symbol of China's rapid rise, but over the next decade it would become a prototype for something even grander: the smart city. Amid skyscrapers that reach the sky like glass spears, drones buzz through the air, delivering packages to high-rise apartments, while underground sensors optimize traffic flow and citizens access public services with a swipe of their smartphones. This scene is not a futuristic fairytale, but the reality that China created in its cities between 2015 and 2025. The change that took place in this decade is not just a technological revolution, but a profound transformation of the way people live, work, and interact with each other. It's a story of ambition, innovation, challenges, and a country determined to meet the urban challenges of the 21st century.

China's path to smart cities didn't begin in 2015, but is rooted in the reforms of the late 1970s, when Deng Xiaoping initiated the country's opening up. Yet it was the second decade of the 21st century that irrevocably changed China's urban landscape. The government realized that the rapidly growing population, increasing urbanization, and the associated problems—traffic chaos, pollution, resource scarcity—could only be addressed through a radical approach. Smart cities, intelligent cities that leverage technologies such as artificial intelligence, the Internet of Things, and big data, became the centerpiece of the national strategy. By 2025, China had initiated hundreds of pilot projects, some of which garnered global attention, while others quietly failed or encountered resistance. This text tells the story of this transformation: from the brilliant visions that drove politicians and entrepreneurs, to the technological breakthroughs that enabled it, to the social and ethical questions it raised.

In 2015, China stood at a crossroads. Urbanization had reached an unprecedented pace: Over 50 percent of the population lived in cities, and this figure was expected to rise to over 70 percent by 2025. Megacities like Shanghai, Beijing, and Guangzhou were grappling with the consequences of this growth. Air quality was often so poor that masks were part of everyday life. Traffic jams stretched for dozens of kilometers, and housing shortages drove property prices to dizzying heights. At the same time, the availability of digital technologies was exploding.

Smartphones were ubiquitous, and companies like Huawei, Alibaba, and Tencent were becoming global tech giants. The government saw this convergence of challenges and opportunities as an opportunity to shape the cities of the future. In 2015, the Ministry of Housing and Urban Development announced that China would launch hundreds of smart city projects by 2020. This announcement was more than a political promise—it was a call to the nation to solve urban problems with technology.

A key moment was the publication of the "Internet Plus" plan in 2015, which pushed for the integration of internet technologies into all areas of life. Cities were to become not only smarter, but also more connected. The idea was that sensors, cameras, and data platforms would create a digital nervous system that governs the urban organism. In Shenzhen, often referred to as China's "Silicon Valley," this vision began to be put into practice. The city became a living laboratory where technologies were tested before being rolled out nationwide.

One example was traffic management: Sensors at intersections collected real-time data, which was analyzed by algorithms to optimize traffic light control. The result was a reduction in congestion times of up to 20 percent in some parts of the city. Such successes made Shenzhen the flagship for China's smart city ambitions.

But Shenzhen was just the tip of the iceberg. Across the country, projects were springing up that could hardly have been more diverse. In Hangzhou, home of Alibaba, the "City Brain" platform was developed, an AI-powered solution that optimized traffic, public safety, and even hospital waiting lists. In Xiong'an, a purpose-built city south of Beijing, the government pursued an even more radical approach: designing a city from the ground up as a smart city, without the legacy of existing infrastructure. This diversity of approaches reflected China's pragmatic approach: There was no one-size-fits-all plan, but rather an experimental field in which various models were tested.

The driving force behind this transformation was the close collaboration between the state, the private sector, and research. The government provided financial resources and political support, while technology companies like Tencent and Baidu contributed the necessary expertise. Universities and research institutes developed new algorithms and sensors specifically tailored to the needs of Chinese cities. This symbiosis made it possible to implement projects at a pace often considered impossible in the West. One example is the rollout of 5G networks, which are essential for smart cities because they enable the rapid transmission of massive amounts of data. By 2019, China already had more 5G base stations than any other country, and by 2025, the network was available nationwide, even in smaller cities.

But the transformation went far beyond technology. It changed people's lives in profound ways. Let's take the example of Zhang Wei, a fictional but typical resident of a smart city like Hangzhou in 2025. In the morning, Zhang is woken up by his smartphone, which not only functions as an alarm clock but also analyzes his sleep data and suggests how to best start his day. On his way to work, he uses a mobility app that suggests the fastest route in real time—a combination of subway and shared bike.

During his lunch break, he orders his food via a platform that controls drones that deliver the food directly to his workplace. In the evening, he attends a concert for which he bought tickets using a digital wallet linked to his social credit score. This score, a controversial system that evaluates citizen behavior, allows him to receive discounts because he regularly recycles and obeys traffic laws. Zhang's life is comfortable, connected, and efficient—yet it is also a life under constant scrutiny.

Widespread surveillance was one of the most controversial aspects of smart city development in China. By 2025, millions of cameras with facial recognition had been installed in cities, not only detecting crimes but also prosecuting everyday violations like running a red light. This technology, developed by companies such as Hikvision and SenseTime, was cited by the government as necessary for public safety. However, critics, both within China and internationally, viewed it as a step toward a surveillance state. The debate about privacy and control was particularly heated in cities such as Urumqi in Xinjiang, where the technology was used to monitor ethnic minorities. These ethical questions cast a shadow over the technical successes and made it clear that smart cities are not just about algorithms and sensors, but also about values and power structures.

Another critical issue was social inequality. While cities such as Shenzhen and Shanghai benefited from the smart city revolution, many smaller towns and rural regions were left behind. The high costs of building smart infrastructure meant that affluent regions were primarily targeted for funding. Migrant workers, who make up a large portion of the urban population, often lacked access to the benefits of new technologies because they lacked the necessary smartphones or digital skills. This led to a digital divide that exacerbated existing social tensions. The government attempted to address this problem with digital education programs and subsidized smartphones, but progress was limited until 2025.

Despite these challenges, China's smart cities had achieved impressive success by 2025. Environmental pollution in many cities had decreased significantly thanks to intelligent energy management systems and electric mobility. In Beijing, once notorious for its smog crises, air quality improved noticeably, not least through the use of sensors that monitored emissions in real time. The efficiency of public services also increased: in Shanghai, citizens could submit requests in minutes via platforms like WeChat that would previously have taken weeks. These advances made China a model for other countries facing similar urban challenges.

But the path was not without setbacks. Many pilot projects failed because they were poorly planned or rushed into implementation. In some cities, millions were invested in technologies that were incompatible with each other, resulting in inefficient systems. One example was a city in Shandong Province, where a traffic management system was installed that was inconsistent with local road conditions and was ultimately shut down. Such failures demonstrated that technology alone is not enough—it also requires careful planning and citizen engagement.

Citizen participation was another issue often neglected in China's smart city development. While the government and companies set the tone, residents had little influence on the design of their cities. This led to resistance in some cases, such as in Guangzhou, where residents protested the installation of surveillance cameras. In other cities, however, citizens were actively involved, for example through apps that allowed them to directly report problems such as potholes or broken streetlights. These examples demonstrated that the success of smart cities depends not only on the technology but also on public acceptance.

A fascinating aspect of the transformation was the cultural adaptation of technologies. In China, smart city solutions were often designed to harmonize with local customs. In Suzhou, a city known for its classical gardens, intelligent lighting systems were integrated in a way that did not disrupt the historical aesthetic. In Chongqing, a mountainous metropolis, drones were developed specifically for the complex topography. These adaptations made it clear that China's smart cities are not just technical constructs but also expressions of the country's diversity and history.

By 2025, China had not only transformed its own cities but also exerted a global influence. The technologies developed in Shenzhen or Hangzhou were exported to countries in Asia, Asia, and Europe as part of the "Digital Silk Road." Cities such as Nairobi and Dubai implemented Chinese monitoring systems, while other countries such as India and Brazil learned from China's experience in traffic management.

At the same time, China faced accusations that its technologies were a tool for expanding geopolitical influence. This debate highlighted that smart cities do not exist in a political vacuum, but are part of global power structures.

Between Control, Service, and Quality of Life

This development was not merely a technical undertaking, but a balancing act between providing efficient services and promoting quality of life. While smart cities were designed to control and optimize everyday urban life through networked technologies, they presented residents with new challenges and opportunities that went far beyond mere functionality. The infrastructural transformation that China underwent during this decade was an attempt to manage its growing population, use resources more efficiently, and simultaneously create a living environment that is not only functional but also livable. This story is characterized by ambitious projects, cultural adaptations, and the tensions that arise when technology meets human needs.

Infrastructure development began with a clear goal: to design urban systems to cope with the growing demand for services such as transportation, energy, water, and waste management. In cities like Guangzhou, where the population grew by millions between 2015 and 2025, this was no small task. The implementation of smart transportation networks was a central component of these efforts. In Shanghai, for example, subway systems were expanded and optimized with AI-powered timetables to ease rush hour congestion. These systems used data from millions of commuters tracked via smartphone apps to adjust train schedules in real time. The result was a reduction in waiting times of up to 30 percent on some lines, noticeably improving everyday life for citizens. But this efficiency came at a price: Many commuters perceive-ed the constant data collection as an invasion of their privacy, and the reliance on apps excluded those without access to modern technology.

Another milestone was the expansion of energy infrastructure. Cities like Hangzhou deployed smart grids that monitored and optimized energy consumption in real time. Sensors in residential buildings recorded individual households' electricity consumption, while algorithms controlled the distribution of solar and wind energy to avoid peak loads. By 2025, Hangzhou had increased the share of renewable energy in its electricity mix to over 40 percent, an impressive achievement in a city once heavily dependent on coal-fired power.

These technological advances not only improved sustainability but also the reliability of the energy supply, which was particularly appreciated during the hot summer months when air conditioning was running at full speed. Nevertheless, some residents complained about rising electricity costs, as the installation and maintenance of the smart systems initially required large investments, which were passed on to consumers.

Water and waste management were other areas where infrastructure underwent transformation. Smart sewage systems were introduced in cities like Chongqing, which struggled with complex topography and heavy rainfall. Sensors monitored water flow in canals and adjusted pumps to prevent flooding. At the same time, recycling programs supported by apps helped citizens sort their waste correctly. In Shenzhen, for example, households received points in their social credit score if they recycled regularly, increasing the recycling rate by 25 percent. These systems improved urban cleanliness and reduced the burden on landfills, but they were not without controversy. Many citizens perceived the linking of recycling to the social credit system as a form of pressure that restricted their freedom, while others found the complexity of the sorting rules overwhelming.

Infrastructural development aimed not only at efficiency but also at improving the quality of life. One example was the creation of green spaces supported by smart technologies. In Beijing, where air pollution had long been a problem, parks were equipped with sensors that monitored air quality and controlled automatic irrigation systems to maintain vegetation. These parks became popular meeting places for families and seniors who appreciated the clean air and tranquility amidst the hectic city. But the reality was not so idyllic everywhere. In many cities, green spaces were sacrificed for new skyscrapers, and the remaining parks were often overcrowded, negatively impacting the quality of life for many residents.

Mobility infrastructure was another area where service and quality of life intersected. In cities like Chengdu, sharing models for electric bicycles and scooters controlled by apps were widely introduced. These systems reduced the need for private cars and relieved road congestion while providing citizens with flexible and cost-effective transportation. At the same time, they created new problems: Improperly parked bicycles blocked sidewalks, and vehicle maintenance was often inadequate, leading to user frustration. Furthermore, the infrastructure was not always designed to meet the needs of all citizens. Older people or people with disabilities often found digital interfaces difficult to access, and physical barriers, such as the lack of ramps at subway stations, remained a problem in many cities.

One particularly ambitious project was the expansion of autonomous transportation systems. In Xiong'an, the model city south of Beijing, self-driving buses controlled by 5G networks were tested. These buses followed set routes and used sensors to detect obstacles, increasing safety and allowing drivers to take a break. For residents, this meant convenient and reliable transportation that reduced the stress of commuting. However, the technology was not flawless: technical failures led to delays, and the high costs of developing and maintaining the systems strained city budgets. Furthermore, the introduction of autonomous vehicles triggered fears of job losses, as drivers and other transport workers feared for their jobs.

Digital infrastructure, especially the 5G network, was the backbone of this transformation. By 2025, China had built a nationwide 5G network that enabled the connectivity of millions of devices, from traffic lights to household appliances. This accelerated the provision of services such as telemedicine, where doctors in Shanghai consulted patients in remote districts via video, and e-government, where citizens completed applications online in minutes. However, the reliance on 5G made cities vulnerable to cyberattacks. An incident in Nanjing, where a hacker attack in 2024 paralyzed the transport network for hours, demonstrated how fragile these systems could be. For residents, this meant not only inconvenience but also a growing distrust of ubiquitous technology.

An often overlooked aspect was social infrastructure, which is crucial to quality of life. In cities like Suzhou, community centers were built equipped with digital platforms to organize events and promote social interactions. These centers offered courses in digital literacy, yoga, or traditional crafts, which helped older residents in particular navigate the modern city. However, funding for such projects was often insufficient, and in many cities, infrastructure focused on commercial projects such as shopping malls, which primarily served the middle class. This led to the alienation of many residents, who no longer felt at home in their own cities.

The cultural dimension of infrastructure was also crucial. In cities like Xi'an, known for their historical heritage, attempts were made to combine modern technologies with traditional elements. Smart lighting systems in historic districts were designed to emphasize traditional architecture, while apps guided tourists through the city and told stories about the past. These efforts strengthened residents' sense of belonging and made the cities more attractive to visitors. But in other cities, such as the rapidly growing Zhengzhou, historic districts were often demolished to make way for new infrastructure, leading to protests and a loss of cultural identity.

The tension between service and quality of life was also evident in residential infrastructure. In cities like Shenzhen, skyscrapers were built with smart systems that automatically controlled heating, lighting, and security. These buildings were a symbol of progress, but high rents made them unaffordable for many. At the same time, millions of migrant workers lived in cramped dormitories on the outskirts of the city, without access to modern amenities. The government launched programs to create affordable housing, but implementation was slow, and many projects were marred by corruption. For residents, this meant that the gleaming infrastructure was often just a facade hiding social problems.

Healthcare infrastructure was another area where progress and challenges converged. In cities like Guangzhou, hospitals were equipped with AI systems that accelerated diagnoses and optimized treatment plans. Telemedicine enabled patients in remote areas to be treated by specialists without having to travel long distances. However, the digitalization of healthcare also led to new inequalities. Older people who were unable to use digital platforms were often disadvantaged, and data security was a growing concern, as health data was a desirable target for hackers.

China's infrastructural development between 2015 and 2025 was an impressive undertaking that revolutionized urban services. But it also demonstrated that technology alone is not enough to ensure quality of life. The reliance on digital systems, the social divide, cultural losses, and security risks made it clear that a sustainable transformation requires more than sensors and algorithms. It requires an infrastructure that is not only efficient but also inclusive and people-centered. In the streets of Shenzhen, where the lights of skyscrapers illuminate the night, the question remains as to how this balance can be found in the coming years. The journey continues, and the world is watching how China shapes this path.

The story of China's urban transformation between 2015 and 2025 is a story of light and shadow. On the one hand, there is unprecedented progress: cities that became more efficient, sustainable, and connected, a country that rapidly developed technologies that set global standards. On the other hand, there are the challenges: surveillance, social inequality, ethical questions, and the role of citizens in an increasingly technological world. This duality is what makes China's smart cities so fascinating. They are neither utopia nor dystopia, but a reflection of the ambitions and contradictions of our time.

Health technology and biotechnology

Over the past decade, from 2015 to 2025, China has undergone remarkable transformation in the fields of health technology and biotechnology. This transformation is not only a story of technological innovation, but also a reflection of the social, economic, and political dynamics that have shaped the country during this time. China has evolved from a country long reliant on foreign technologies and innovations to a global player, even surpassing the United States and Europe in some areas of biotechnology. This development is the result of a combination of government planning, massive investment, international cooperation, and a relentless pursuit of technological independence. But how did this transformation come about? What milestones, challenges, and visions drove this process? Let's explore this fascinating journey through a decade of breakthroughs and upheavals.

The story begins in 2015, a time when China's healthcare system faced enormous challenges. The population was aging rapidly, healthcare spending was rising relentlessly, and dependence on imported medicines and technologies was a thorn in the government's side. Average life expectancy was around 76 years, and infant mortality, although declining, was still a problem in rural areas. At the same time, demand for high-quality medical care in urban centers like Shanghai and Beijing had increased dramatically. The government recognized that the healthcare system needed to be reformed to meet the needs of a modern, urbanized society. This marked the start of a series of ambitious plans that placed healthcare technology and biotechnology at the heart of the national development strategy.

A pivotal moment was the adoption of the "Healthy China 2030" plan in 2016. This plan was more than just a policy document; it was a blueprint for the future of Chinese healthcare. The goal was to increase life expectancy to 79 years by 2030, improve healthcare across the board, and reduce dependence on foreign technologies. The plan emphasized the importance of innovation in medicine, especially biotechnology, and set clear priorities: biopharmaceutical development, medical technology, digital health, and preventive measures. It was an ambitious undertaking that required both government support and the mobilization of the private sector.

The foundation for this transformation had already been laid several years earlier, when China began investing heavily in research and development. In 2015, the budget for biotechnology research amounted to several billion yuan, and by 2023, this amount had increased to at least 20 billion yuan (about 2.6 billion euros). These investments flowed into universities, research institutes, and private companies specializing in areas such as genomics, gene therapy, and artificial intelligence in medicine. A prominent example is the Beijing Genomics Institute (BGI) in Shenzhen, which became a global leader in genome sequencing. BGI was not only a symbol of China's scientific ambition, but also proof that the country was capable of competing on an international level.

Parallel to these investments, the Chinese government pursued a comprehensive reform of the healthcare system. One of the biggest challenges was the unequal distribution of medical resources between urban and rural areas. Between 1993 and 2011, the urban-rural healthcare gap had narrowed, but was still noticeable. The introduction of Diagnosis Related Groups (DRGs) was an attempt to standardize healthcare billing and combat corruption. Physicians, who had previously been vulnerable to bribery due to low salaries, were to be better compensated through a more transparent compensation system. This reform was not only a technological advancement, but also a social step to strengthen public trust in the healthcare system.

Another focus was strengthening intellectual property protecttion. Until 2015, China had often been criticized for providing inadequate protection for Western companies' patents. This changed with a series of reforms that began in 2017. The introduction of a Patent Term Extension (PTE) program and the membership of the Chinese Food and Drug Administration in the International Council for Harmonization of Technical Requirements for Pharmaceuticals for Human Use (ICH) signaled a new era. International pharmaceutical companies could now be confident that their innovations were protected in China, leading to an increase in the launch of innovative medicines. This was a crucial step in attracting foreign investment while strengthening the domestic industry.

The "Made in China 2025" strategy, published in 2015, also played a key role. Although it did not focus exclusively on health technology, biotechnology was a central component of this initiative. The strategy aimed to make China more self-reliant in key industries such as medical technology, biopharmaceuticals, and artificial intelligence. One specific goal was to increase the proportion of domestically produced medical devices in Chinese hospitals. By 2025, 70 percent of high-end medical technology was to come from Chinese manufacturers, and as many as 95 percent by 2030. This was a clear signal to foreign companies that they had to adapt to the new rules, whether through joint ventures, local production, or partnerships with Chinese companies.

A vivid example of this transformation is the story of Simeon Medical, a German company that entered the Chinese market in 2010 through a distributor. Five years later, in 2015, the company established a subsidiary in Shanghai to meet the growing demand for service and sales. Simeon Medical supplied surgical lights, camera systems, and ceiling supply units for hospitals, and by 2025, the company generated approximately 6 to 8 percent of its revenue in China. This demonstrates how foreign companies benefited from the growing opportunities, but also the importance of adapting to local conditions.

While medical technology was advancing, biotechnology was experiencing a veritable boom. China set new standards, particularly in the field of biopharmaceutical research. The focus was on the development of antibody-drug conjugates (ADCs), cell therapies, and innovative antibodies. One example is Legend Biotech, a Chinese company that developed the cancer treatment Carvykti in collaboration with the US company Johnson & Johnson. This drug, which generated sales of $900 million in 2024, became a symbol of China's ability to compete on a global level. The partnership with Johnson & Johnson also demonstrates how important international collaborations were to its success, especially in areas with high development costs.

The role of artificial intelligence (AI) in healthcare technology cannot be underestimated. Starting in 2015, China began to use AI on a large scale in medicine, whether in image analysis, drug discovery, or personalized medicine. Companies like iCarbonX used big data and AI to create patient health profiles and promote preventative measures. By 2025, the market for AI-based healthcare technologies was estimated at nearly $20 billion, with applications ranging from diagnosing rare diseases to optimizing clinical trials. These developments were not only technically impressive but also had a profound impact on the way healthcare was organized in China.

But the path was not without obstacles. One of the biggest challenges was its dependence on international markets for advanced biotechnology products. While China made significant strides in research and development, many of its advanced therapies, such as cell therapies, relied on exports to Western markets because domestic demand was often insufficient. This created a certain vulnerability, as geopolitical tensions and trade restrictions made access to these markets difficult. At the same time, China faced the challenge of reducing the cost of innovative therapies to make them affordable for the general population. This was particularly important in a country where healthcare spending was expected to rise from $543.5 billion in 2014 to a projected $2.5 trillion in 2035 if no reforms were implemented.

Another obstacle was the shortage of skilled workers. Despite massive investments in education and research, there was a shortage of highly skilled biotechnology professionals in the early years of transformation. Universities such as Tsinghua University and Fudan University began offering specialized programs in biotechnology and biomedical engineering, but it took several years for these programs to produce sufficient graduates. By 2025, the situation had improved, but demand for experts in fields such as genomics and AI-assisted medicine remained high.

Despite these challenges, China continued its rise. A key factor was its ability to embrace global trends and adapt them to its own needs. The introduction of 5G technologies in the early 2020s revolutionized telemedicine, especially in rural areas. Hospitals in remote regions could now collaborate in real time with experts in Beijing or Shanghai, significantly improving the quality of care. At the same time, the digitalization of healthcare enabled better management of patient data, which in turn accelerated research and development.

Another example of China's innovative strength was the development of vaccines during the COVID-19 pandemic. Companies like Sinovac and Sinopharm played a key role in the rapid development and production of vaccines that were used not only in China but also worldwide. This experience strengthened confidence in the Chinese biotech industry and demonstrated the country's ability to act quickly in times of crisis. The pandemic also served as a catalyst for investment in biosecurity, an area that also played a key role in the "Healthy China 2030" plan.

International cooperation remained a central component of the transformation. As China aimed to become more technologically independent, it recognized the value of partnerships with Western companies. AstraZeneca's acquisition of Gracell Biotechnology in 2023 was an example of this dynamic. Such collaborations enabled Chinese companies to access global markets, while Western companies benefited from China's research capabilities and cost-efficient manufacturing capabilities. At the same time, reforms in the drug approval process led to an increasing number of Chinese-developed drugs, such as Fruzaqla and Ryzneuta, being approved in the US and Europe.

The role of synthetic biology cannot be overlooked in this context. Researchers in China developed new technologies to control cells with high precision, opening up applications in tissue engineering and drug development. These advances were not only scientifically significant but also had the potential to fundamentally change the way diseases are treated. One example was the work on nanotechnology solutions, such as nanorobots that could specifically target cancer cells. Such innovations, which sounded like science fiction in the early 2010s, were increasingly becoming reality in China.

The societal impact of this change was enormous. In cities, the adoption of digital health platforms led to easier patient access to doctors and diagnoses. Mobile apps that monitored health data in real time became standard, and wearable devices that monitored vital signs such as blood sugar or heart rate were commonplace in many households. In rural areas, telemedicine improved access to high-quality care, although challenges remained, particularly with regard to infrastructure.

Another exciting chapter in this story was the role of genomics. China invested heavily in genome sequencing, not only for medical purposes, but also for agriculture and the environment. The development of transgenic crops that were more resistant to disease and climate change was one area in which China made significant progress. These innovations had the potential to improve food security, a critical issue in a country of over 1.4 billion people.

Despite all these successes, the question of the ethical dimension of biotechnology research remained. Between 2015 and 2025, China faced repeated criticism, particularly following the scandal surrounding scientist He Jiankui, who created gene-edited babies in 2018. This incident sparked a global debate about the limits of genetic engineering and forced China to tighten its regulations. By 2025, the country had implemented a robust system for monitoring biotechnology research to ensure that innovations were both safe and ethical.

The economic impact of the change was also significant. The healthcare market in China grew from 10.2 trillion yuan in 2020 to a projected 14.09 trillion yuan by 2023. This growth was due not only to the rising demand for healthcare services but also to the increasing importance of prevention and wellness. Companies investing in digital health solutions, such as telemedicine platforms and fitness apps, saw a boom, driven by the growing middle class and their interest in health and quality of life.

A look ahead shows that China will continue its course toward technological independence and global leadership. The "Healthy China 2030" plan and the "Made in China 2025" strategy have laid the foundation for an era in which China is not just a consumer but also an innovator in health technology. But this transformation is not just a story of numbers and technology. It is a story of people—of scientists tirelessly conducting research, of patients benefiting from new therapies, and of a government with a clear goal in mind: a healthier, stronger China.

The years 2015 to 2025 were a time of upheaval, challenges, and triumphs. China has proven that it is capable of setting global standards while simultaneously considering its unique cultural and economic circumstances. The journey is far from over, but the progress made this decade is a testament to the potential of a country determined to shape its own future. The story of China's transformation in health technology and biotechnology is one of innovation, ambition, and the unwavering belief that science can change the world.

Ethical and Moral Implications in Transition

A key aspect shaping the transformation in health technology and biotechnology in China was the question of the ethical and moral implications of this rapid development. In the early 2010s, the ethical debate surrounding biotechnology research in China was still underdeveloped. The pace of scientific advances often outpaced the ability of society and regulators to create appropriate ethical frameworks. This became particularly clear in 2018, when scientist He Jiankui attracted worldwide attention by creating gene-edited babies designed to be resistant to HIV. This incident marked a turning point in the history of Chinese biotechnology and sparked an intense national and international debate about the limits of genetic engineering.

The He Jiankui scandal was a shocking moment that exposed the weaknesses in China's regulatory and ethical system. At the time, guidelines for human gene editing were patchy, and oversight of research institutes was often inadequate. He Jiankui used the CRISPR-Cas9 technology to edit the genes of embryos, which was not only ethically questionable but also scientifically controversial, as the long-term consequences of such interventions were unknown. The international community reacted with sharp criticism, and in China itself, the incident triggered a wave of outrage. Many citizens were torn between pride in the country's scientific prowess and concern about the moral implications of such experiments.

The Chinese government's response was swift and decisive. He Jiankui was sentenced to three years in prison, and the government introduced new, stricter regulations to control research on human embryos. By 2020, the country had implemented a comprehensive set of rules that strictly regulated the application of gene editing technologies to humans. These regulations not only prohibited gene editing for non-medical purposes but also required transparent documentation and ethical review of all research projects.

This was a clear step toward more responsible science, one that took into account both progress and society's moral concerns. Social acceptance of biotechnological innovations in China also evolved during these years. In the early 2010s, the public was often skeptical of new technologies, especially those related to genetics or artificial intelligence. This skepticism was partly culturally conditioned, as traditional values and fear of the unknown played a significant role. However, rapid urbanization and a growing middle class led to a shift in thinking. Younger, educated Chinese, particularly in cities like Beijing, Shanghai, and Shenzhen, were increasingly open to technological innovations, especially if they promised concrete benefits such as better healthcare or personalized medicine.

The COVID-19 pandemic of 2020-2022 played a crucial role in promoting social acceptance of health technologies. The rapid development of vaccines by companies like Sinovac and Sinopharm showed the public that biotechnology could save lives in times of crisis. At the same time, the pandemic led to wider adoption of digital health solutions such as telemedicine and health apps. In rural areas, where access to doctors was often limited, platforms such as WeDoctor became an indispensable tool. These platforms enabled patients to consult with doctors online, which not only improved care but also increased trust in technological solutions.

Nevertheless, tensions between technological advancements and ethical concerns persisted. One example was the use of AI in healthcare. While AI-based diagnostic systems were capable of detecting diseases such as lung cancer or rare genetic disorders with high accuracy, there were concerns about data privacy. In China, where state surveillance was pervasive, many citizens feared that their health data could be misused. This concern was partially alleviated by the introduction of stricter data protection laws, such as the Personal Information Protection Law (PIPL) of 2021. Nevertheless, the question of how health data could be used securely and ethically remained a hotly debated topic.

Another aspect of the ethical debate was the question of social justice. While the urban middle class benefited from advances in health technology, rural communities often had limited access to these innovations. The government attempted to reduce this imbalance by investing in infrastructure and promoting telemedicine, but the gap persisted. This led to discussions about the moral obligation to make technological advances accessible to all segments of the population, regardless of their social or economic status.

Synthetic biology, another area in which China made signifycant progress, also raised ethical questions. The ability to design cells or even entire organisms opened up new perspectives for medicine, agriculture, and environmental protection. However, the prospect of creating "artificial life" made many people uneasy. In China, where traditional values such as harmony and respect for nature played an important role, the acceptance of such technologies was not a given. The government responded by launching public consultations and educational campaigns to educate the population about the benefits and risks of synthetic biology.

By 2025, the ethical landscape in China had changed signifycantly. While the early years of change were characterized by a "progress at any cost" mentality, the country emerged as a player that increasingly recognized the importance of ethical considerations. This was evident not only in the stricter regulations but also in the way scientists and companies began to proactively address ethical issues. Research institutes established ethics committees, and universities integrated ethics modules into their biotechnology and medical degree programs.

Societal acceptance of health technologies and biotechnology was closely linked to trust in these systems. In the early 2010s, trust in the healthcare system was low, partly due to corruption scandals and unequal care. However, through reforms such as the introduction of DRGs, improving infrastructure, and promoting transparency, the healthcare system gained credibility. The pandemic reinforced this trend as the population experienced the tangible benefits of biotechnological innovations. At the same time, the ethical debate remained a dynamic process, shaped by past experiences, present challenges, and visions for the future.

International cooperation remained a central component of the transformation. While China aimed to become more technologically independent, it recognized the value of partnerships with Western companies. AstraZeneca's acquisition of Gracell Biotechnology in 2023 was an example of this dynamic. Such collaborations enabled Chinese companies to access global markets, while Western companies benefited from China's research capabilities and cost-efficient manufacturing capabilities. At the same time, reforms in the drug approval process led to an increasing number of Chinese-developed drugs, such as Fruzaqla and Ryzneuta, being approved in the US and Europe.

The role of synthetic biology cannot be overlooked in this context. Researchers in China developed new technologies to control cells with high precision, opening up applications in tissue engineering and drug development. These advances were not only scientifically significant but also had the potential to fundamentally change the way diseases are treated. One example was the work on nanotechnology solutions, such as nanorobots that could specifically attack cancer cells. Such innovations, which sounded like science fiction in the early 2010s, were increasingly becoming reality in China.

The societal impact of this change was enormous. In cities, the introduction of digital health platforms led to easier patient access to doctors and diagnoses. Mobile apps that monitored health data in real time became standard, and wearable devices that monitored vital signs such as blood sugar or heart rate were commonplace in many households. In rural areas, telemedicine improved access to quality care, although challenges remained, particularly in terms of infrastructure.

Another exciting chapter in this story was the role of genomics. China invested heavily in genome sequencing, not only for medical purposes but also for agriculture and the environment. The development of transgenic crops that were more resistant to disease and climate change was one area in which China made great strides. These innovations had the potential to improve food security, a critical issue in a country of over 1.4 billion people.

The economic impact of the change was also significant. The healthcare market in China grew from 10.2 trillion yuan in 2020 to a projected 14.09 trillion yuan by 2023. This growth was driven not only by rising demand for healthcare services, but also by the increasing importance of prevention and wellness. Companies investing in digital health solutions, such as telemedicine platforms and fitness apps, saw a boom, driven by the growing middle class and its interest in health and quality of life.

A look ahead shows that China will continue its course toward technological independence and global leadership. The "Healthy China 2030" plan and the "Made in China 2025" strategy have laid the foundation for an era in which China will be not only a consumer but also an innovator in healthcare technology. But this transformation is not just a story of numbers and technology. It is a story of people—of scientists tirelessly conducting research, of patients benefiting from new therapies, and of a society learning to balance innovation with ethical considerations.

The years 2015 to 2025 were a time of upheaval, challenges, and triumphs. China has proven capable of setting global standards while simultaneously addressing its unique cultural and economic circumstances. The journey is far from over, but the progress made this decade is a testament to the potential of a country determined to shape its own future. The story of China's transformation in health technology and biotechnology is one of innovation, ambition, and the unwavering belief that science can change the world when coupled with responsibility and respect for society.

Space travel and China's reach for the stars

The world watched in 2015 as a nation once known for its earthly triumphs turned its eyes to the heavens. Spaceflight, long the playing field of superpowers like the United States and Russia, began to transform, and China emerged with a confidence that inspired both admiration and concern. In the following decade, up to 2025, China's space program would not only achieve technical milestones but also make geopolitical, economic, and cultural ripples that reached far beyond the Earth's surface. This is the story of China's reach for the stars, an excursion marked by ambition, precision, and a clear vision, but also by challenges, competition, and a world wondering what this new era means.

The roots of China's space ambitions run deep into 20th-century history. As early as the 1950s, when the young People's Republic was still grappling with the aftermath of war and poverty, a small group of scientists dreamed of rockets that could pierce the skies. Qian Xuesen, a brilliant engineer trained in the United States before being expelled during the McCarthy era, laid the foundation for China's rocket technology. His return to China was a turning point, a moment that sowed the seeds for what would blossom decades later. But by 2015, China was no longer a rising nation but an economic superpower with a space program ready to take to the world stage.

That year, the world looked to the Chang'e-3 mission, which two years earlier had landed a rover called Yutu, the "Jade Rabbit," on the moon. It was the first soft lunar landing by a country since the 1970s, a technical triumph that demonstrated that China could not only catch up but also innovate. But

Chang'e-3 was just the beginning. The program, named after the mythological moon goddess, was part of a larger plan that extended far beyond Earth's orbit. China had a roadmap that was as precise as it was ambitious: its own space station, lunar bases, Mars missions, and perhaps even bolder goals. What the world saw in 2015 was a nation not just knocking on the door of the space elite, but forcefully opening it.

The driving force behind China's space program was the China National Space Administration (CNSA), an agency closely aligned with the military and government. Unlike Western space agencies like NASA, which often suffered from public scrutiny and budget fluctuations, the CNSA operated with a long-term vision supported by the Communist Party. This centralized control allowed China to pursue projects with a continuity often lacking in other countries. But it wasn't just the organization that drove China forward. It was a combination of national pride, technological innovation, and the desire to establish itself as a global leader.

A key moment in this decade was the launch of the Tiangong space station. The first Tiangong station, Tiangong-1, was launched in 2011, but by 2015 it was already a relic, destined to return to Earth unchecked. The real story began with Tiangong-2, launched in 2016, and culminated in the modular space station taking shape in Earth orbit starting in 2021. Tiangong, meaning "Heavenly Palace," was more than a technical achievement. It was a symbol of China's ability to achieve great things independently of international collaborations such as the International Space Station (ISS), operated by the US, Russia, Europe, and others. China had been excluded from the ISS, partly due to US security concerns, and this rejection became a catalyst. Instead of asking for participation, China built its own platform.

The Tiangong Station was a marvel of engineering. With a core module called Tianhe, launched in 2021, and additional modules added in the following years, it could accommodate three taikonauts, as China's space travelers were known. The station was equipped with cutting-edge technology, includeing robotic arms, laboratories for scientific experiments, and systems that enabled a long-term presence in space. For the taikonauts, Tiangong was a home away from Earth, a place where they spent months conducting experiments ranging from weightlessness to plant cultivation. These missions were not only scientific but also political. Each successful crew rotation was celebrated in China as a testament to the nation's strength.

But Tiangong was only part of the story. At the same time, China was forging ahead with its lunar program. Following the success of Chang'e-3, further missions followed, includeing Chang'e-4, which set a historic milestone in 2019. This probe landed on the far side of the Moon, an area never before directly explored by a spacecraft. The challenge was enormous: Since the far side cannot communicate directly with Earth, China had to launch a relay satellite, Queqiao, into a special orbit to enable data transmission. The Yutu-2 rover, which landed with Chang'e-4, rolled across the lunar surface, collecting data that astonished scientists around the world. This mission demonstrated not only China's technical capabilities but also its willingness to take risks and explore new territory.

The lunar missions were part of a larger plan that became increasingly clear by 2025. China not only wanted to visit the

Moon, but to use it as a springboard for the future. Plans for an International Lunar Research Station (ILRS), to be developed in collaboration with partners such as Russia, began to take shape. This station, to be realized in the 2030s, would enable a permanent presence on the Moon, with habitats, laboratories, and even resource utilization. The Moon is rich in helium-3, an isotope that could serve as fuel for future fusion reactors, and China saw this as a strategic opportunity. While the United States pursued similar goals with its Artemis program, a quiet but intense race for lunar dominance developed.

In addition to the Moon, China set its sights on Mars. The Tianwen-1 mission, launched in 2020, was a bold undertaking. It included an orbiter, a lander, and a rover called Zhurong, named after the Chinese god of fire. In May 2021, Zhurong landed on the Martian surface in Utopia Planitia, a region known for its geological diversity. The rover explored the terrain, analyzed soil samples, and searched for traces of water that may have once flowed on Mars. Tianwen-1 was a milestone, as China became the second nation after the United States to successfully land a vehicle on Mars. The mission was a testament to China's ability to master complex interplanetary projects and sent a clear message to the world: China was not just a player, but a serious competitor.

What made China's space program so successful? One factor was massive government support. The government invested billions in space exploration without the volatility that often plagued Western programs. This funding made it possible to advance projects like Tiangong, Chang'e, and Tianwen at a speed that surprised other nations. Another factor was the integration of civilian and military technology. China's space program was closely linked to the People's Liberation Army, which made it possible to pool resources and expertise. But it wasn't just money and organization. China had a new generation of scientists and engineers who worked with passion and precision. Many of them had been trained abroad but had chosen to make an impact at home, driven by national pride and the prospect of making history.

A less tangible but equally important aspect was the cultural dimension. In China, space exploration was not just a technical endeavor but a symbol of the nation's rise. The names of the missions—Tiangong to Chang'e—were deeply rooted in Chinese culture and evoked images of myth and legend. The media reported extensively on each mission, and the public followed the successes with enthusiasm. For many Chinese, space travel was proof that their country had found its place among the stars. This mixture of pride and progress gave the program a momentum that was hard to ignore.

But China's rise was not without controversy. The international community, especially the United States, observed developments with a mixture of respect and suspicion. Security concerns played a major role. Many Western analysts saw China's space program as not only scientific, but also military. Satellites used for navigation or communications could also be used for military purposes. Tests of anti-satellite weapons, such as the one in 2007 in which China destroyed its own satellite, had sparked global concern, highlighting the danger of space debris and the militarization of space. The close link between civilian and military space travel also fueled skepticism.

Another problem was the issue of international cooperation. While China was willing to cooperate with countries like

Russia and developing nations, it remained a loner in many areas. Its exclusion from the ISS had left its mark, and although China invited other nations to participate in projects like the ILRS, many Western countries were reluctant. This led to a fragmentation of global space efforts, with competing blocs—led by China and the US—pursuing their own visions. For science, this was a missed opportunity, as joint projects often enable greater progress. But for China, independence was a strategic advantage that weighed heavily.

The issue of transparency was also at stake. While the CNSA regularly reported its successes, there were often few details about the exact objectives or technologies. Failures, such as the uncontrolled crash of Tiangong-1 in 2018, were downplayed by China, leading to criticism. Space debris was a global problem, and China's contributions to it—particularly following anti-satellite tests—contradicted its assurances of peaceful use of space. These tensions reflected the larger geopolitical dynamics in which China, as a rising power, aroused both admiration and opposition.

Despite these challenges, China's 2025 space program was an impressive testament to human endeavor. From the Tiangong Station, which orbited Earth like a lighthouse, to the rovers on the Moon and Mars, and now plans for a lunar base, China had achieved a series of milestones few had thought possible. But what did this rise mean for the world?

For many, China's space program was an inspiration. Countries like India, which also pursued their own programs, saw China as a role model. Developing countries that gained access to Chinese satellites or technologies benefited from cooperation, often as part of the Belt and Road Initiative, which also had a space component. Scientists around the world used data from missions like Chang'e-4 to better understand the universe. Competition with the United States and other spacefaring nations led to a new "space understanding" that spurred innovations in technology, robotics, and sustainability.

For others, China's rise was a challenge. The United States, seeking to redefine space with its Artemis program and private companies like SpaceX, saw China as a competitor threatening its dominance. Europe, wavering between cooperation and competition, sought its own role in this new era. Russia, once a pioneer of space exploration, found itself in an uncertain partnership with China that presented both opportunities and risks. Space, once a place of cooperation, increasingly became a site of geopolitical rivalries.

But beyond these tensions, China's space exploration was also a story of inspiration. For a young female engineer in Shanghai, a student in a small town in Guangxi, or a scientist in Beijing, looking to the stars held promise. It was a reminder that a nation once grounded had now reached the heavens. The stories of taikonauts like Liu Yang, the first Chinese woman in space, or of missions like Tianwen-1 that pushed the boundaries of possibility inspired a generation to dream big.

The Differences in Space Exploration: China vs. the West

A comparison between China's space program, led by the China National Space Administration (CNSA), and the efforts of NASA and SpaceX, the leading private space company in the United States, reveals profound differences in organization, funding, objectives, and approach. These differences are not only technical in nature but also reflect the cultural, political, and economic contexts in which these programs operate. To illuminate the most striking differences, it is worthwhile to examine the areas of organizational structure, funding, technological strategies, international cooperation, and cultural narratives in more detail.

A key difference lies in the organizational structure. The CNSA is a government agency closely linked to the Chinese government and the People's Liberation Army. This centralized control enables unified, long-term planning, with projects like the Tiangong Space Station and the Chang'e lunar missions pursuing a clear roadmap. Decisions are made centrally, and space priorities are closely linked to the strategic goals of the Communist Party, whether boosting national pride or securing geopolitical advantage.

In contrast, NASA is officially a civilian agency funded by the US government but often subject to the whims of political priorities and budget cuts. NASA must regularly justify itself to Congress, which can lead to delays or changes in projects like the Space Launch System (SLS). SpaceX, on the other hand, is a private company driven by the vision and entrepreneurial spirit of its founder, Elon Musk. SpaceX operates with an agile, market-oriented structure that allows the company to respond quickly to market needs, but is also dependent on the profitability of its projects. These different structures lead to remarkable dynamism: While China plans with a stable, long-term perspective, NASA struggles with political uncertainty, and SpaceX relies on speed and innovation, often with a focus on commercial applications.

Funding is another area where the programs differ significantly. China's space program is supported by massive government investments, the exact amounts of which are often difficult to track because budgets are not as transparent as in Western countries. Estimates suggest that between 2015 and 2025, China invested billions in projects such as Tianwen-1, Tiangong, and the lunar missions, without the fluctuations common in democratic systems. This financial stability allows the CNSA to pursue high-risk projects with long-term goals, such as the planned International Lunar Research Station (ILRS).

NASA, on the other hand, operates with an annual budget of approximately $25 billion in 2025, but often has to be divided between different projects, creating conflicting priorities. SpaceX finances itself through a combination of private capital, contracts with NASA, and commercial customers, such as satellite launches or tourist flights. This reliance on external revenue forces SpaceX to develop cost-effective solutions, such as the reusable Falcon and Starship rockets, which have drastically reduced the cost of accessing space. Thus, while China relies on state resources, NASA balances public funding with political pressure, and SpaceX pursues a market-driven approach that combines innovation with profitability.

Technologically, the three players pursue different strategies. China has focused on perfecting proven technologies while exploring new frontiers. The Chang'e missions demonstrate a combination of precision and risk-taking, for example, by landing on the far side of the Moon, which required a complex communications infrastructure. China's rockets, such as the Long March series of launch vehicles, are reliable but less innovative than SpaceX's approaches. The CNSA values self-reliance and develops its technologies largely independently of Western suppliers, which is both an advantage and a limitation.

NASA, on the other hand, relies on a mix of its own research and partnerships with industry. Projects such as the Artemis program, which aims to return to the Moon, rely heavily on private companies such as Boeing and SpaceX, making NASA flexible but also dependent on external players. SpaceX has revolutionized space travel with its reusable rockets, particularly the Falcon 9 and Starship, which is designed for interplanetary missions. This technology has significantly reduced the cost per launch and increased the frequency of missions, giving SpaceX a competitive advantage. While China focuses on continuity and self-reliance, SpaceX drives innovation through radical cost reduction and scalability, and NASA seeks to combine both worlds.

A particularly striking difference is the attitude toward international cooperation. China was excluded from the International Space Station (ISS), prompting the CNSA to build its own space station, Tiangong. A key difference lies in the organizational structure. The CNSA is a government agency closely linked to the Chinese government and the People's Liberation Army. This centralized control enables unified, long-term planning, with projects like the Tiangong Space Station and the Chang'e lunar missions pursuing a clear roadmap. Decisions are made centrally, and space priorities are closely linked to the strategic goals of the Communist Party, whether boosting national pride or securing geopolitical advantage.

In contrast, NASA is officially a civilian agency funded by the US government but often subject to the whims of political priorities and budget cuts. NASA must regularly justify itself to Congress, which can lead to delays or changes in projects like the Space Launch System (SLS). SpaceX, on the other hand, is a private company driven by the vision and entrepreneurial spirit of its founder, Elon Musk. SpaceX operates with an agile, market-oriented structure that allows the company to respond quickly to market needs, but is also dependent on the profitability of its projects. These different structures lead to remarkable dynamism: While China plans with a stable, long-term perspective, NASA struggles with political uncertainty, and SpaceX relies on speed and innovation, often with a focus on commercial applications.

Funding is another area where the programs differ signifycantly. China's space program is supported by massive government investments, the exact amounts of which are often difficult to track because budgets are not as transparent as in Western countries. Estimates suggest that between 2015 and 2025, China invested billions in projects such as Tianwen-1, Tiangong, and the lunar missions, without the fluctuations common in democratic systems. This financial stability allows the CNSA to pursue high-risk projects with long-term goals, such as the planned International Lunar Research Station (ILRS).

NASA, on the other hand, operates with an annual budget of approximately $25 billion in 2025, but often has to be divided between different projects, creating conflicting priorities. SpaceX finances itself through a combination of private capital, contracts with NASA, and commercial customers, such as satellite launches or tourist flights. This reliance on external revenue forces SpaceX to develop cost-effective solutions, such as the reusable Falcon and Starship rockets, which have drastically reduced the cost of accessing space. Thus, while

China relies on state resources, NASA balances public funding with political pressure, and SpaceX pursues a market-driven approach that combines innovation with profitability.

Technologically, the three players pursue different strategies. China has focused on perfecting proven technologies while exploring new frontiers. The Chang'e missions demonstrate a combination of precision and risk-taking, for example, by landing on the far side of the Moon, which required a complex communications infrastructure. China's rockets, such as the Long March series of launch vehicles, are reliable but less innovative than SpaceX's approaches. The CNSA values self-reliance and develops its technologies largely independently of Western suppliers, which is both an advantage and a limitation.

NASA, on the other hand, relies on a mix of its own research and partnerships with industry. Projects such as the Artemis program, which aims to return to the Moon, rely heavily on private companies such as Boeing and SpaceX, making NASA flexible but also dependent on external players. SpaceX has revolutionized space travel with its reusable rockets, particularly the Falcon 9 and Starship, which is designed for interplanetary missions. This technology has significantly reduced the cost per launch and increased the frequency of missions, giving SpaceX a competitive advantage. While China focuses on continuity and self-reliance, SpaceX drives innovation through radical cost reduction and scalability, and NASA seeks to combine both worlds.

A particularly striking difference is the attitude toward international cooperation. China was excluded from the International Space Station (ISS), prompting the CNSA to build its own space station, Tiangong.

Another difference lies in the speed and flexibility of implementation. China's space program is characterized by its patience and long-term focus. Projects like the ILRS or the Mars missions are part of a plan spanning decades, and failures are often dealt with internally without disrupting the momentum. NASA, on the other hand, is vulnerable to delays caused by political or bureaucratic hurdles, such as the SLS, which was years behind schedule. SpaceX is unique in this respect, operating at a speed unusual in the space industry. The development of Starship, despite some spectacular failures, demonstrates a "fail fast, learn fast" mentality that is hardly conceivable in government spaceflight. This agility has enabled SpaceX to transform from a newcomer to a dominant player in just a few years, while China and NASA are committed to slower but more stable progress.

Their approach to risk is also different. China takes calculated risks, as demonstrated by the landing of Chang'e-4, which was a technical gamble but mastered with precise planning. NASA is more risk-averse because failures are highly criticized in public, leading to a conservative approach. SpaceX, on the other hand, embraces risks, as demonstrated by the explosions during Starship tests, viewing them as learning opportunities. These different risk cultures shape the way innovations emerge: China focuses on perfection, NASA on safety, and SpaceX on bold experiments.

Finally, there are differences in goals. China pursues a mix of scientific exploration and resource utilization, for example, through the exploration of helium-3 on the Moon. NASA has similar scientific goals but is more focused on international cooperation and advancing human presence in space, as demonstrated by the Artemis program. SpaceX has a unique goal: to colonize Mars and create a multi-planetary civilization. While China and NASA seek a balance between science, politics, and exploration, SpaceX's vision is more radical and less tied to national interests.

In summary, China's space program is characterized by state control, long-termism, and national symbolism, while NASA operates within a democratic framework that emphasizes cooperation and scientific excellence but is constrained by political constraints. SpaceX distinguishes itself through its private, agile, and risk-taking nature, focused on commercial efficiency and a visionary future. These differences not only reflect their respective systems but also shape the future of space, in which China, NASA, and SpaceX are pursuing different paths to the stars. How these paths intersect or diverge will define the coming decades.

In 2025, China not only stands on the cusp of new worlds but also faces new questions. How will the world react to a permanent Chinese presence on the Moon? What role will China play in a future space ecosystem? And how could humanity collectively benefit from this new age of exploration? The answers to these questions still lie in the future, but one thing is certain: China's reach for the stars has changed the world forever.

The journey continues. From the dusty plains of Mars to the craters of the Moon, from the laboratories in Beijing to the dreams of a new generation – China has found its place in the cosmos. And the stars, quiet and independent, continue to shine, inviting new adventures to those who dare to reach for them.

Renewable energies and green technologies

Over the past decade, from 2015 to 2025, China has transformed from a country known primarily for its coal-fired power plants and thick smog into a global leader in renewable energy and green technologies. This transformation is not only a technical and economic achievement, but also a story of political will, social change, and a nation reinventing itself at an unprecedented pace. It is a story of contradictions, challenges, and triumphs that demonstrates how a country of 1.4 billion people and one of the world's largest economies is taking the leap into a more sustainable future—and sweeping the world along with it.

The starting point of this transformation was anything but promising. As recently as 2015, China struggled with air quality that was almost unbearable in many cities. In Beijing and other major cities, the skies were often shrouded in a gray blanket of smog, a visible sign of the country's dependence on fossil fuels. At that time, coal-fired power plants provided around 70 percent of the world's electricity, and China was the world's largest emitter of carbon dioxide. The health consequences were severe: respiratory diseases increased, and life expectancy in particularly polluted regions fell. But in the midst of this crisis, an awareness emerged, supported by both the government and the population: Something had to change. This was the moment China began to rethink its future.

The turning point began with a combination of political decisions and technological innovations. 2015 marked the year in which China signed its commitments to the Paris Climate Agreement. The government set ambitious goals:

CO_2 emissions were to peak by 2030, and the share of renewable energies in the energy mix was to increase significantly. But words alone were not enough – China relied on action. The government initiated massive investments in renewable energies, the scale of which was unique in the world. Between 2015 and 2020, over $400 billion was invested in the expansion of wind, solar, and hydropower. These sums were invested not only in infrastructure projects but also in research and development to make China more independent of foreign technologies.

A key moment was the rapid expansion of solar energy. At the beginning of 2015, China's installed solar capacity was around 28 gigawatts—respectable, but far behind the US and Germany. But within a few years, China catapulted itself to the top. By 2025, the country had reached an installed capacity of over 400 gigawatts, more than twice that of any other country. These figures are impressive, but they only tell part of the story. Behind the bare numbers are the people who made this transformation possible.

In the Gobi Desert, where sandstorms once swept across barren land, gigantic solar farms have sprung up, resembling glittering oases of glass and steel. Workers like Zhang Wei, a former farmer from Gansu Province, found new employment in these projects. Zhang, who once struggled to grow crops, learned to install and maintain solar panels. His income tripled, and he became part of a new generation of workers who saw a future in China's green economy.

Wind energy experienced a similar boom. Wind farms sprang up along coastal regions and on the windy steppes of Inner Mongolia. China became the largest market for wind turbines, and domestic companies like Goldwind and Sinovel began to conquer the global market. But this progress was not without challenges. In the early years of expansion, China struggled with inefficient power grids. Many wind and solar plants produced electricity that could not be fed into the grid because of outdated infrastructure. This problem, known as "curtailment," resulted in up to 20 percent of renewable energy generated going unused in some regions. The government responded with a multi-billion-dollar power grid modernization program, delivering far-reaching improvements by 2025. Smart grids powered by AI-powered technology optimized distribution and reduced losses. It was a technical feat that demonstrated how China combined its industrial strength with innovation.

In addition to wind and solar power, hydropower also played a central role. China was already the world's largest producer of hydropower in 2015, thanks to massive projects like the Three Gorges Dam. But in the years that followed, the country focused on building smaller, more sustainable hydroelectric power plants that required less environmental impact. At the same time, existing facilities were modernized to increase their efficiency. These efforts helped ensure that hydropower continued to provide a stable share of the energy mix while gradually reducing reliance on coal.

Another crucial factor was the electrification of transportation. China's cities, once dominated by gasoline and diesel vehicles, experienced a revolution on the roads. In 2015, there were approximately 300,000 electric vehicles in China—by 2025, this number had risen to over 20 million. Companies like BYD and NIO became global market leaders, and cities like Shenzhen electrified their entire bus fleets. This development was driven by massive government subsidies and strict regulations on combustion-engine vehicles. But it wasn't just a matter of policy—people themselves drove the change. In Shanghai, for example, charging electric cars became as easy as charging a smartphone. Charging stations sprouted up on every corner, and innovative business models like battery swap stations made electric mobility practical and affordable.

But the transformation wasn't limited to the energy sector. Green technologies permeated nearly every aspect of the economy. In agriculture, precision technologies using satellite data and AI led to more efficient use of water and fertilizers. Cities like Hangzhou experimented with "smart" buildings that optimized their energy consumption in real time. Even the textile industry, long a polluter, began using sustainable materials like recycled polyester. These developments were often the result of collaborations between government, businesses, and research institutions, sparking a unique dynamic in China.

Of course, there were also setbacks. The rapid industrialization of green technologies led to new environmental problems. The production of solar panels and batteries for electric vehicles required rare earths and other raw materials, the extraction of which was often associated with environmental degradation. In Jiangxi Province, for example, communities suffered from pollution caused by lithium and cobalt mining. The government responded with stricter environmental regulations, but balancing economic growth and environmental protection remained a challenge. Voices also criticized the social costs of change. In coal-mining regions such as Shanxi, thousands of workers lost their jobs when power plants were shut down. Retraining these workers for jobs in the green economy was a complex process that did not always go smoothly.

Despite these obstacles, China demonstrated a remarkable ability to learn from mistakes and adapt. One example is the circular economy, which has gained momentum in recent years. Recycling programs for batteries and solar panels were introduced across the board to reduce environmental impact. At the same time, China relied on international cooperation. As part of the Belt and Road Initiative, the country exported green technologies to developing countries, from solar panels in Africa to wind farms in Central Asia. These projects were not without criticism—some accused China of using them to secure geopolitical influence—but they helped accelerate the global transition to renewable energy.

The role of society in this transformation cannot be underestimated. Young Chinese, especially millennials and Generation Z, developed a strong environmental consciousness. In cities like Beijing and Guangzhou, they organized campaigns for clean air and sustainable consumption. Social media platforms like WeChat and Douyin became forums where ideas for a greener life were shared. At the same time, the middle class drove demand for sustainable products, from electric cars to biodegradable packaging. This societal pressure intensified political and economic efforts, transforming change into a collective movement.

China's transition to renewable energy and green technologies over the past decade is not only a story of technological and economic achievements, but also sheds light on the dynamics of political decision-making. The way China has driven this transformation differs fundamentally from the processes in democratic systems. Party-political administrative decision-making, as made in China's centralized system, contrasts with Western-style democratic decision-making common in Western countries. Both approaches bring specific advantages and problems that have significantly shaped the course and effectiveness of China's green transition.

A key advantage of party-political administrative decision-making in China is its speed and efficiency. The Chinese Communist Party (CCP) has the authority to implement long-term strategies without lengthy parliamentary debates or public consultations. When the government decided to massively expand renewable energy in 2015, billions of dollars in investment were mobilized within a few months. Projects such as the solar farms in the Gobi Desert or the modernization of the power grid were implemented with a speed that is almost unimaginable in democratic systems. In countries like Germany or the USA, large infrastructure projects often have to go through years of approval processes and public consultations, which can be delayed by citizen initiatives or political disputes. In China, however, centralized control enabled decisions to be implemented quickly, giving the country a head start in the global energy transition.

This efficiency is also reflected in the ability to pool resources. The CCP was able to coordinate state-owned enterprises, local governments, and private actors to advance national goals such as the expansion of wind energy or the electrifycation of transport. One example is the city of Shenzhen, which electrified its entire bus fleet by 2017 – a process that would have taken years or even decades in other countries. This central planning made it possible to exploit economies of scale and reduce costs. For example, prices for solar modules fell by over 50 percent between 2015 and 2025, not least because China promoted large-scale production. In democratic systems, where decisions often depend on compromises between different interest groups, such coherent and rapid mobilization of resources can be difficult.

Another advantage of the Chinese system is long-term planning security. Five-year plans developed by the CCP provide a clear roadmap for decades. Companies and investors could rely on the government's consistent pursuit of its renewable energy goals. This created a stable environment for innovation and investment, for example in battery technology, where companies like CATL became global market leaders. In democratic systems, however, political priorities can fluctuate with each change of government. In the US, for example, changing administrations over the same period repeatedly led to uncertainty in climate policy, making long-term planning more difficult.

But these advantages come at a price. Party-political and administrative decisions in China are often accompanied by a lack of transparency and public participation. While democratic systems create broader legitimacy through discussions and elections, decisions in China are made behind closed doors. In some cases, this led to projects that, while technically impressive, were socially or environmentally problematic. The construction of hydropower plants in ecologically sensitive regions such as the Qinghai-Tibet Plateau, for example, sparked protests from local residents who were largely ignored. In a democratic system, such projects might have been stopped or adjusted through public pressure or legal action. In China, however, such concerns were often overlooked in favor of national priorities, undermining public confidence in some regions.

Another problem with centralized decision-making is the risk of misallocation. Without oversight by independent institutions or a critical public, resources can flow into inefficient or poorly designed projects. In the early years of the solar boom, for example, China invested in numerous solar parks in remote regions without creating the necessary grid infrastructure, leading to high curtailment rates. Democratic systems, although slower, often benefit from a broader debate that can uncover such errors early on. In Germany, for example, public discussion about the expansion of wind energy led to a greater focus on grid stability and citizen participation, which promoted more sustainable solutions in the long term.

Reliance on party-political directives can also hamper innovation. While China's top-down approach enabled large projects, it was often state-supported large companies that were favored. Smaller, innovative startups had a harder time competing with powerful state-owned companies. In democratic systems, however, competition often fosters a greater diversity of ideas. Silicon Valley, for example, spawned numerous disruptive technologies because it provided an environment where independent entrepreneurs could experiment freely. In China, by contrast, innovations were often tied to government regulations, which brought stability but sometimes also a lack of imagination.

Another aspect is social justice. In China, workers in the coal industry, such as in Shanxi Province, were often laid off without adequate retraining programs, leading to social tensions. In democratic systems, where unions and civil society organizations have a stronger voice, such transitions can be better managed through negotiations and social protections. The EU, for example, has created mechanisms to support workers in fossil fuel industries with the "Just Transition Fund" – an approach that has only slowly gained traction in China.

Despite these weaknesses, China's transformation demonstrates that a centralized system can deliver extraordinary results in times of crisis. The urgency of the climate crisis required swift and decisive action, and China was able to deliver it. Democratic systems, on the other hand, score points for their ability to create broader social acceptance and develop more balanced long-term solutions, even if this takes time. Both approaches have their strengths and weaknesses, and China's success in the energy transition is proof that centralized power can be effective in certain contexts – but also that it carries risks without checks and balances.

China's transformation between 2015 and 2025 demonstrates how profoundly political systems influence the path to a sustainable future. While partisan efficiency catapulted China to the forefront of green technologies, questions of transparency, social justice, and long-term sustainability sometimes remain unresolved. For the world, China's example is both an inspiration and a warning: speed and decisiveness are essential, but without the involvement of society, new imbalances threaten. The path to a green future requires both vision and responsibility – and China has shown that it combines both, albeit in its own unique way.

Nevertheless, or perhaps precisely because of this, China in 2025 looks back on a decade marked by unprecedented progress. The share of coal in the energy mix has fallen to below 40 percent, while renewable energies account for almost half of electricity production. Air quality in cities has improved significantly, and China is well on its way to achieving its climate goals. But the road is far from over. New challenges, such as the decarbonization of heavy industry and the integration of hydrogen technologies, lie ahead. At the same time, the question remains how China can further expand its global leadership in the green economy without making social or environmental compromises.

China's recent history is the story of a country that reinvented itself amid global challenges—not perfectly, but with a determination that changed the world. For people like Zhang Wei, who now works in the Gobi Desert under clearer skies, this transformation is tangible. And for the world, China is an example that change is possible—if the will is there.

Quantum communication: The next dimension

On a clear August night in 2016, high above the Gobi Desert, a tiny dot flashed in the sky, barely visible to the naked eye. It wasn't a star, or an airplane, but Micius, the world's first quantum satellite, named after an ancient Chinese philosopher. This satellite marked a turning point in the history of communications technology and was a bold step for China into a future where information could be transmitted not only quickly but also with absolute security over vast distances. Micius was more than a technical masterpiece; it was a symbol of China's ambitions to push the boundaries of science and establish itself as a leader in quantum technology.

In the years between 2015 and 2025, China transformed from a country often considered a laggard in the global scientific landscape into a pioneer rewriting the rules of digital communication. This chapter tells the story of this transformation, explaining the principles of quantum communication in a way that will fascinate even non-physicists, and illuminating the geopolitical, economic, and technological implications of a decade that changed the world.

Quantum communication is not science fiction, but a technology based on the fascinating and often counterintuitive laws of quantum mechanics. Imagine two people trying to send each other a secret message without a third party being able to intercept it. In classical communication—such as an email or a phone call—this is a problem. Even the best encryption methods, such as those used today in banks or government networks, could theoretically be cracked by a sufficiently powerful computer. Quantum computers, which could become ubiquitous in the coming decades, pose a threat to these classical encryptions because they are capable of solving complex mathematical problems currently considered unbreakable in seconds. This is where quantum communication comes into play, based on principles such as quantum entanglement and the so-called no-cloning theorem. These principles guarantee security that is not based on computing power, but on the immutable laws of physics.

Quantum entanglement is one of the most fascinating phenomena in quantum mechanics. Imagine two dice that are magically linked. If you roll one and it shows a six, the other will immediately show a six as well—regardless of whether they are in the same room or on different continents. This connection remains until a measurement is made that changes the state of the dice. Albert Einstein once called this phenomenon "spooky action at a distance" because it challenges classical notions of space and time. In quantum communication, this entanglement is used to generate secret keys used to encrypt messages. The no-cloning theorem ensures that a quantum state cannot be copied without changing it. Every attempt at eavesdropping leaves traces because measuring a quantum state inevitably disrupts it. This makes quantum communication theoretically secure against eavesdropping—a promise that sounds like a holy grail in a world where cyberattacks and data leaks are commonplace.

China's journey into the world of quantum communication did not begin in 2016 with the launch of Micius, but years earlier in the laboratories of the University of Science and Technology of China (USTC) in Hefei. There, Professor Jian-Wei Pan, a physicist often referred to as the "father of Chinese quantum physics," led a team determined to translate basic research into practice. Pan had studied in Vienna under Nobel laureate Anton Zeilinger, whose groundbreaking work on quantum entanglement laid the foundation for many subsequent developments. Back in China, Pan brought with him not only scientific know-how but also a vision: to transform quantum communication from a theoretical curiosity into a technology that secures the digital infrastructure of the future. In 2015, China was still an outsider in quantum research. While countries like the US, Japan, and European nations like Austria and Germany were also working on quantum technologies, China had the advantage of centrally controlled scientific funding and a government willing to invest billions in strategic technologies.

The launch of Micius in August 2016 was a milestone that caught the world's attention. The satellite, named after the philosopher Mozi, who pondered light and optics in the 5th century BC, was the centerpiece of the Quantum Experiments at Space Scale (QUESS) project. The goal was to demonstrate that quantum entanglement is possible over long distances and that quantum key distribution (QKD)—the method used to exchange secure keys via quantum channels—also works via satellites. Micius was equipped with high-precision optical systems that could send entangled photons from an orbit 500 kilometers above the Earth to ground stations in China.

The challenge was enormous: The photons had to be sent through the atmosphere, where they could be disrupted by air turbulence, light pollution, or weather conditions. But Jian-Wei Pan's team overcame this hurdle. In June 2017, the team published the results of an experiment in the journal Science in which entangled photons were transmitted over a distance of 1,200 kilometers between two ground stations in Delingha and Lijiang. It was the first time such a feat had been achieved and proved that satellite-based quantum communication was not only possible but also practical.

This achievement was more than a scientific triumph; it was a geopolitical statement. While the US and Europe were still working on ground-based quantum networks, China was ahead of the game by bringing the technology into space. The significance of this development can hardly be overstated. At a time when cyberattacks on governments, businesses, and critical infrastructure are on the rise, quantum communication offers a solution that not only counters today's threats but also the future dangers posed by quantum computers. China recognized early on that control over this technology would bring not only economic but also strategic advantages. A secure communications network is invaluable for military and government purposes, and China used this insight to strengthen its position in the global technology arena.

Parallel to the satellite project, China was building an impressive terrestrial quantum network. In 2017, the so-called Beijing-Shanghai Quantum Communication Backbone, a fiber optic network more than 2,000 kilometers long connecting Beijing and Shanghai, went into operation. This network, consisting of 32 nodes, was the first of its kind and demonstrated that quantum communication is possible even over long distances on Earth. Transmitting quantum keys over fiber optic cables is technically challenging because photons can be attenuated or lost due to interference as they travel through the cable. Nevertheless, the Chinese researchers succeeded in developing a system robust enough to be used for real-world applications. Banks, government agencies, and companies began using this network for secure data transmissions, such as financial transactions or the transmission of sensitive documents.

The significance of this network went beyond the technology. It was a testament to China's ability to implement large-scale projects quickly and efficiently—a contrast to the often hesitant and fragmented efforts in Western countries. While Europe and the US struggled with regulatory hurdles, funding issues, and coordination between different research institutes and companies, China was able to act quickly thanks to its centralized planning and generous government support. The 14th Five-Year Plan (2021–2025), a central document of Chinese economic and technological policy, emphasized the strategic importance of quantum technologies and allocated significant funds for research. This enabled China to lead not only in basic research but also in the practical application of quantum communication.

Another milestone followed in 2021 when Chinese researchers in Shanghai demonstrated that quantum communication is possible even in a metropolitan environment. In a city with millions of lights, air pollution, and constant electromagnetic interference, quantum codes were successfully transmitted directly through the air for kilometers using light pulses. This was a breakthrough, as most previous experiments had taken place in remote areas to minimize interference. The ability to realize quantum communication in an urban environment demonstrated that the technology is not only suitable for specialized applications but can also be integrated into everyday life.

Imagine banks in Shanghai or government agencies in Beijing exchanging sensitive data over a quantum network without fear of eavesdropping. This progress brought the vision of a global quantum internet one step closer.

In 2025, China reached another peak when a quantum communication link was established between China and South Africa. This intercontinental link, realized via the Micius satellite and later via the Jinan-1 microsatellite, spanned 12,900 kilometers and was the longest quantum link ever established. The collaboration with Stellenbosch University in South Africa demonstrated that quantum communication is not just a national, but a global technology. With a key generation rate of 1.07 million secure bits per satellite overpass, the experiment proved that quantum key distribution is feasible even over long distances. The use of a compact microsatellite and portable ground stations reduced costs and made the technology more accessible, opening the door to further international collaborations.

But what makes quantum communication so special, and why is China investing so heavily in this technology? To understand this, it's worth looking at the basics of quantum key distribution (QKD). Imagine two parties, often referred to in the literature as "Alice" and "Bob." Alice wants to send Bob a secret message. In a classical system, Alice would encrypt the message with a key that she sends to Bob on a separate channel. If an eavesdropper, say "Eve," intercepts this key, she could decrypt the message without either Alice or Bob noticing. In quantum communication, however, Alice sends individual photons encoded in specific quantum states (e.g., polarization) to Bob.

These photons carry the information for the key. When Eve attempts to intercept the photons, she changes their state because she needs to measure them to obtain the information.

This change is noticed by Alice and Bob, who compare a portion of the data after transmission to determine if an attempt has been made to eavesdrop. If everything is secure, they use the key to encrypt the actual message. If an attempt is detected, they discard the key and start over. This process is not only secure but physically impossible to crack as long as the laws of quantum mechanics apply.

However, the practical implementation of this technology is fraught with challenges. One of the biggest problems is the transmission rate. While classical communication systems can transmit data at speeds of gigabits per second, the transmission rate for quantum keys is often in the range of bits per second. For the connection between China and South Africa, the rate was only 0.1 bits per second—far too slow for practical applications such as video streaming or large data transfers. Nevertheless, this speed is sufficient for transmitting keys, as these keys only need to be a few bits long to enable secure encryption.

Another challenge is range. Photons sent through fiber optic cables or the atmosphere lose intensity, making transmission over long distances difficult. This is where quantum repeaters come into play: devices that amplify the quantum signal without destroying the quantum state. While such repeaters are being developed in China and other countries, they are not yet commercially ready, limiting the scaling of quantum networks.

Despite these challenges, China made impressive progress between 2015 and 2025. A key factor in this success was the close collaboration between academia, industry, and government. While in Western countries, research is often driven by private companies or university institutions competing for limited funding, China has pursued a centralized strategy. The Chinese Academy of Sciences, the USTC, and other institutions are working hand in hand with government agencies such as the National Development and Reform Commission (NDRC) to realize projects such as Micius and the Beijing-Shanghai network. This centralized planning made it possible to efficiently pool resources and implement projects in record time. A comparison with the construction of the new airport in Beijing, which was completed in just a few years, shows how effectively China tackles large-scale projects – an approach that often encounters bureaucratic hurdles in the Western world.

Another aspect that explains China's success is its investment in talent. Jian-Wei Pan is just one of many scientists who have studied abroad and brought their knowledge back to China. The government has launched programs to cultivate young talent and attract foreign experts. At the same time, China has educated a generation of students who excel in the natural sciences, particularly computer science and physics. In 2019, reports indicate that about 30 percent of all Chinese students studied IT-related subjects, a sign of the prioritization of technological innovation. This investment in human capital has paid off: China leads not only in the number of patent applications in the field of quantum communications (15% of global patent applications between 2015 and 2025), but also in the number of scientific publications.

However, China's advances in quantum communications are not without controversy. In a world marked by geopolitical tensions, the technology is often viewed as part of a larger competition for technological supremacy. The United States, which passed the National Quantum Initiative Act in 2018, has invested over $1.2 billion in quantum research to keep pace with China. Europe also has ambitious plans, such as the QuNet initiative, which aims to build a Europe-wide quantum communications network. But while Western countries often struggle with the fragmentation of their research landscapes, China benefits from its ability to centrally control resources and priorities. At the same time, there are concerns about the military applications of quantum communications. A secure network could be used not only for civilian purposes such as banking or healthcare, but also for military communications, raising security questions at a time of increasing global tensions.

One example of these geopolitical implications is the Belt and Road Initiative, under which China is exporting its quantum communications technology to other countries. The collaboration with South Africa is a step in this direction, but there are plans to establish similar connections with other partner countries. This could provide China with not only economic but also political advantages, as countries that rely on Chinese technology could become more closely tied to China. Critics warn of "technological dependence," similar to the proliferation of 5G technology by Chinese companies like Huawei. But proponents argue that quantum communications is a global technology that benefits all countries by increasing the security of digital infrastructures.

Despite the impressive progress, many hurdles remain on the path to a global quantum internet. One of the biggest is the development of quantum repeaters, which enable quantum signals to be transmitted over thousands of kilometers without loss. While China has made progress in this area, such devices are not yet commercially ready. Another problem is the vulnerability of quantum satellites to interference. One study indicated that a moderately powered ground-based laser could disrupt a satellite's key generation by increasing the quantum bit error rate. This shows that even quantum communications are not completely impervious and that the race for next-generation security has already begun.

A look at market forecasts shows that quantum communications has enormous economic potential. According to a study by the Fraunhofer Institute and Saarland University, global revenue was approximately €1.7 billion in 2023 and could rise to €5.8 billion by 2030, with annual growth rates between 15 and 25 percent. China is well positioned to capture a significant share of this market, not least through companies like ID Quantique, which, although originating in Switzerland, is part of a Korean group and works closely with Chinese partners.

However, the commercialization of the technology is still in its early stages. High costs and the need for specialized equipment such as single-photon detectors or cryogenic systems currently make quantum communication unaffordable for many applications. However, advances in miniaturization, such as the development of compact chips for random number generation, could change this in the coming years.

The cultural and societal impact of quantum communication in China is also remarkable. In a country where control over information and data plays a central role, quantum communication offers a way to strengthen the security of digital infrastructure without compromising citizens' privacy. At the same time, it raises questions about how this technology is being used. While Western media often criticize the Chinese government's surveillance capabilities, Chinese scientists argue that quantum communication primarily serves to protect sensitive data, for example in the healthcare or financial industries. The ability to transmit patient data or financial transactions securely could strengthen trust in digital systems and enable new applications.

A vivid example is its application in healthcare. In rural areas of China, where access to medical care is often limited, quantum communication could enable the secure transmission of patient data between hospitals and specialists. A pilot project in Anhui Province demonstrated how quantum key distribution can be used to transmit medical data in real time, for example, for remote consultations with doctors. Such applications could not only improve healthcare but also demonstrate how quantum communication directly impacts people's lives.

In 2025, China will be at the forefront of quantum communication, but the road is far from over. The vision of a global quantum internet, where entangled photons exchange data between continents, is still years away. However, the progress of the past decade shows that China has the resources, expertise, and will to make this vision a reality. Collaborations with international partners, such as Stellenbosch University and Austrian researchers, demonstrate that quantum communication is not just a national, but a global endeavor. At the same time, the technology remains a theater of geopolitical rivalries in which China, the US, Europe, and other players vie for supremacy.

To the layperson, quantum communication may seem like magic, but it is the result of hard scientific work and strategic planning. It promises a future in which our data is more secure than ever before, in which banks, governments, and hospitals can operate without fear of cyberattacks. For China, it is a symbol of its rise to technological superpower, proof that the country can not only keep up with the big players, but surpass them. The story of Micius and the Beijing-Shanghai network is just the beginning—a first step into a new dimension of communication that will change the world forever.

Education and digital learning platforms

The People's Republic of China, long known for its industrial strength and economic dynamism, had set itself an ambitious goal: to assume a leading role in the global digital landscape by 2025, not only in technology but also in education. Education has always been a central pillar of social and economic progress in China, but the integration of digital learning platforms into the education system between 2015 and 2025 marked a turning point that permanently changed both the way knowledge was imparted and the social structures. This transformation was not only technological but also cultural and political. It tells a story of ambition, innovation, challenges, and a country striving towards the digital future at unprecedented speed while simultaneously confronting the downsides of this development.

The story begins at a time when China was already a global powerhouse, but with an education system deeply rooted in traditional structures. The Chinese education system was known for its rigor, its focus on performance, and the central role of the Gaokao, the national college entrance examination, which determined the future of millions of students. But as the world immersed itself in the digital age, the Chinese government recognized that education needed to be reformed to keep pace with the demands of a modern, technology-driven economy.

The "Made in China 2025" and "Internet Plus" strategic plans, launched in 2015, were not only economic blueprints but also a call to transform the education system through digital technologies. These plans aimed to make China a global leader in areas such as artificial intelligence, big data, and digital platforms. Education was seen as key to preparing the next generation for this future.

In the classrooms of metropolises like Shanghai and Beijing, as well as in remote provincial schools, the landscape began to change. Digital learning platforms, initially conceived as a supplement to traditional classes, quickly became an integral part of the education system. Companies like Alibaba, Tencent, and ByteDance, which already dominated other sectors, entered the education market and brought their technological expertise with them. Platforms like Xueersi, Yuanfudao, and VIPKid grew rapidly, offering personalized learning content, interactive courses, and AI-powered learning analytics. These platforms promised to make education more accessible, efficient, and personalized—a promise that resonated particularly in a country of 1.4 billion people with a strong focus on educational equity.

The story of Wang Kun, a physical education teacher at Qingzhen Middle School in Guiyang, vividly illustrates this shift. Passionate about objective assessment and performance, Wang dreamed of eliminating human error in the assessment process. His school introduced digital tools that not only recorded students' performance in real time but also analyzed their engagement and concentration. AI-powered cameras monitored students' movements during physical education classes, while algorithms assessed their progress. This technology, developed by companies like Guizhou Jingshi City Investment Smart Education, was part of a larger vision to revolutionize education through digital precision.

But Wang's story also highlights the ambivalence of this development: While the technology enabled more objective assessments, it also led to unprecedented surveillance of students, raising questions about data privacy and ethics.

The driving force behind this transformation was the Chinese Communist Party (CCP), which viewed education as a strategic tool to achieve its economic and political goals. The "National Informatization Strategy" (2016–2020) called on companies to go global and help shape the "Digital Silk Road." Education was a central component of this strategy. The CCP promoted domestic technology companies like Baidu, Alibaba, and Tencent (BAT) through protectionism, keeping foreign competitors like Google and Facebook out of the market. This created a protected space in which Chinese companies could flourish. At the same time, the government invested heavily in digital infrastructure, from broadband networks to 5G, laying the foundation for the widespread use of digital learning platforms.

Between 2015 and 2020, the e-learning market in China grew rapidly. According to data from iiMediaResearch and iResearch, revenue in the education sector exceeded €50 billion in 2020, a sign of the growing importance of digital platforms. These platforms primarily targeted students in rural areas, where access to quality education has traditionally been limited. The idea was to improve educational opportunities through standardized content and online courses, particularly for the gaokao, which was the same for all students, regardless of whether they attended school in Beijing or in a remote province like Guizhou.

Platforms such as NetEase Cloud Classroom and Tencent Classroom enabled teachers to stream courses in real time, while AI tools analyzed learning progress and assigned personalized assignments. This development was particularly important in a country where 85 percent of students lived in rural areas, where qualified teachers were often lacking.

The story of Li Mei, a student from a small village in Sichuan Province, shows how these platforms changed lives. Li Mei, a farmer's daughter, had limited access to the tutoring that was ubiquitous in cities. But through an app called Yuanfudao, she was able to attend online classes taught by Shanghai-based teachers in the evenings after school. The platform used AI to identify her weaknesses in math and assign her tailored exercises. Within two years, she improved her grades so significantly that she passed the gaokao with flying colors and earned a place at a prestigious university. Her story is just one of millions that demonstrate how digital learning platforms have advanced educational equity in China—at least at first glance.

But the transformation was not without challenges. Rapid digitalization led to a commercialization of the education sector, creating new inequalities. While platforms like VIPKid offered affordable courses, many premium services were expensive, favoring wealthy families in cities. The cost of tutoring rose, and parents felt compelled to invest ever more money in their children's education to compete for the best gaokao scores. This development led to a paradoxical effect: On the one hand, digitalization was intended to democratize education, but on the other, it increased the pressure on families and students, especially in the middle class.

In 2021, the Chinese government intervened to break this dynamic. With a surprise education reform, it banned private education companies from making profits and prohibited extracurricular classes on weekends for children under six. These measures were aimed at reducing financial pressure on families and promoting educational equity. Companies like New Oriental Education & Tech Group, whose share prices plummeted 65 percent following the announcement, suddenly faced an existential crisis. The reform was a clear expression of state control over the education sector and an attempt to curb commercialization. But it also had side effects: Many teachers lost their jobs, and the black market for tutoring flourished as parents continued to seek ways to support their children.

Another aspect of digitalization was the integration of artificial intelligence into teaching. Schools like Qingzhen Middle School in Guiyang introduced "smart" classrooms where cameras monitored students' attention and algorithms analyzed their learning progress. These technologies promised to make teaching more efficient by reducing the burden on teachers and providing students with tailored content. But they also raised ethical questions. The widespread surveillance of students, the collection of health data, and the analysis of facial expressions led to concerns about data privacy. Critics argued that China was creating a "digital panopticon" where students were constantly monitored and assessed. This development reflected the broader trend of surveillance in China, where technologies such as the social credit system already controlled citizens.

Despite these challenges, the 2018 PISA study showed that China ranked first in reading, mathematics, and science, a testament to the strength of its education system. Digitalization played a key role in this. In cities tested in the study, such as Beijing and Shanghai, schools used advanced technologies to provide individualized support to students. The gross enrollment ratio in tertiary education doubled to 50 percent between 2011 and 2018, and in 2019, nearly 47 million students were enrolled in Chinese higher education institutions, many of them using online courses and digital platforms. These figures underscore the success of the digitalization strategy, but also the need to further refine it to include all segments of the population.

The story of Zhang Youyou, a developer at Guizhou Jingshi City Investment Smart Education, illustrates the ambition behind these technologies. Zhang worked in a glass office tower in Guiyang, developing AI tools that would revolutionize teaching. His vision was to combine neuroscience with digital technology to make learning more efficient and cost-effective. But as he and his colleagues worked on "smart" classrooms, they faced criticism that their technologies violated students' privacy. Zhang himself was convinced that the benefits outweighed the risks, but the debate about the ethical implications persisted.

Another key player in this development was ByteDance, the company behind TikTok, which entered the education sector with its Dali smart lamp. Equipped with a touchscreen and cameras, this lamp was designed to help parents support their children with homework, even from a distance. But the lamp became a symbol of the ambivalence of digitalization: On the one hand, it offered practical support, while on the other, it increased the pressure on children and parents to constantly perform. The lamp was just one example of the many innovations that flooded the education market between 2015 and 2025, from interactive whiteboards to virtual classrooms.

The pandemic of 2020 to 2022 significantly accelerated the digitalization of education in China. When schools closed, digital platforms became the lifeline of education. Platforms like DingTalk and Tencent Classroom made it possible to continue classes online, while AI tools helped teachers keep track of hundreds of students. This period demonstrated how robust China's digital infrastructure had become, but also how much its dependence on technology had grown. In rural areas, where not all students had access to fast internet or modern devices, the limitations of digitalization became apparent. The government responded by investing in infrastructure to connect even remote regions to the digital grid.

By 2025, China had created an education system that was unique in the world. The combination of state guidance, technological innovation, and a relentless focus on performance had placed the country at the forefront of the global education landscape. But this success came at a price. The comercialization of the education sector, the surveillance of students, and the ethical issues surrounding AI and data privacy remained unresolved challenges. The story of China's educational transformation is one of triumph and contradictions, of progress and control, of individual success stories like Li Mei's and the systemic tensions created by digitalization.

The role of teachers also changed. In traditional classrooms, teachers were often the unchallenged authority, but with the introduction of digital platforms, they became more of a facilitator of the learning process. AI tools took over tasks such as grading tests or creating learning plans, giving teachers more time to provide individualized support to students. At the same time, using these technologies required new skills. Teachers like Wang Kun had to undergo training to navigate the new systems, which wasn't always easy. In rural areas, where technical equipment was often outdated, teachers faced the challenge of using digital tools with limited resources.

Parents also played a crucial role in this transformation. In China, where education is often seen as the key to social advancement, parents were willing to invest significant sums in their children's education. The introduction of digital platforms increased this pressure, as parents now had access to a wealth of online courses and tutoring services. But the 2021 reform forced many families to rethink their strategies. Instead of expensive tutoring courses, parents sought cost-effective alternatives, leading to a boom in free or low-cost platforms supported by government institutions.

The international perspective on China's educational transformation is also noteworthy. While countries like Germany and the USA developed their own digitalization strategies, China was often seen as a model for the rapid and comprehensive integration of technology into education. However, the strong state control and surveillance of students also led to criticism. European experts, such as researchers Kristin Shi-Kupfer and Mareike Ohlberg of the Mercator Institute for China Studies, pointed out that China's digital offensive presented not only opportunities but also challenges for the global education landscape. The dominance of Chinese companies like Huawei in 5G technology and their role in digital infrastructure increased concerns that China could set global standards that did not always align with Western values such as data protection and individual freedom.

The future of education in China remains uncertain. By 2025, the country had made enormous progress, but the challenges have not yet been resolved. The balance between technological innovation and ethical standards, between educational equity and commercialization, and between state control and individual freedom will shape the coming years. The story of China's educational transformation is not yet over, but it shows how a country with steely determination and technological vision can redefine the way knowledge is imparted. It's a story of progress, but also of caution—a reminder that technology is both a tool and a responsibility.

Robotics and industrial automation

In 2015, China was at a crossroads. Long known as the workshop of the world, the country was confronted with a changing global economy. Labor costs were rising, its demographic dividend—a large, young, and low-cost workforce—was dwindling, and international competition for technological dominance was intensifying. At the same time, pressure was growing to increase productivity, reduce environmental impact, and lessen its dependence on foreign technology. In this context, China began transforming its industrial landscape through an unprecedented use of robotics and automation.

The years from 2015 to 2025 marked an era of rapid technological progress, during which China not only accelerated the automation of its industries but also established itself as a global leader in robotics. This transformation was characterized by ambitious policies, enormous investments, technological breakthroughs, and a profound transformation of the world of work. But it also brought challenges: social tensions, ethical questions, and the need to balance innovation with sustainability. This chapter tells the story of this transformation—a story of ambition, progress, and the complex interactions between technology, business, and society.

At the beginning of this decade, China's industry was still heavily reliant on manual labor. Millions of migrant workers toiled in the vast factories of Guangdong and Zhejiang provinces, flocking from rural areas to the booming cities to work in manufacturing. Textiles, electronics, toys—virtually everything that landed on the shelves of Western supermarkets bore the "Made in China" label. But times were changing. Wages rose as workers demanded higher salaries and better working conditions. At the same time, the young population shrank due to the decades-long one-child policy, limiting the availability of cheap labor. For a country whose economy was based on low-cost mass production, this posed an existential challenge. Added to this was international pressure: countries like Vietnam and India began to catch up as alternative manufacturing locations, while Western nations sought to strengthen their own industries through "reshoring" – the relocation of production facilities.

Amid these challenges, the Chinese leadership realized that the future of industry lay in automation. In 2015, the government announced the ambitious "Made in China 2025" program, a strategic initiative aimed at transforming China from a manufacturing base for simple goods into a global center for high-tech innovation. Robotics and automation were at the heart of this plan. The goal was to increase productivity, improve product quality, and reduce dependence on foreign technologies. It was a wake-up call for industry: modernize or fall behind. The government supported this goal with massive subsidies, tax breaks, and investments in research and development. At the same time, companies were encouraged to invest in automation technologies, whether by purchasing industrial robots or developing their own solutions.

The early years of this transformation were marked by a veritable boom in the use of industrial robots. According to the International Federation of Robotics (IFR), China became the world's largest market for industrial robots in 2013, and this trend accelerated in the following years. In 2015, China installed approximately 68,000 robots, more than any other country. By 2020, this number had grown to over 150,000 per year, and by 2025, China had more industrial robots in operation than the United States, Japan, and Germany combined. These robots were used not only in large state-owned enterprises but also in small and medium-sized businesses that gained access to this technology thanks to falling costs and government support. In factories like those of Foxconn, the world's largest contract manufacturer of electronics, assembly lines once operated by hundreds of workers were increasingly replaced by robotic arms that operated around the clock with precise efficiency. One example that captures the dynamics of this time is the story of Li Wei, a factory worker from Shandong Province. In 2015, Li worked in an automotive parts factory, where he spent eight hours a day screwing screws into metal parts. The work was monotonous, physically demanding, and poorly paid. When the factory began introducing robotic arms in 2017, Li feared for his job.

But instead of being laid off, he was trained to maintain and program the new machines. Within a few years, he was promoted to technician, with higher pay and better working conditions. Li's story is exemplary of many workers in China who were offered new opportunities during this transition period—but also of the challenges faced by those who couldn't adapt quickly enough.

The rapid proliferation of robots, however, was only part of the story. At the same time, China was developing its own robotics industry. In the early 2010s, the country was heavily dependent on foreign manufacturers such as ABB (Switzerland), Fanuc (Japan), and Kuka (Germany). These companies supplied most of the robots installed in Chinese factories. But "Made in China 2025" set a clear goal: to promote domestic manufacturers. Companies such as Siasun, Estun, and DJI (better known for drones, but also active in robotics) began developing their own robots, which were often more cost-effective than their Western counterparts. By 2025, China not only had the largest market for robots, but also a thriving domestic industry producing for both the domestic market and export.

A key factor in this success was the close integration of government, industry, and academia. Universities such as Tsinghua University in Beijing and Zhejiang University in Hangzhou worked closely with companies to develop new technologies. Research centers for artificial intelligence (AI) and robotics mushroomed, funded by government funds and private investment.

These centers focused not only on traditional industrial robots but also on new applications such as collaborative robots (cobots) that could work side by side with humans and service robots used in areas such as logistics, healthcare, and hospitality. One example is the city of Shenzhen, which evolved from a center for low-cost electronics into a hotspot for robotics innovation. This is where startups emerged that developed robots for everything from autonomous delivery vehicles to robot dogs that patrolled warehouses.

But the path was not without obstacles. Rapid automation led to social tensions. In some regions, particularly in less developed provinces, workers lost their jobs without adequate retraining programs in place. The gap between highly skilled technicians and unskilled workers widened, exacerbating social inequality. In cities like Chongqing, where traditional industries like steel production were being automated, protests erupted from workers who felt overwhelmed by the technological wave. The government responded with retraining and social support programs, but implementation was often uneven and met with criticism.

Another problem was the dependence on foreign components. While China made progress in developing its own robots, many key components such as precision motors, sensors, and semiconductors continued to come from abroad. This made the Chinese robotics industry vulnerable to international trade tensions, particularly during the trade war with the US in the late 2010s. The government therefore invested heavily in developing its own semiconductor industry, but by 2025, China lagged behind the global market leaders in some areas.

Despite these challenges, progress was impressive. By 2025, China had not only multiplied the number of robots it deployed, but also increased the quality and variety of applications. In the automotive industry, one of the most highly automated sectors, robots worked with a precision that human workers could hardly match. In electronics manufacturing, robots enabled the production of increasingly complex devices, from smartphones to 5G base stations. Even in traditionally labor-intensive industries such as textiles, automated systems began to take over tasks such as sewing or dyeing fabrics.

A particularly fascinating example is the development of the "smart factory." In cities such as Shanghai and Suzhou, almost fully automated production facilities emerged. These factories used not only robots but also the Internet of Things (IoT) to connect machines, robots, and logistics systems. Sensors monitored every stage of the production process in real time, while AI algorithms optimized efficiency and predicted errors before they occurred. One such example is Haier's factory in Qingdao, which was recognized as one of the World Economic Forum's first "Lighthouse Factories" in 2020. Here, household appliances such as refrigerators and washing machines were produced with a level of customization previously unimaginable – customers could configure their appliances online, and production was automatically adjusted.

But automation wasn't limited to industry. In cities, robots began to shape everyday life. In Beijing and Shenzhen, autonomous delivery robots became a familiar sight, delivering packages, groceries, or even coffee to customers. In hospitals, robots assisted medical staff by distributing medicines or performing disinfection tasks – a development that received a boost during the 2020 COVID-19 pandemic. This pandemic served as a catalyst for robotics: As social distancing and hygiene became top priorities, China accelerated the use of robots in public spaces.

The role of artificial intelligence in this context cannot be overestimated. AI was the brain behind many of the robots deployed during this decade. From machine learning, which enabled robots to learn from mistakes, to computer vision, which enabled them to recognize objects with high precision, AI drove robotics to new heights.

Chinese companies such as Baidu, Tencent, and Alibaba invested billions in AI research, and these technologies quickly found their way into industry. One example is the use of AI-controlled robots in logistics: In massive warehouses at companies such as JD.com, hundreds of robots moved autonomously, sorting packages and optimizing the supply chain with an efficiency that human workers could not achieve.

But this progress also brought with it ethical questions. How would automation change the world of work in the long term? While some, like Li Wei, benefited from automation, others faced uncertainty. Fears of job losses were pervasive, especially in industries that relied heavily on manual labor. At the same time, the question arose as to how China could close the growing gap between highly skilled and unskilled workers.

Education and retraining became key themes, and the government launched large-scale programs to prepare the population for the demands of the new economy. However, implementation was complex, and many regions lacked the resources to implement these programs across the board.

The environment was another issue. Automation promised to make production more efficient and less resource-intensive. Smart factories did indeed lead to a reduction in waste and energy consumption. But the production of robots itself—especially the manufacture of batteries and electronic components—had a significant ecological footprint. Already struggling with air pollution and other environmental problems, China faced the challenge of balancing technological progress with sustainability. By 2025, the country had made progress, for example, by introducing stricter environmental regulations for industry, but it remained a balancing act.

Internationally, China's rise in robotics was viewed with a mixture of admiration and concern. On the one hand, the country was an indispensable partner in global supply chains, but on the other, Western nations viewed China's growing technological independence as a threat. The trade war with the US and the sanctions against Chinese technology companies such as Huawei had demonstrated how geopolitical tensions could influence technological development. But China was undeterred. Through investments in research and development and strategic partnerships with countries along the "New Silk Road," the country further expanded its position as a global technology leader.

The Impact on the Chinese Labor Market

China's transformation through robotics and automation brought about profound changes in the labor market, creating both opportunities and challenges for the population. While automation increased productivity and created new career fields, it forced millions of workers to adapt to a rapidly changing world of work. The impact on the labor market was multifaceted: it ranged from the creation of highly skilled jobs and the displacement of traditional jobs to new social and economic challenges.

At the same time, prospects opened up for a future in which education, training, and social security would play a central role in preparing the population for the demands of the automated economy. This chapter continues this chapter and examines how China dealt with these changes, the consequences it had to cope with, and what the labor market of the future might look like.

The wave of automation that swept across China in the years after 2015 fundamentally changed the structure of the labor market. In industries such as the automotive industry, electronics manufacturing, and logistics, robots and AI-controlled systems took over tasks previously performed by humans. Welding robots in car factories, automated sorting machines in warehouses, and self-learning manufacturing systems in electronics production significantly reduced the need for unskilled labor. For many workers who had performed repetitive tasks for years, this meant an uncertain future. In cities like Dongguan, the heart of China's manufacturing industry, thousands of migrant workers lost their jobs as factories switched to robots. These workers, often without formal training, faced the challenge of navigating an economy that increasingly demanded technical skills.

But automation brought not only job losses, but also new opportunities. Between 2015 and 2025, job fields emerged that had previously barely existed. Programmers for robotics systems, data analysts for AI-assisted manufacturing processes, and technicians for the maintenance and optimization of automation technologies were urgently needed.

Companies like BYD, a leading manufacturer of electric vehicles, created thousands of jobs for engineers and software developers capable of designing and operating complex automated production lines. These new jobs offered not only higher salaries but also better working conditions compared to the often strenuous work in traditional factories. For people like Zhang Mei, a young engineer, automation represented an opportunity to work in a dynamic environment. After graduating with a degree in robotics from Northwestern Polytechnical University, she found a job at a startup in Shenzhen in 2022, where she worked on developing cobots for use in small workshops. Her career demonstrates how automation opened new doors for highly skilled professionnals.

Nevertheless, the transition was difficult for many workers. The gap grew between those who benefited from the new opportunities and those who were left behind. Particularly in rural areas and less developed provinces such as Henan or

Guizhou, the resources to comprehensively retrain workers were lacking. Many of the laid-off factory workers were in their 40s or 50s and lacked the time or means to acquire new skills. This led to a polarization of the labor market: on the one hand, there were highly skilled professionals in demand in booming tech centers such as Beijing, Shanghai, and Shenzhen, and on the other, a growing number of workers stranded in precarious employment or unemployment. This social inequality became one of the biggest challenges China faced in this decade.

The Chinese government recognized the need to respond to these developments and launched extensive retraining and upskilling programs. Starting in 2018, vocational training centers were established nationwide, offering courses in robotics, programming, and data analytics. These programs were often conducted in collaboration with companies such as Huawei and Alibaba, which contributed their expertise to curriculum development.

In Jiangsu Province, for example, the local government collaborated with Siasun, a leading robotics company, to train former factory workers to become technicians for the maintenance of industrial robots. Such initiatives were successful but not widely available. Many regions lacked qualified teachers, modern equipment, or sufficient funding, which limited the effectiveness of the programs.

Another aspect was the need to adapt the education system to the demands of the automated economy. Until 2015, the Chinese education system was heavily focused on academic performance and exams, with little room for practical, technical training. This changed in the following years.

Universities and vocational schools expanded their offerings in the fields of robotics, AI, and mechanical engineering. At the same time, partnerships with industry were expanded to equip students with practical skills at an early stage. In cities like Hangzhou, so-called "innovation hubs" emerged, where students, startups, and established companies collaborated to develop new technologies. These centers became breeding grounds for talent that drove the next generation of automation.

Social security was another critical issue. As automation boosted the economy, concerns grew that some segment of the population could be permanently excluded from its economic benefits. To prevent this, China experimented with new models of social security. In some cities, such as Shenzhen and Guangzhou, pilot projects for a universal basic income were tested to provide a transition period for workers who had lost their jobs. However, these programs were controversial because of their high costs and raised questions about their long-term financial viability. At the same time, the government invested in expanding the pension and healthcare systems to guarantee basic benefits for older workers affected by automation.

The future of China's labor market will depend heavily on the ability to ensure skills and employment opportunities for all segments of the population. By 2025, it became apparent that the labor market would evolve in two directions. On the one hand, there would be a growing demand for highly skilled professionals capable of developing, maintaining, and optimizing complex systems.

These professionals would be concentrated in urban centers, where they would have access to world-class education and infrastructure. On the other hand, creating employment opportunities for less skilled workers would remain a challenge. One possible solution could be to promote service occupations that are difficult to automate, such as nursing, education, or the creative sector. In Shanghai, for example, the need for caregivers grew as the aging population played a larger role—an area where human empathy and interaction remained essential.

Another approach for the future could be to promote entrepreneurship. Automation reduced production costs and enabled small businesses to enter manufacturing with lower investment. In cities like Chengdu, the government supported startups that used automated technologies to manufacture customized products for niche markets. These companies created jobs that combined creativity and technical skills, offering workers the opportunity to reinvent themselves in a dynamic economy.

The international dimension cannot be overlooked. China's advances in robotics and automation made the country an attractive destination for highly skilled professionals from around the world. At the same time, China exported its technologies to countries along the New Silk Road, creating new job opportunities for Chinese overseas. Engineers and technicians from China increasingly worked in countries like Pakistan and Kenya to implement automated infrastructure projects. This not only strengthened China's global position but also offered new career paths for highly skilled workers.

The consequences that China will have to address in the coming years are complex. The growing inequality between urban and rural areas, and between highly skilled and unskilled workers, requires targeted policies to avoid social tensions. The government will need to continue investing in education and retraining to ensure that the population is equipped with the necessary skills. At the same time, social security will play a key role in supporting those disadvantaged by automation. The environmental issue also remains central: While automation increases efficiency, China must ensure that the production of robots and AI systems is sustainable to minimize environmental impact.

China's future labor market will likely be a mix of high-tech professions, creative and social services, and entrepreneurial initiatives. The government will play a central role in creating the framework by investing in education, infrastructure, and social security. For the population, this represents an opportunity to be part of one of the world's most dynamic economies, but also the need for continuous training and adaptation. The story of China's automation is not only a story of machines, but also of people learning to navigate a new world—with all its opportunities and challenges.

By 2025, China had transformed from the world's workshop into a center of innovation. Robotics and automation had profoundly changed not only industry but also society. In factories, humans and machines worked ever more closely together, while robots shaped everyday life in cities. The challenges—social inequality, environmental pollution, geopolitical tensions—remained, but China's ambition and the speed of its transformation were impressive. The story from 2015 to 2025 is a story of vision, perseverance, and the recognition that technological progress always has a human dimension. For China, this was only the beginning of an even greater transformation, the effects of which would reach far beyond the country's borders.

China's Agricultural Technological Revolution

In the heart of Shandong Province, where the fields shimmer golden in the morning light and the breeze gently caresses the rice stalks, a farmer named Li Wei stands in front of a drone hovering silently over his fields. Holding a tablet, he watches as the device collects precise data on soil moisture, nutrient levels, and pest infestation. Just ten years ago, Li Wei would have paced the fields with a hoe in hand to check the health of his plants.

Today, his work is a blend of technology and tradition, a reflection of the agricultural technological revolution China is undergoing as part of the Made in China 2025 initiative. This revolution, which encompasses far more than just agriculture, is an ambitious quest for technological self-sufficiency and global leadership that has radically changed the way China cultivates its fields. It is a story of innovation, challenges, and the pursuit of a sustainable future that reveals both the strengths and contradictions of a nation balancing tradition and modernity.

The Made in China 2025 initiative, launched by the Chinese government in 2015, was initially intended as a blueprint for industrial transformation, with the goal of transforming China from the world's workshop into a global innovation leader. Ten key industries, including robotics, artificial intelligence, and new energies, were the focus. But agricultural technology, often viewed as a marginal topic, evolved into a central pillar of this strategy. Why? Because agriculture in China is not just an economic issue, but also an existential one. With 1.4 billion people to feed and only about 10 percent of its land suitable for arable farming, China faces a unique challenge: How can it sustainably feed a growing population with limited resources? The answer lies in a technological revolution that modernizes agriculture without uprooting the cultural roots of rural communities.

The agricultural technology revolution began with a clear vision: to increase productivity, reduce environmental impact, and minimize dependence on foreign technologies. In the early 2000s, China relied heavily on imported agricultural technologies, from seeds to farm machinery. This posed not only an economic burden but also a geopolitical risk, as global supply chains are vulnerable to trade conflicts and sanctions. Made in China 2025 addressed this issue by encouraging massive investments in research and development to develop domestic technologies. Companies like DJI, originally known for consumer drones, began producing agricultural drones that are now used worldwide. These drones, equipped with high-resolution cameras and AI-assisted image processing, can analyze the condition of crops in real time and apply pesticides or fertilizers in a targeted manner, drastically reducing resource use.

Li Wei, a farmer from Shandong, is a typical example of the impact of these technologies. His drone, manufactured by a Chinese startup that benefited from government subsidies, has increased his yields by 20 percent while reducing water consumption by a third. Such stories are not isolated. In the vast plains of Heilongjiang, China's breadbasket in the northeast, autonomous tractors, guided by satellite navigation, drive in precise paths across the fields. These machines, developed by companies like XAG, are part of a larger trend: precision agriculture. By combining sensors, satellite data, and AI, farmers can make decisions based on real-time information instead of relying on experience or intuition. The result is agriculture that is more efficient, sustainable, and resilient to climate change.

But the agricultural revolution is not just a story of technology, but also of people. In China's villages, where generations of farmers have tilled the fields, the change brings both opportunities and challenges. For young people like Zhang Mei, an agronomist from Sichuan, the revolution has opened up new perspectives. After graduating from Chengdu Agricultural University, she returned to her home village to establish a cooperative using modern technologies. With the support of government loans, her cooperative purchased drones and sensors that optimize tea cultivation.

Today, the cooperative exports high-quality tea to Europe, a success that would have been unthinkable without technological advances. But not all farmers share this enthusiasm. Older farmers unfamiliar with digital technologies often feel overwhelmed. In many regions, training to bridge the gap between traditional agriculture and modern technology is lacking. This highlights one of the central challenges of the revolution: How can we ensure that progress is inclusive and leaves no one behind?

The role of the state in this transformation should not be underestimated. Made in China 2025 is a state-led initiative, and agricultural technology is no exception. The government has launched multi-billion dollar funding programs to support startups, research institutes, and established companies. In cities like Shenzhen, China's Silicon Valley, agritech companies are springing up, benefiting from venture capital and government subsidies. At the same time, the government has pushed ahead with infrastructure projects to better connect rural areas to the digital grid. 5G towers now stand out even in remote villages, and broadband internet is standard in many regions. These investments have laid the foundation for the spread of agricultural technologies, from IoT sensors that monitor soil conditions to blockchain platforms that ensure food traceability.

But strong government control also has its downsides. Critics argue that centralized planning often leads to inefficient resource allocation. In some regions, expensive technologies have been introduced without farmers being adequately trained to use them. Overcapacity in the production of agricultural drones or sensors is also a problem, as many companies were lured by subsidies without developing long-term market strategies. There are also concerns about data security. The widespread use of sensors and drones generates enormous amounts of data that is collected by companies and government agencies. While this improves decision-making, there are questions about farmers' privacy and control over this data. In a nation where the government has a strong influence on the technology industry, such concerns are not unfounded.

Another aspect of the agricultural technology revolution is sustainability. China faces enormous environmental challenges: soil pollution, water scarcity, and the effects of climate change threaten agricultural production. Made in China 2025 has made sustainability a priority, and the results are promising. Precision agriculture reduces the use of pesticides and fertilizers, which lowers environmental impact. In Jiangsu Province, farmers are experimenting with vertical farms powered by LED lighting and hydroponic systems. These farms, often built in former industrial buildings, use less water and land than traditional agriculture and could serve as a model for the future. At the same time, the government is promoting the development of biodegradable materials for agricultural applications, from mulch films to packaging. But the challenges remain significant. The transition to sustainable agriculture requires not only technology but also a shift in the mindset of farmers and society. In a culture where high yields have often taken priority over environmental protecttion, this is a long-term process.

The global dimension of the agricultural technology revolution must not be overlooked. Made in China 2025 is not only a national plan but also a geopolitical statement. By exporting agricultural technologies, China is strengthening its influence in developing countries, particularly in Africa and Southeast Asia. Chinese companies like DJI and XAG supply drones and autonomous machines to countries seeking to modernize their agriculture.

These exports are part of the Belt and Road Initiative, which is expanding China's economic and political presence worldwide. But exporting technology also brings with it responsibility. In some countries, there are concerns that reliance on Chinese technologies could threaten national sovereignty in the long term. At the same time, international competition has forced China to raise its standards. Companies like John Deere and Bayer are strong competitors, and Chinese firms must deliver quality and innovation to compete in the global market.

Back in Shandong, where Li Wei lands his drone in the field, it becomes clear that the agricultural technology revolution is more than a set of technologies. It is a story of change, of people adapting, and of a nation shaping its future. For Li Wei, the revolution means not only higher yields but also the hope that his children will one day live in a world where food security and environmental protection go hand in hand. But the road there is not without obstacles. The tension between state control and entrepreneurial freedom, between tradition and modernity, between local needs and global ambitions characterizes the revolution. Made in China 2025 has transformed China's agriculture, but the question remains: Can this transformation create a sustainable, inclusive future that empowers both the fields and the people?

The agricultural technology revolution is a microcosm of the larger goals of Made in China 2025. It demonstrates how profoundly technology can transform a society, but also how complex the implementation of such changes is. The coming years will show whether China can meet the challenges: closing the digital divide, protecting the environment, and simultaneously achieving global leadership. For farmers like Li Wei and agricultural scientists like Zhang Mei, the revolution is already a reality. Their stories are a testament to the human spirit striving for progress amidst change and uncertainty.

And as drones fly over the fields, sensors collect data, and tractors autonomously ply their trades, a new kind of agriculture is growing in China—one that honors the past, embraces the present, and shapes the future.

The agricultural technology revolution, however, is not without its critics. The long-term effects of strong government control are often debated in academic circles and international forums. While centralized planning has enabled China to scale quickly, there are concerns that it limits the creativity and flexibility of some companies. In some cases, technologies were introduced that were not tailored to farmers' specific needs, leading to inefficient investments. For example, in some regions, state-of-the-art drones were delivered that were designed to work on large, flat fields but were unsuitable for the hilly terraced fields. Such missteps demonstrate the difficulties of applying a one-size-fits-all strategy to a country with such diverse geographies and cultural characteristics.

Another critical issue is social justice. While young, well-educated farmers like Zhang Mei are benefiting from the revolution, many older farmers feel excluded. In rural areas, where literacy and digital literacy rates are often low, the adoption of new technologies remains a challenge. While the government has introduced training programs, these do not always reach the most remote regions. In some villages, there are reports of farmers going into debt to purchase expensive technologies without the necessary support to use them effectively. This social divide between those benefiting from progress and those left behind is a key issue affecting the long-term sustainability of the revolution.

The environment remains another focus. China faces enormous environmental challenges, from soil pollution to water scarcity. Precision agriculture has helped reduce the use of pesticides and fertilizers, which has lessened environmental impact. In Jiangsu Province, for example, farmers are experimenting with vertical farms powered by LED lighting and hydroponic systems. These farms use less water and land than traditional agriculture and could serve as a model for the future. But the transition to truly sustainable agriculture requires more than just technology. It requires a cultural shift in which environmental protection becomes as important as high yields. In a society where maximizing production has long been a priority, this is a long-term process.

The global dimension of the agricultural technology revolution is also significant. By exporting agricultural technologies, China is strengthening its influence in developing countries, particularly in Africa and Southeast Asia. Chinese companies supply drones and autonomous machines to countries seeking to modernize their own agriculture. These exports are part of the Belt and Road Initiative, which is expanding China's economic and political presence worldwide. But exporting technology also brings with it responsibility. In some countries, there are concerns that long-term dependence on Chinese technologies could threaten national sovereignnty. At the same time, international competition has forced China to improve its standards. Companies like John Deere and Bayer are strong competitors, and Chinese firms must deliver quality and innovation to survive in the global market.

The agricultural technology revolution is a microcosm of the larger goals of Made in China 2025. It demonstrates how profoundly technology can transform a society, but also how complex the implementation of such changes is. The coming years will show whether China can overcome the challenges: closing the digital divide, protecting the environment, and achieving global leadership. For farmers like Li Wei and Zhang Mei, the revolution is already a reality. Their stories are a testament to the human spirit striving for progress amidst change and uncertainty. And as drones fly over fields, sensors collect data, and tractors autonomously ply their trades, a new kind of agriculture is growing in China—one that honors the past, embraces the present, and shapes the future.

The agricultural technology revolution is an ongoing process that brings both successes and challenges. For China, it is an opportunity not only to feed its own people but also to set a model for the world. The balance between technology and tradition, between government direction and individual initiative, between local needs and global ambitions will be crucial. The story of Li Wei, Zhang Mei, and millions of other farmers is proof that change is possible, but only if it is managed thoughtfully and compassionately. China's fields are not just a place of production, but a symbol of a nation striving for a sustainable, just and innovative future.

Acceptance and criticism among the population

The question of the Chinese population's acceptance or criticism of their own country's development seems pointless, given the centralized rule of the Communist Party. Nevertheless, it must be asked and will prove entirely appropriate in the course of this chapter.

Over the past decade, the country has developed into a global superpower, shaping the world stage not only economically, but also culturally and technologically. But while China has been admired for its rapid progress on the one hand, there has been growing criticism on the other – both within its own population and internationally. The acceptance and rejection of this change are reflected in the hopes, fears, and expectations of the people who have witnessed this process. This chapter sheds light on the complex facets of this change, the reactions of the population, and the tensions that have developed between progress and control, pride and doubt, and tradition and modernity.

In 2015, China stood at a turning point. Under the leadership of President Xi Jinping, the country had already made significant progress since its decision to pursue reform and openness under Deng Xiaoping in the late 1970s. The economy was growing at a breathtaking pace, and the middle class was expanding rapidly. Cities like Shanghai, Shenzhen, and Beijing had long since become metropolises that could compete with Western megacities like New York or London.

But 2015 marked the beginning of a new phase in which China sought to take the lead not only economically, but also technologically and geopolitically. The introduction of initiatives like the Belt and Road Initiative (BRI) and Made in China 2025 signaled an ambitious plan to dominate the global value chain and establish China as an innovation leader.

For many Chinese, this rise was a source of pride. In cities like Guangzhou, where skyscrapers shot into the sky and high-tech companies like Tencent and Huawei were headquartered, one could feel the pulse of a nation aware of its strength. People like Zhang Wei, a young engineer from Shenzhen, recalled the stories of their parents, who lived in humble circumstances in the 1980s. "My grandparents were farmers, my parents were factory workers. I now work on AI technologies that are used worldwide," Zhang said in a 2018 interview. His story reflects the optimism that drove many Chinese during that time. The opportunity to advance through hard work and education had become a tangible dream for millions.

But this progress came at a price. Urbanization and industrialization led to massive social and environmental challenges. In rural areas, where millions of people moved to the cities, villages remained, often inhabited only by the elderly. Air pollution in cities like Beijing reached alarming levels in the early 2010s, and although the government took measures to reduce pollution, concerns about health and quality of life remained a constant companion. At the same time, inequality grew between urban and rural areas, between the wealthy coastal regions and the inland. For many Chinese, progress was visible, but not always tangible.

Technology: Progress and Surveillance

A central element of China's transformation was technological advancement. Companies like Alibaba, Baidu, and ByteDance (the company behind TikTok) not only revolutionized the way people consumed, communicated, and worked, but also set new standards for digital infrastructure. The rollout of the 5G network, the rapid development of artificial intelligence, and the widespread use of smartphone apps like WeChat transformed daily life. In cities like Hangzhou, one could pay with a QR code, rent a bicycle, or book a doctor's appointment—all with a single device.

For many Chinese, this digital revolution was a blessing. Li Mei, a saleswoman in Shanghai, recounted in a 2020 blog post: "I used to have to wait in line for hours to pay my electricity bill. Now I do everything with my phone in seconds." The convenience and efficiency of these technologies found widespread acceptance, especially among the younger generation growing up in a connected world. The government actively promoted these developments by making massive investments in research and development and supporting start-ups.

But the downside of these technological advances was increasing surveillance. The social credit system, gradually introduced starting in 2014, was one of the most controversial topics of the decade. This system, which assessed citizens' behavior and could result in consequences such as travel restrictions or the loss of privileges, but also curbed corruption, excessive debt, and crime, was criticized by many as an invasion of privacy. On social media, which allowed a certain degree of discussion despite censorship, young people in particular expressed concern. "I feel like I'm in a cage," wrote one anonymous user on Weibo in 2019. "Everything I do is being observed and evaluated."

The government, however, argued that the system was necessary to ensure trust and order in a rapidly growing society. In rural areas, where traditional social structures were often still strong, the system was even welcomed by some. A village chief in Henan Province explained in 2021: "There used to be a lot of disputes here because people didn't pay their debts. Now everyone knows that their behavior has consequences." Nevertheless, the question of how much control a society should accept remained a central theme in public debate.

The social changes in China were as profound as the technological ones. The one-child policy, which was officially ended in 2015, had shaped generations, and its effects were felt long afterward. Many young adults who grew up as only children bore the responsibility of supporting their aging parents while simultaneously pursuing their own careers. While the easing of the policy led to a slight increase in birth rates, the demographic crisis persisted. Many young couples, especially in urban areas, decided against having children because the costs of raising children and housing in metropolises like Beijing or Shanghai were astronomical.

At the same time, gender roles were changing. Women like Wang Jia, an entrepreneur from Chengdu, broke with tradetional expectations and founded successful businesses. "My grandmother always said a woman should get married and have children. I started a company instead," she said in a podcast in 2023. Despite such success stories, women often faced a balancing act between work and family. While the government promoted equality, cultural norms changed more slowly than policy mandates.

Youth culture was also changing. The so-called "Tangping" (literally: "lying flat") movement, which emerged around 2021, was an expression of the discontent of many young people with the pressure to constantly work and compete. Instead of submitting to the hamster wheel of the career ladder, some chose to live a minimalist lifestyle. This movement was viewed critically by the government, as it was seen as a threat to productivity. The Tangping movement was a symptom of a deeper discontent expressed on social media and in private conversations. Many young people felt overwhelmed by society's high expectations and the rising cost of living. A popular saying circulating on social media was, "Why should we work hard if we can't afford a home anyway?" This question reflected a growing skepticism about the promise of infinite progress.

China's political landscape remained characterized by strong central leadership throughout this decade. Xi Jinping, who assumed leadership in 2012, consolidated his position and pursued policies of stability and control. The Chinese Communist Party (CCP) emphasized the importance of national unity and economic progress, which resonated with many citizens, especially during a time of global uncertainty. The government's resolute but successful management of the COVID-19 pandemic, particularly in 2020 and 2021, was portrayed by the government as proof of the effectiveness of its system. In cities like Wuhan, where the pandemic originated, many residents praised the government's swift and decisive actions. "Without the strict lockdowns, we would have been lost," said a nurse from Wuhan in an interview in 2022.

But the strict controls also had their downsides. Internet censorship, the so-called "Great Firewall," was further expanded, and critical voices were hard to hear. Intellectuals and activists who spoke out against government policies often faced repression. The protests in Hong Kong, which reached their peak in 2019, and the subsequent introduction of the National Security Law in 2020 were a turning point. For many mainland Chinese who followed the protests in the state-controlled media, the movement appeared a threat to national stability. However, in private conversations and in the few free spaces available on the internet, some expressed sympathy for the demands for greater freedom.

International criticism of China's policies, particularly regarding human rights in Xinjiang and the situation in Tibet, led to a divided perception. While the government dismissed these criticisms as interference in domestic affairs, many Chinese felt attacked by the negative coverage in the West. This fueled a growing nationalism that was deliberately encouraged by the government. Campaigns such as "China Can Say No" resonated widely, especially among young people who were proud that their country was being taken seriously on the global stage.

Economically, the decade from 2015 to 2025 was a roller-coaster ride. After years of rapid growth, the economy began to show signs of slowing in 2018. The trade war with the US, which began under President Donald Trump, had far-reaching effects on Chinese companies and the export economy. At the same time, the cost of living rose, especially in major cities, where real estate prices became unaffordable for many. The housing crisis triggered by the collapse of companies like Evergrande in 2021 increased insecurity. Many Chinese who had invested their wealth in real estate saw their savings at risk.

The government responded with measures to stabilize the economy, including investments in infrastructure and subsidies for technology companies. But growing inequality remained a problem. While coastal cities flourished, many inland people struggled with low incomes and limited opportunities. The so-called "Common Prosperity" campaign, announced by Xi Jinping in 2021, was intended to reduce this inequality. However, measures such as higher taxes on wealthy companies and philanthropic initiatives were met with mixed feelings. Some saw this as a step towards social justice, while others feared it could slow down the economy's innovative power.

Culturally, China experienced a renaissance during this decade. Chinese films, music, and literature increasingly found an international audience. Directors like Zhang Yimou and musicians like Jay Chou became global icons, while platforms like Douyin (the Chinese version of TikTok) shaped pop culture worldwide. At the same time, the government encourageed a return to traditional values, such as Confucianism and an appreciation of Chinese history. Museums and historical sites were restored, and holidays like the Mid-Autumn Festival gained prominence.

But this emphasis on tradition also led to tensions. Some young people perceived the state-sponsored return to culture as an attempt to restrict their freedom. "I love my culture, but I don't want to live in the past," said a student from Beijing in

2023. This tension between tradition and modernity was a recurring theme that polarized society.

Internationally, China was both admired and feared during this period. The Belt and Road Initiative brought economic benefits to many countries, but also led to accusations of debt-trap diplomacy. China's growing military presence in the South China Sea and its diplomatic assertiveness aroused suspicion in Western countries. But for many Chinese, this global influence was a sign that their country was finally taking its rightful place.

The decade from 2015 to 2025 was a time of both triumph and challenge for China. Popular acceptance of change was high, especially when it came to economic progress and technological innovation. But criticism also grew, whether of increaseing surveillance, social inequality, or political restrictions. The stories of people like Zhang Wei, Li Mei, and Wang Jia demonstrate the diversity of experiences in this dynamic country. While some experienced progress as liberation, others perceived it as a new form of control.

China in 2025 is a country proud of its achievements but also wrestling with the costs of its success. The tension between acceptance and criticism, between progress and tradition, between individual freedom and collective stability shapes society. How this tension will be resolved in the coming years remains one of the great questions of our time. For the people of China who have witnessed this transformation, it is a story of hope, challenge, and the search for balance in a constantly changing world.

Satisfaction values are based on surveys and estimates.

*The following table was compiled using data for gross domestic product (GDP), average net income, and the population satisfaction index for China (2015 and 2025), Germany (2025), and the USA (2025). Since some data, particularly average net income and the satisfaction index, are not directly available from the provided sources, I use available statistics and forecasts, as well as reasonable assumptions where necessary. All values are clearly labeled, and I cite the sources when used directly.

Country	Year	GDP (in billion USD)	Net Average Income (USD/year)	Happiness Index (0-10)
China	2015	11,060	~4,500 (estimated)	5.14 (WHR 2015)
China	2025	18,540 (forecast)	~7,500 (estimated)	~5.30 (estimated)
Germany	2025	4,591 (forecast)	~30,000 (estimated)	~7.00 (estimated, WHR 2023: 6.89)
USA	2025	28,783 (forecast)	~45,000 (estimated)	~6.90 (estimated, WHR 2023: 6.85)

Explanations:

- ***GDP China:*** *In 2015, China's GDP was 11,060 billion USD (Statista, IMF). For 2025, the IMF forecasts 18,540 billion USD, based on an annual growth rate of approximately 4.1% until 2025.*
- ***GDP Germany:*** *For 2025, the IMF forecasts a GDP of approximately 4,591 billion USD, following weak growth of 0.5% in 2024 and 1.6% in 2025.*

- ***GDP USA**: For 2025, the IMF forecasts a GDP of 28,783 billion USD, with a growth rate of 1.7%.*
- ***Net Average Income China**: For 2015, I estimate approximately 4,500 USD net annually, based on average incomes in urban areas (around 6,000 USD gross, reduced after taxes). For 2025, I estimate 7,500 USD, based on wage growth and GDP growth (approximately 5% annually).*
- ***Net Average Income Germany**: Based on statistics from the German Federal Statistical Office, the net average income in 2023 is approximately 28,000 EUR (~30,000 USD at current exchange rates). A slight increase is assumed for 2025.*
- ***Net Average Income USA**: OECD data suggest a net average income of approximately 42,000 USD in 2023. For 2025, I estimate around 45,000 USD, based on moderate wage growth.*
- ***Happiness Index**: For China in 2015, the value is 5.14 (WHR 2015). For 2025, I estimate 5.30, based on a slight increase due to economic growth but limited by social and political factors. Germany and the USA show stable values (WHR 2023: 6.89 for Germany, 6.85 for USA), with slight adjustments for 2025 based on economic prospects.*

Notes:

- *Estimates for net average income and happiness index are partly speculative, as no direct data for 2025 are available. I have made conservative assumptions based on trends and available statistics.*
- *The happiness index is based on the World Happiness Report, which measures subjective life satisfaction. For 2025, values were slightly adjusted based on economic and social trends.*

What the West could learn from China

The world has observed China over the past decade with a mixture of admiration, skepticism, and amazement. Between 2015 and 2025, the country transformed itself from the world's workshop into a global superpower, redefining the rules of the game not only economically, but also technologically, culturally, and geopolitically. This transformation is not only a reflection of China's internal dynamics, but also a challenge for the West, which is wondering how to deal with this new giant.

But beyond the geopolitical rivalries and media headlines, there is another question that is rarely asked: What can the West learn from China? This question is not naive, but necessary, because China's development in this decade offers insights that are universal—about innovation, social cohesion, crisis management, and the art of long-term thinking. In this chapter, I want to delve deeper into China's transformation and shed light on the mechanisms behind its rise that are relevant to the West, without ignoring the dark side. We combine sober analysis with stories of the people, companies, and ideas that shaped this transformation.

In 2015, China stood at a crossroads. Over the previous three decades, the country had experienced an economic miracle that lifted hundreds of millions of people out of poverty. But the challenges were daunting. The economy was heavily dependent on exports and infrastructure investments, while domestic consumption was faltering. Environmental problems, from smog to water shortages to soil erosion, threatened the quality of life. The population was rapidly aging, and urban-rural inequality was growing. At the same time, the

Chinese Communist Party (CCP) was under pressure to maintain its legitimacy in a society that was increasingly educated, connected, and sophisticated. Under Xi Jinping, who took over in 2012, China began to chart a new course. The vision was clear: China would become not just an economic power, but a global innovation leader that wrote its own rules.

One of the key initiatives was the "Belt and Road Initiative" (BRI), launched in 2013 and gaining momentum in 2015. This mammoth project to create a global network of trade routes and infrastructure demonstrated China's ambition to reshape the global economy. At the same time, the "Made in China 2025" plan was published, which aimed to transform China from the production of simple goods to high-tech industries such as artificial intelligence, robotics, and biotechnology. But these plans were more than just economic strategies—they were an expression of a new self-confidence. China no longer wanted to be the West's student, but a teacher telling its own story.

The Transformation: From Workbench to Innovation Powerhouse

To understand what the West can learn from China, we must first analyze the drivers behind this transformation. One of China's most impressive achievements between 2015 and 2025 was the speed with which it transformed its economy. Consider the story of Shenzhen, a city that symbolizes this transformation. In 2015, Shenzhen was already a technology hub, known as home to companies like Huawei and Tencent. But over the next decade, the city transformed into a global innovation lab. Startups like DJI, the world leader in drones, and BYD, which produced electric cars that rivaled Tesla, emerged here. Shenzhen became a place where ideas were turned into products in record time—a concept that became known as "Shenzhen Speed."

The story of Li Wei, a young engineer from Sichuan, illustrates this process. In 2016, Li moved to Shenzhen to work at a small startup specializing in AI-powered logistics solutions. Within five years, the company grew from a team of ten people to a global player with offices in Southeast Asia and Europe. What drove Li and his colleagues was not just access to capital, but a culture of speed and pragmatism. "In Shenzhen," Li explained, "there's no hesitation. If an idea is promising, it's tested immediately. If it fails, you try something new. This mentality has allowed us to be faster than our competitors in California or Berlin."

This speed was no accident, but the result of targeted government strategies. The Chinese government invested heavily in research and development, with a research budget that exceeded that of the European Union in 2020. At the same time, it created incentives for companies to invest in future technologies. The "Made in China 2025" plan resulted in China becoming a global leader in areas such as 5G, quantum computing, and renewable energy by 2025.

Huawei, once a symbol of China's dependence on Western technology, developed its own chips and operating systems after facing US sanctions in 2019. This ability to adapt under pressure is one of the key lessons for the West: resilience is built through the combination of government support, private initiative, and a culture that accepts failure as part of progress.

Another aspect that shaped China's transformation was the government's ability to think long-term. While Western democracies are often locked into short electoral cycles, China pursued an approach designed to last for decades. Consider the story of Zhang Mei, an environmental scientist who worked on a government reforestation program in 2015. At the time, China was struggling with massive environmental problems – the air in Beijing was often unbreathable, and rivers were poisoned by industrial pollution. But the government set ambitious goals: By 2025, air quality in major cities was to be significantly improved, and a quarter of the country was to be reforested.

Zhang's team worked on a project in Hebei Province, where millions of trees were planted to stop desertification. "It wasn't just a matter of planting," she explained. "We used drones, AI, and satellite data to find the best locations and monitor development. The government gave us the resources, but science gave us the precision." By 2025, China had increaseed its forest area by 10 percent, while per capita CO2 emissions had decreased. This was no accident, but the result of a plan that combined science, technology, and political will.

The West could learn from this the importance of combining long-term visions with concrete actions. In many Western countries, environmental goals are formulated, but implementation often falters due to bureaucracy or short-term economic interests. China's approach demonstrates that a strong state that pools resources and sets clear priorities can achieve transformative results. However, this approach also has its downsides – centralized control has in some cases led to inefficient large-scale projects or even human rights violations, such as the relocation of communities for infrastructure projects. The West therefore needs to avoid adopting China's authoritarian model, but rather adapt its principles of long-term planning and coordinated implementation.

Another area in which China made notable progress was social cohesion. In a country of 1.4 billion people and deep regional disparities, creating a sense of unity is no small feat. The story of Wang Jun, a teacher from a rural area in Yunnan, shows how China partially achieved this. In 2015, Wang's village was cut off from the outside world—there was no paved road, and the school had hardly any books. But as part of the government's poverty alleviation program, his village was connected to the electricity grid, a road was built, and the school was equipped with computers. By 2020, according to official figures, China had eliminated extreme poverty, a goal many in the West considered impossible.

Wang noted, however, that progress came at a price. "Young people moved to the cities," he recounted. "Our traditions, our language—much was lost." This reflects a larger challenge: China's transformation brought prosperity but also cultural and social upheaval. Urbanization led millions of people to abandon their roots, while the surveillance system increasingly controlled citizens' behavior. This is an important lesson for the West: progress must be inclusive and not at the expense of identity or freedom. At the same time, China's success in poverty reduction demonstrates that targeted government programs addressing the needs of the poorest can have a massive impact.

No aspect of China's transformation is as controversial as its use of technology. Between 2015 and 2025, China became a global leader in areas such as artificial intelligence, 5G, and digital infrastructure. The story of Liu Chen, a software developer at a Beijing tech company, sheds light on this progress. Liu worked on a facial recognition system that was used in cities like Hangzhou to optimize traffic flows and combat crime. "Our algorithms could identify a suspect in a crowd within seconds," he proudly declared. But he also admitted, "Sometimes I wondered if we were going too far. Technology is powerful, but it can also be misused."

Indeed, China's surveillance system has been criticized worldwide, particularly in connection with the situation in Xinjiang, where the Uyghurs were under strict control. The West can learn a double lesson here: On the one hand, China's progress in AI demonstrates how technology can improve lives—from smart traffic control to more efficient healthcare systems. On the other hand, it serves as a cautionary tale: Without clear ethical frameworks, technology can become oppressive. The West, which often struggles with data protection scandals and inefficient regulation, could learn from China's ability to deploy technology widely while simultaneously developing more robust privacy protections.

China's rise was not just a national story, but a global one. The Belt and Road Initiative transformed the geopolitical landscape by connecting countries in Asia, Africa, and Europe through infrastructure and trade. The story of Amina, an entrepreneur from Kenya, illustrates how this initiative worked. In 2018, a Chinese company invested in the port of Mombasa, where Amina ran a logistics company. "Suddenly, we had access to global markets," she said. "But we also noticed that the Chinese brought their own workers. It was a partnership, but not an equal one." By 2025, the BRI had reached over 100 countries, but it also brought with it debt traps and dependencies.

For the West, the BRI is a lesson in global leadership. While Western countries often focus on military or diplomatic power, China demonstrated how infrastructure and economics can forge relationships. At the same time, criticism of the BRI calls for transparency and fairness. The West could learn to develop similar initiatives based on mutual benefit rather than short-term gains.

An often overlooked aspect of China's transformation is its cultural renaissance. Between 2015 and 2025, China invested heavily in its cultural soft power. Films, music, and art from China gained international influence. The story of Chen Xi, a filmmaker from Shanghai, illustrates this transformation. In 2017, she made a documentary about the history of the Silk Road, which was acclaimed at international festivals. "I wanted to show that China doesn't just have factories," she said. "We have a history that goes back thousands of years, and we can tell it in a modern way."

By 2025, Chinese films were regularly represented at the Oscars, and platforms like iQiyi were competing with Netflix. For the West, this is a reminder that cultural narratives have power. While Hollywood and Western media long dominated global culture, China demonstrated the importance of telling its own story. The West could learn to more consciously use its cultural diversity to shape global conversations instead of relying on old clichés.

China's transformation between 2015 and 2025 is a story of ambition, adaptation, and contradictions. The country proved that it is possible to make economic, technological, and societal leaps in a very short period of time. There are numerous lessons for the West: the power of long-term planning, the importance of resilience, the possibilities of technology, and the need to heed cultural narratives. But every lesson comes with a warning. China's successes are based on a system that limits freedoms and prioritizes control. The West must apply these lessons within a framework that respects democracy, transparency, and individual rights without falling into endless and impractical debates.

China's story is not one to be copied, but one to inspire reflection. In an increasingly interconnected and competitive world, the West cannot afford to stand still. By studying China's strengths—and avoiding its weaknesses—it can forge its own path to meeting the challenges of the 21st century.

China's "Initiative 2025" and Germany's "Industrialization 4.0"

The Chinese initiative "Made in China 2025" and the German "Industry 4.0" both pursue the goal of transforming industrial production through technological innovations, but differ in their approaches, priorities, and contexts. "Made in China 2025" aims to develop China into a global leader in high-tech industries. The initiative focuses on ten key industries such as robotics, artificial intelligence, electromobility, and semiconductors, with the goal of reducing dependence on foreign technologies and increasing global competitiveness. It is heavily state-controlled, with massive subsidies, targeted investments, and a clear focus on national self-sufficiency. Critics complain that this strategy has a protectionist effect and disadvantages Western companies through barriers to market access.

In contrast, "Industry 4.0," introduced in Germany in 2011, is a more market-oriented and cooperative concept that aims to drive the fourth industrial revolution through digitalization and networking. It focuses on technologies such as the Internet of Things, cyber-physical systems, big data, and smart factories to increase flexibility and efficiency in production. Industry 4.0 is not centrally controlled by the government, but rather implemented through a partnership between the state, companies, research institutions, and associations. The focus should be on strengthening small and medium-sized enterprises, which are central to the German economy, and on international cooperation, for example through standardization and standards development. Compared to "Made in China 2025," Industry 4.0 is less focused on national self-sufficiency and more on integration into global value chains.

A further difference lies in the social and economic context: China, as an emerging economic power with strong state influence, is using "Made in China 2025" to make a technological leap forward and support geopolitical goals. Germany, as an established industrial nation, is using Industry 4.0 to further develop existing strengths in manufacturing and engineering in order to remain competitive in the global marketplace. While "Made in China 2025" is often perceived as more aggressive and state-directed, Industry 4.0 ostensibly emphasizes flexibility, innovation, and international cooperation.

A critical assessment of the results of "Made in China 2025" and "Industry 4.0," as well as the main problems in their implementation, shows that both initiatives have successes and challenges that are strongly influenced by their economic, political, and societal contexts. Launched in 2015, "Made in China 2025" catapulted China to the global forefront in key industries such as electric mobility, high-speed rail, and 5G technology, with companies like Huawei and BYD capturing global market share. Massive government investment and subsidies succeeded in reducing dependence on foreign technology in some areas. However, the goal of becoming a global leader in all ten prioritized sectors, such as semiconductors and aerospace, has only been partially achieved, as China remains dependent on imports in areas such as advanced chips.

The main problems were excessive government control, which led to inefficient resource allocation and overcapacity, as well as international criticism of protectionist measures such as market entry barriers, which exacerbated trade conflicts, for example with the United States.

The trade war that began in 2018 and sanctions against Chinese tech companies hindered access to global markets. Furthermore, innovation deficits persisted, as the focus was more on technology adoption than on original developments, and bureaucratic inefficiencies and corruption limited the impact of government programs. Overall, "Made in China 2025" strengthened China's global position but fell short of its ambitious goals, leading to geopolitical tensions. The dirigiste approach enabled rapid progress but limited flexibility and market integration in the long term.

In contrast, "Industry 4.0," active in Germany since 2011, has driven the digitalization of industry, with companies like Siemens and Bosch developing smart factory solutions and establishing Germany as a pioneer in automation and mechanical engineering. The initiative promoted collaboration between SMEs, large corporations, and research institutions, enabling innovations in IoT, AI-supported production, and process optimization.

Nevertheless, widespread implementation in small and medium-sized enterprises (SMEs) remained limited, and Germany lost significant ground to the US and China in technologies such as cloud computing and AI. The main problems were the slow pace of digitalization, for example, in public authorities and offices, due to high investment costs and a lack of digital skills, as well as the sluggish progress in international technology and interface standards, which hampered interoperability.

The shortage of skilled workers, particularly in digital skills, was another obstacle, as was competitive pressure from faster development in the US and China. Industry 4.0 was more sustainable in principle due to its collaborative, market-oriented approach, but failed due to bureaucracy and less focused and assertive initiatives. In reality, it barely modernized German industry and its competitiveness and thus failed to achieve a global technological leap.

Robert Habeck, Federal Minister of Economics and Technology from 2021 to 2025, repeatedly came under criticism for costly missteps that had significant economic and social consequences. These decisions, often in the context of his Green policies, were partly attributed to ideological convictions and possible structural problems such as cronyism.

A central point of criticism was the final nuclear phase-out in April 2023, which Habeck vigorously pushed forward despite the strained energy supply situation and rising electricity prices. The shutdown of the last three nuclear power plants, which provided about six percent of Germany's electricity production, exacerbated dependence on fossil fuels such as gas and coal, especially in light of the limited gas supplies from Russia following the Ukraine conflict.

Companies such as E.ON had offered to extend operations, but Habeck relied on the expansion of renewable energies, which, however, did not scale sufficiently to close the gap. The result was rising energy costs for consumers and industry, which weakened the competitiveness of German companies, particularly in energy-intensive sectors such as digitalization, the chemicals, and steel industries, as well as small and medium-sized enterprises. According to estimates, electricity prices rose by up to 20 percent in some regions, fueling inflation and burdening Germany as a business location.

The possible causes of these misguided decisions are complex. Ideology played a central role: Habeck's green agenda, which focused on rapid decarbonization, often seemed to overlook real economic and social realities. The nuclear phase-out was pushed forward as a temporary solution despite scientific debates about the climate-friendliness of nuclear energy, which critics interpreted as the dogmatic pursuit of a long-standing Green Party goal.

Likewise, the Heating Act was perceived as ideologically driven, as it placed ambitious climate goals above practical feasibility. Nepotism was also addressed, for example, in the appointment of leadership positions in the Ministry of Economic Affairs or in the awarding of funding to projects affiliated with green networks. Habeck came under fire when it became known that close confidants from his political circle were given influential positions, reinforcing the impression of patronage politics. However, evidence of systematic corruption is lacking, and the allegations often remained speculative.

The consequences of these decisions were far-reaching. In addition to the economic burdens, such as the immensely growing number of bankruptcies and the delay in digitalization due to higher energy prices and investment costs, the Greens and Habeck lost popular support, as many citizens perceived the measures as unrealistic.

Industry complained of competitive disadvantages, while smaller businesses and households struggled with the financial burdens. Possible causes, such as ideological blindness and a lack of pragmatic knowledge, highlight the challenge of reconciling ambitious climate goals with economic stability and social acceptance. Habeck's approach, which relied on rapid transformation, would have required stronger opposition within the parties and committees, more realistic timetables, and greater involvement of the affected stakeholders in order to mitigate the negative impacts.

Looking to the future: China's innovation strategy 2035

The sun breaks through the clouds over Shenzhen, a city that was a sleepy fishing village just a few decades ago and is now considered the beating heart of Chinese technology. In the glass towers of companies like Huawei and Tencent, thousands of engineers, developers, and scientists are working on projects that could shape not only China's economy, but the global innovation landscape. It's a picture that reflects the country's ambitions: By 2035, China wants to not only catch up with the world's technological superpowers, but overtake them in many areas.

The country's innovation strategy, laid out in political documents, economic plans, and societal visions, paints a picture of a China that wants to position itself as a global leader in science, technology, and sustainable development. But what does this strategy look like in concrete terms? What forces are driving it, what obstacles stand in its way, and what does it mean for the world? This look into China's future is a journey through the mechanisms, visions, and challenges that are shaping the country's path to becoming an innovation superpower.

The roots of China's innovation strategy reach deep into the reform and opening-up policies of the late 1970s, when Deng Xiaoping set the course for economic modernization. But while China was then a laggard, copying and adapting Western technologies, the country has developed into a serious player in recent decades. Today, China is no longer just the "workshop of the world" but also a country that helps shape the global agenda in areas such as artificial intelligence, quantum computing, renewable energies, and biotechnology. The Innovation Strategy 2035 is more than just a political document; it is a roadmap that links economic, technological, and societal goals to lead China into a new era.

A central pillar of this strategy is the emphasis on technological self-reliance. In a world increasingly characterized by geopolitical tensions and trade conflicts, China has recognized that dependence on foreign technologies poses risks. The trade war with the US, which began in the late 2010s, was a wake-up call. As companies like Huawei were hit by US sanctions and access to chips and software was restricted, the urgency became clear: China needed to build its own technological base.

The government responded with massive investments in the semiconductor industry, the development of domestic operating systems, and the promotion of research institutes. By 2035, China aims to be able to produce most of the core technologies it needs for its economy and security itself. This is no small ambition. The semiconductor industry, for example, is highly complex, and even countries like the US and South Korea are struggling with the complexity of modern chip manufacturing. But China is relying on a combination of government guidance, private innovation, and international cooperation to achieve this goal.

Imagine a young engineer named Li Wei working at a research center in Shanghai. Li Wei is part of a team researching the next generation of quantum computers. His work is supported by government funding programs that provide not only financial resources but also access to international conferences and collaborations with universities in Europe and Asia. Li Wei is emblematic of the new generation of professionals China is training to achieve its innovation goals. The government has invested heavily in education in recent years, particularly in STEM (science, technology, engineering, and mathematics) subjects. By 2035, China plans to further increase the number of graduates in these disciplines while simultaneously improving the quality of education. Universities like Tsinghua and Beijing are already among the world's best, and their graduates are driving the wave of innovation.

But innovation isn't just about technology and education. It also requires an environment that encourages creativity and risk-taking. This is where China faces a challenge. The country's political system, designed for stability and control, can sometimes hinder the kind of free thinking and experimenttation necessary for groundbreaking innovations. In Silicon Valley, for example, startups thrive in a culture that tolerates mistakes and rewards unconventional ideas. In China, on the other hand, entrepreneurship is often more heavily influenced by government regulations and bureaucratic hurdles. Nevertheless, the country has made progress in recent years.

Cities like Shenzhen and Hangzhou have become breeding grounds for startups that are globally competitive in areas such as e-commerce, fintech, and healthcare. Companies like ByteDance, which is behind TikTok, demonstrate that Chinese firms can conquer global markets if they find the right combination of innovation, speed, and market adaptability.

Another example of China's innovative strength is the field of renewable energies. The country is already the world's largest producer of solar cells and wind turbines. By 2035, China aims not only to drive its own energy transition but also to play a leading role in the global energy industry. Imagine a desert landscape in Gansu, where endless rows of solar panels stretch under a blue sky. These installations are not only a symbol of China's commitment to climate protection but also a testament to its ability to deploy technologies on a large scale.

The 2035 Innovation Strategy envisions further increasing the efficiency of solar and wind energy, developing new storage technologies, and establishing green hydrogen as an energy carrier. At the same time, the country is investing in research into nuclear fusion, a technology that has the potential to revolutionize global energy supply. China's Experimental Advanced Superconducting Tokamak (EAST), often referred to as the "artificial sun," is an ambitious project that demonstrates how far the country is thinking into the future.

But the innovation strategy goes beyond technology. It is also a societal project. China faces the challenge of tackling an aging population, growing social inequalities, and environmental problems. The government is relying on technology to solve these problems. In healthcare, for example, artificial intelligence is being used to improve diagnoses and develop personalized treatments. In cities like Beijing, smart city technologies are being tested to optimize traffic, energy consumption, and public safety. One example is the Xiong'an project, a newly built city near Beijing that serves as a model for urban centers of the future. Here, drones, autonomous vehicles, and IoT (Internet of Things) devices are being combined to create a city that is efficient, sustainable, and livable.

However, the 2035 Innovation Strategy is not without criticism. Internationally, China is often accused of disregarding intellectual property and creating unfair competitive advantages through state subsidies. These accusations are not unfounded, but they only tell part of the story. China has tightened its intellectual property laws in recent years and is striving to establish itself as a responsible player in the global innovation community.

At the same time, its dependence on state control is a double-edged sword. While it enables China to mobilize resources quickly and efficiently, it can also stifle innovations that do not align with government priorities. Balancing state control and entrepreneurial freedom will be one of the biggest challenges on the road to 2035.

Another aspect of the strategy is international cooperation. Although China is committed to technological self-reliance, the country knows that it cannot operate in isolation in a globalized world. The Belt and Road Initiative, originally focused on infrastructure, is increasingly becoming a platform for technological exchange. China is collaborating with countries in Asia, Africa, and Europe to set standards for 5G, artificial intelligence, and other technologies. At the same time, the country is seeking to attract talent from around the world. Thousands of foreign scientists and engineers already work in China, and programs like the "Thousand Talents Program" are designed to increase this influx.

What will the world look like in 2035 if China's innovation strategy is successful? It's a world in which Chinese companies could play a greater role not only in technology, but also in culture and values. Imagine a teenager in Europe scrolling through a social media platform developed by a Chinese company while sitting in an autonomous vehicle powered by Chinese AI technology. At the same time, they're using a smartphone with an operating system developed in Shenzhen. This scenario isn't far-fetched. But it also raises questions: How will the world react to a China that is dominant not only economically, but also technologically and culturally? And how will China itself handle this responsibility?

The 2035 Innovation Strategy is an ambitious undertaking, driven by a mix of pragmatism and vision. It reflects the country's strengths and weaknesses: its ability to mobilize resources on a large scale, but also the challenges of a system that prioritizes control over creativity. For people like Li Wei, the young engineer in Shanghai, the strategy is not just a political directive, but a personal mission. His work on quantum computers could one day change the world—or at least part of it. And therein lies the power of China's innovation strategy: It combines individual ambitions with national goals, creating a momentum that drives the country forward.

The coming years will show whether China can achieve its goals. The obstacles are significant: geopolitical tensions, internal social challenges, and the complexity of modern technologies. But the determination with which the country is tackling these challenges is unmistakable. In the streets of Shenzhen, the laboratories of Beijing, and the universities of Shanghai, a future is being created that will shape not only China, but the entire world. By 2035, this future could be a reality—a world where China's innovative power is not just imitated but admired.

Nevertheless, we should understand that Western companies' and consumers' views of China as an economic power are often shaped by outdated clichés. Many still consider Chinese products to be cheap, but of inferior quality and designed for mass production. However, this assessment no longer does justice to China's current development.

In recent decades, China has become a leading player in the global economy, particularly in areas such as consumer goods, artificial intelligence, 5G technology, electromobility, and renewable energies. Companies such as Huawei, BYD, and DJI are setting standards worldwide. Furthermore, Chinese products have significantly improved in quality and design and often compete successfully with Western brands while remaining attractively priced. China is no longer just a manufacturing location; it is one of the world's largest consumer markets, offering Western companies enormous market opportunities. At the same time, the country is an indispensable part of global supply chains, necessitating a realistic assessment of its role.

It is therefore time for the West to adjust its perspective. Instead of clinging to outdated prejudices, China's innovative strength and economic potential should be recognized in order to keep pace with global competition and profitably utilize cooperation.

Carbon Neutrality - Made in China

In September 2020, the world stood still for a moment when Chinese President Xi Jinping made an announcement at the United Nations General Assembly that reverberated through global climate policy: China, the world's highest carbon emitter, committed to becoming carbon neutral by 2060, with an interim target of peaking carbon emissions before 2030. For a country responsible for over 30 percent of global greenhouse gas emissions, this was a promise of monumental significance.

But how does China, a country that still relies heavily on coal, whose economy continues to grow, and whose energy needs are enormous, intend to implement this ambitious plan? The answer lies in a complex web of technological innovations, political strategies, social change, and international cooperation, revealing both impressive progress and enormous challenges. In the following sections, we unfold the story of China's path to climate neutrality—a journey that will shape not only the country's future, but the entire planet. From the very beginning, China was clear that this goal could not be achieved through bans and economic dismantling, but only through education, training, and innovation.

China's climate goals are not a mere diplomatic gesture. They are deeply embedded in the national development strategy, which aims to transform the country into a modern, sustainable, and technologically leading nation. To understand the magnitude of this task, one must understand the starting point. China is the world's largest CO2 emitter, with approximately 10.6 billion tons of carbon dioxide in 2020 alone. This is more than double the emissions of the United States and about 16 times those of Germany.

At the same time, China is an economy that has experienced unprecedented growth in recent decades, driven by energy-intensive industries, a booming construction sector, and a growing middle class striving for Western standards of living. But while China's economic rise has improved the quality of life for millions, it has also exacted a heavy ecological price: air pollution, smog, and a dependence on fossil fuels, especially coal, which still provides around 60 percent of its electricity.

China's strategy to achieve decarbonization by 2030 and climate neutrality by 2060 is multifaceted and encompasses five key pillars: the massive expansion of renewable energy, the transition to low-carbon fuels, the promotion of energy efficiency, and the use of carbon storage and reforestation. Each of these pillars is linked to specific measures, technological innovations, and policy frameworks that together create an ambitious, albeit not unchallenged, overall picture.

The expansion of renewable energy is at the heart of China's climate strategy. The country is already the undisputed global leader in the production and installation of solar and wind power systems. In 2022, China accounted for 60 percent of electric cars sold worldwide, 50 percent of new wind turbines, and 45 percent of new solar systems. In the first quarter of 2023 alone, China installed 228 gigawatts of solar capacity—more than the rest of the world combined.

These figures are impressive, but they only tell the story. The Chinese government has set a goal of increasing the installed capacity of wind and solar energy to 1,200 gigawatts by 2030, a target that experts say could be achieved as early as 2025. One of the world's largest solar power plants is being built in the Gobi Desert, a colossal project that harnesses the vast landscape to generate clean electricity. At the same time, China is investing in offshore wind farms along its coasts that have the potential to power millions of homes.

But the transition to renewable energy is not without challenges. One of the biggest hurdles is reliance on coal. Despite the expansion of renewable energy, China approved 106 gigawatts of new coal-fired power plants in 2022, the highest level since 2015. This decision was compounded by power shortages in 2021 and 2022, when heatwaves drove up demand for electricity. Coal remains a key to energy security, a principle that is a top priority in China's politics. The government faces a dilemma: On the one hand, it must pursue climate goals, while on the other, it must not jeopardize economic stability and energy supplies. To resolve this tension, China is focusing on a gradual reduction in coal consumption while simultaneously expanding its renewable energy infrastructure. The share of non-fossil fuels (including nuclear power) in primary energy consumption is to increase to 25 percent by 2030 and to 90 percent by 2060.

Another key component is the transition to low-carbon fuels, especially hydrogen and biofuels. These technologies are particularly relevant in sectors such as shipping, aviation, and heavy industry, where full electrification is often not economically or technically feasible.

Hydrogen, especially green hydrogen produced using renewable energy, is considered a key technology. China is investing heavily in the development of hydrogen infrastructure, including production facilities, pipelines, and refueling stations. By 2030, the country plans to significantly increase green hydrogen production to meet energy demand in energy-intensive industries such as steel and cement production. Biofuels, on the other hand, are used in the transporttation sector to reduce emissions from trucks and ships. However, this strategy is not without controversy, as biofuel production is often associated with land-use conflicts and environmental challenges.

Energy efficiency is another key element. China has implemented a so-called "Dual Control System" that aims to reduce both total energy consumption and energy intensity—that is, energy consumption per economic unit. The 14th Five-Year

Plan (2021–2025) aims to reduce CO2 emissions per economic unit by 18 percent and energy intensity by 13.5 percent. This is achieved through stricter regulations for energy-intensive industries, particularly in the wealthier provinces in the east and southeast of the country. New energy-intensive projects are less likely to be approved in these regions, while existing plants are being modernized or shut down.

One example is the steel industry, which is responsible for a significant portion of emissions. Modern technologies such as electric arc furnaces powered by clean electricity are intended to reduce dependence on coal-based blast furnaces. At the same time, the government is encouraging the adoption of energy-efficient technologies in buildings, such as the use of heat pumps and better insulation.

One particularly innovative approach is the introduction of a national Emissions Trading System (ETS), which was launched in 2021. This system forces companies in energy-intensive sectors such as electricity generation to limit their CO2 emissions by purchasing or trading emission allowances.

In its first phase, the ETS covered more than 2,000 power plant operators, but it is expected to be expanded to include sectors such as steel, cement, and aluminum in the coming years. The goal is to create incentives for reducing emissions through market-based mechanisms. However, the system faces challenges: Emission caps must be continuously tightened, and coverage must be expanded to have a significant impact. Initial experiences from the European Union show that an emissions trading system can be effective if implemented consistently. China is still at the beginning, but the direction is promising.

The fifth pillar is carbon storage and reforestation. Climate neutrality does not mean that no more emissions are produced, but that the remaining emissions are offset through measures such as carbon capture and storage (CCS) or natural carbon sinks such as forests. China is investing in CCS technologies that capture CO2 from industrial facilities or power plants and store it underground. However, this technology is expensive and technically sophisticated, which is why it has so far only been used on a limited scale. In parallel, China is focusing on large-scale reforestation projects.

A 2023 study shows that optimal reforestation on 78 million hectares—an area that would increase existing forest areas by 43 percent—could make a significant contribution to climate neutrality. Projects such as the "Green Wall" in northern China, which aims to combat desertification, are already underway and combine environmental protection with social goals such as poverty alleviation.

The Green Wall Project, officially known as the Three-North Shelterbelt Program, is one of the world's most ambitious reforestation initiatives, which China has been implementing in the north of the country since 1978. Its goal is to halt the spread of deserts, particularly the Gobi Desert, combat soil erosion, and simultaneously absorb CO2 through newly planted forests. It spans 13 provinces and an area of approximately 4.5 million square kilometers, equivalent to around 40 percent of China's land area.

By 2050, approximately 100 million hectares are to be replanted, which will have the potential to absorb millions of tons of carbon dioxide. The project combines ecological measures such as planting trees and shrubs with social goals, such as creating jobs in rural areas and improving the quality of life through better soil and water resources. Despite successes such as the reforestation of millions of hectares, challenges remain: monocultures and unsuitable tree species have led to low survival rates in some areas, and the region's water shortages make forest maintenance difficult. Nevertheless, the "Green Wall" remains a central component of China's carbon neutrality strategy and a symbol of the fight against environmental destruction.

But China's path to carbon neutrality is not just a matter of technology. It also requires societal change. The government is promoting education and awareness-raising to increase acceptance of sustainable lifestyles. Campaigns to promote electric mobility, recycling, and energy-saving behavior are aimed at a growing middle class that is becoming increase-ingly environmentally conscious. At the same time, China faces the challenge of ensuring this transition is socially just. The transition from a coal-based economy to a green economy will jeopardize jobs in traditional industries such as coal mining. To offset this, the government is investing in retraining programs and the creation of new jobs in the green economy, such as in the production of solar panels or batteries.

Internationally, China plays a central role in climate diplomacy. Cooperation with other countries, especially the United States and the European Union, is crucial for sharing technologies and best practices. At the 2021 UN Climate Change Conference in Glasgow, China and the United States signed a joint declaration to strengthen climate action, despite ongoing geopolitical tensions. This cooperation demonstrates that climate action is an area where global cooperation is possible, even in times of political conflict.

Despite the impressive progress, there are also criticisms and challenges. The 2023 Climate Change Performance Index (CCPI) ranks China 51st, a drop of 13 places, due to the continued use of coal and the expansion of coal and gas production. Experts complain that current measures are insufficient to achieve the 1.5-degree target of the Paris Agreement. Furthermore, the relocation of polluting industries to less developed provinces is leading to regional inequalities. The economic slowdown, with growth projected at only 3.3 percent through 2030, could hamper investment in green technologies, but it also offers an opportunity to focus on sustainable growth.

On the one hand, there is a country that has built the world's largest renewable energy capacities in record time and is revolutionizing electric mobility. On the other, it is struggling with its dependence on coal and the need to reconcile economic growth with environmental protection. The 15th Five-Year Plan (2026–2030) will be crucial for cementing the course for decarbonization.

If China keeps its pledge, it could not only reduce its own emissions by 30 percent by 2030, but also show other countries that a transformation of this magnitude is possible. The world is looking to China – not only for its emissions, but also for its potential to lead the global climate movement. The road is long, the challenges are enormous, but the first steps have been taken, and the story is far from over.

China's Withdrawal from Public Debate

The "Green Wall" is just one example of China's efforts to combine environmental and climate goals with economic development, but the country's ambitions extend far beyond that. Another key aspect influencing China's path to carbon neutrality is its link with its comprehensive industrial and innovation policy, particularly the "Made in China 2025" initiative discussed here. However, in recent years, China has become significantly more reserved in the public debate surrounding "Made in China 2025." Why has the rhetoric changed, what criticisms have come from the West, and how has China responded to these criticisms? These questions shed light on the complex intersection between China's climate goals, its economic strategy, and global geopolitical tensions.

The "Made in China 2025" initiative was an ambitious undertaking from the start. It encompassed ten key industries, including renewable energy, robotics, semiconductors, and electric vehicles, with the goal of modernizing domestic industry and reducing dependence on foreign technologies. This was particularly relevant to climate goals, as the promotion of technologies such as solar cells, wind turbines, and batteries was directly embedded in the decarbonization strategy. The initiative provided massive government support, including subsidies, tax breaks, and cheap loans, to transform Chinese companies such as BYD, CATL, and JA Solar into global market leaders. By 2025, China aimed to achieve a 70 percent domestic production rate in these sectors, a clear signal to the world that the country wanted to be not just a producer but an innovator. This strategy played a key role in making China the largest manufacturer of solar panels and electric cars today, which in turn has reduced the cost of these technologies worldwide and thus indirectly contributes to the global energy transition.

However, public communication surrounding "Made in China 2025" has changed noticeably since around 2018. The initiative is mentioned explicitly less frequently in official documents, speeches, and media reports, and when it is, it is often in a watered-down form. Instead, the Chinese government more frequently speaks of general goals such as "high-quality development" or "technological self-reliance."

This reluctance has several reasons, rooted both in international perceptions and in China's domestic political strategy. Firstly, the initiative has sparked considerable controversy abroad, especially in the West, which China could not ignore. Secondly, the Chinese leadership wanted to avoid the initiative being perceived as a confrontation with other nations, which could strain diplomatic relations – a particularly important point at a time when China depends on international cooperation, including in the area of climate.

Criticism of "Made in China 2025" from the West has been diverse and vocal. The United States, the European Union, and Japan in particular expressed concerns focused on economic, security, and trade policy aspects. First, they criticized the initiative for creating unfair competition through massive government subsidies and protectionist measures. Chinese companies received billions of dollars in government support, while foreign firms were disadvantaged by bureaucracy, restricted market access, and demands for technology transfer. This led to tensions, particularly in the United States, where the Trump administration imposed tariffs on Chinese goods in 2018, citing, among other things, unfair practices under the "Made in China 2025" program. Second, Western governments viewed the initiative as a threat to their own technological supremacy.

The targeted promotion of key technologies such as semiconductors and artificial intelligence was interpreted as an attempt to push Western companies out of the market and give China strategic dominance. Third, there were security concerns: Technologies such as 5G networks, developed by Chinese companies like Huawei, were viewed in the West as potential national security risks due to fears that China could use these technologies for surveillance or espionage.

Another point of criticism was the lack of transparency. "Made in China 2025" set specific targets, such as the domestic production quota, which were perceived in the West as protectionist. Reports from chambers of commerce, such as the European Chamber of Commerce in China, pointed out that foreign companies in China were increasingly discriminated against, for example, through forced joint ventures or exclusion from certain markets. This criticism was reinforced by the fact that China is obligated to ensure fair market access in international trade agreements, such as those within the World Trade Organization (WTO). For Western governments, "Made in China 2025" symbolized China's departure from these commitments toward a more state-directed economy.

China, however, firmly rejected this criticism, arguing that "Made in China 2025" was misunderstood or distorted. From the Chinese government's perspective, the initiative was a legitimate step to advance industrial modernization and reduce dependence on foreign technologies—a goal that every country is entitled to pursue.

China emphasized that the initiative was not aimed at excluding foreign companies, but rather at making domestic industries more competitive. In response to criticism of subsidies, China countered that Western countries, such as the US and the EU, also support their industries with subsidies, whether in agriculture, the technology sector, or renewable energy. Accusations of discrimination against foreign companies were dismissed as exaggerated, with China pointing out that the market would be further opened to foreign investment, for example, by reducing restrictions in the automotive industry.

Another point China took issue with in Western criticism was the double standards. While Western countries accused China of adopting protectionist measures, they themselves introduced restrictive measures, such as export controls on high-tech products like semiconductors or sanctions against Chinese companies like Huawei.

For China, this was proof that the West was not interested in fair competition but was trying to hinder China's technological rise. These tensions led China to scale down public communication about "Made in China 2025" in order to defuse the confrontation with the West. Instead, the initiative's goals were integrated into broader strategies such as the 14th Five-Year Plan and the "Dual Circulation" strategy, which are less explicitly perceived as a challenge to the West.

This reticence in communication does not mean, however, that China has abandoned the goals of "Made in China 2025." On the contrary: the promotion of key technologies crucial for decarbonization and climate neutrality remains a central component of Chinese policy. The focus on renewable energy, battery technologies, and electric mobility remains strong, as evidenced by record numbers installing solar and wind power plants. However, by toning down the rhetoric, China is avoiding unnecessary geopolitical tensions that could hinder international climate cooperation. Climate goals require global cooperation, and China recognizes that it relies on technology exchanges and foreign investment to achieve its ambitious targets.

The controversy surrounding "Made in China 2025" demonstrates how closely China's climate goals are linked to its economic and geopolitical strategy. While the initiative has helped establish China as a leading force in green technology, it has also aroused suspicion in the West. The Chinese government has responded by adjusting its communications without abandoning its underlying goals.

This balancing act between national ambition and international diplomacy will be crucial to achieving decarbonization by 2030 and carbon neutrality by 2060. The coming years will show whether China can defuse tensions with the West without compromising its vision of a sustainable, technologically advanced future. In a world that urgently needs solutions to the climate crisis, China's ability to combine innovation and cooperation could make all the difference.

PS: The Chinese word for "crisis," 危机 (wēijī), indeed carries a profound duality with its syllables: 危 (wēi) meaning "danger" and 机 (jī) meaning "opportunity." This concept invites reflection on how crises, while inherently risky, can also open doors to new possibilities. It's a reminder of the balance between challenge and potential in life's pivotal moments. What are your thoughts on this perspective?

Also published by me:

Elon Musk - Ideas & Visions - How a man is transforming our civilization

Elon Musk is undoubtedly one of the most influential figures of the 21st century. His name is inextricably linked to groundbreaking technologies, bold ambitions and a radical approach to solving the biggest problems of our time. Whether it's promoting sustainable energy, enabling interplanetary travel or revolutionising the way we interact with machines, Musk operates at the intersection of science, technology and visions for the future of humanity.

The story of Elon Musk is a fascinating mix of brilliance, tenacity and unconventionality. Born in Pretoria, South Africa, the son of an engineer and a nutritionist, Musk showed extraordinary curiosity and intelligence from an early age. At the age of twelve, he programmed his first computer game and sold it for a small sum - a harbinger of the entrepreneurial energy that would later change the world. But Musk was not just a child prodigy with technical talent; he was also a dreamer who found inspiration in books such as The Hitchhiker's Guide to the Galaxy and The Lord of the Rings. These works shaped his imagination and fostered his belief that humanity could play a more significant role in the universe.

What sets Musk apart from other successful entrepreneurs is his ability to think the unthinkable and turn it into reality.

While many in the technology industry focus on incremental improvements to existing products, Musk strives for fundamental change. His projects, from Tesla and SpaceX to Neuralink and The Boring Company, demonstrate an unparalleled willingness to take risks and push the boundaries of what is possible. It is not just his technical brilliance that sets him apart, but also his ability to inspire teams and achieve extraordinary things in an often chaotic environment.

In this introduction, however, I want to not only shed light on Elon Musk's achievements and ambitions, but also raise the deeper questions that surround his life and work. How far can a visionary mind go to achieve its goals? What ethical compromises are involved in radical progress? And how do Musk's ventures affect society - not just technologically, but also philosophically?

Analyzing Musk's life is not simply a journey through technological milestones; it is also a reflection on what it means to dream and act in a world full of challenges. Musk often refers to himself as an "engineer," a term that describes both his technical orientation and his ability to solve problems. But behind this sober label lies a complexity that goes far beyond the role of a classic engineer. He is a visionary who believes in a future that others consider impossible and an entrepreneur who is willing to pursue his dreams with an almost ruthless determination.

His critics accuse him of being a ruthless workaholic who exploits employees and resources to the limit to advance his visions. Others see him as a modern hero, a man who refuses to passively accept the world's problems and instead finds solutions that have the potential to change billions of lives. Both perspectives are important to understanding Musk and his legacy. Because the truth often lies somewhere in between - in the gray areas between idealism and pragmatism, between genius and madness.

Elon Musk challenges us to think beyond the limits of what is possible. His projects invite us to question our idea of progress and consider the consequences of technological change. This text will not only highlight the highlights of his career, but also explore the philosophical and societal questions his work raises. What does it mean to create a sustainable future? Is the colonization of Mars a noble dream or an escape from Earth's problems? And how does the fusion of man and machine change our understanding of identity and humanity?

The journey through Musk's life is an invitation not only to consider the future, but also to critically question the present. In a world marked by climate change, resource scarcity and technological upheaval, his ideas are both a glimmer of hope and a warning. Musk shows us what is possible when we harness the power of science - but also the risks involved.

In the following text, we will examine Musk's greatest achievements, analyze his visions and motivations, and shed light on the challenges and controversies that have shaped his path. In doing so, we will not only try to understand Elon Musk as a person, but also to grasp the profound impact his work has had on our world. It is a story of courage, intelligence, and the irrepressible will to change the world - and an invitation to ask ourselves what role we want to play in this rapidly changing world.

Elon Musk's rise to fame did not begin with rockets or electric cars, but with software. After moving from South Africa to the USA via Canada, he first made a name for himself in the tech industry. With Zip2, a kind of precursor to Google Maps, Musk and his brother Kimbal developed a company that combined local business directories with digital maps. The sale of Zip2 to Compaq in 1999 netted him $22 million—a sum that not only gave him financial flexibility but also paved the way to his next big venture.

That next step was X.com, an online payment system that eventually became PayPal. Musk's vision was to revolutionnize traditional banking by moving payments online and simplifying the process for users. But his time at PayPal was not without conflict. Musk, known for his authoritarian leadership style and high demands, often clashed with his partners. He was ultimately ousted as CEO before the company was sold to eBay for $1.5 billion. Nevertheless, the sale secured him a financial gain that enabled him to move on to his bigger dreams.

While many of his contemporaries would have chosen a quiet life after such success, Musk saw the PayPal episode as merely a stepping stone. For him, the transition from software to hardware was a logical consequence of his ambition to solve problems at a deeper level. Software alone, he seemed to believe, would not be enough to tackle the great challenges facing humanity.

When Musk invested in Tesla and later took over the helm, the electric car industry was considered dead. Previous attempts to establish electric vehicles had failed and the automotive industry seemed determined to stick with fossil fuels. But Musk saw the potential to make electric cars not only environmentally friendly but also desirable. With the Tesla Roadster, a sports car based on the Lotus Elise, he managed to change the perception of electric cars. Suddenly they were no longer just an environmentally motivated choice, but a statement of innovation and progress.

The models that followed - the Model S, Model X, Model 3 and finally the Model Y - built on this foundation. Tesla transformed from a niche player into one of the most valuable car manufacturers in the world. But the path was anything but easy. Production problems, skeptical investors and fierce competition took a huge toll on Musk and his team. There were moments when Tesla was on the brink of bankruptcy, and Musk even invested his personal fortune to keep the company alive. This period, which Musk described as "production hell," showed his unwavering belief in Tesla's vision and his willingness to risk everything to make it a reality.

While Tesla focused on Earth, Musk set his sights on the stars with SpaceX. SpaceX was founded in 2002 with the ambitious goal of drastically reducing the cost of space travel and ultimately enabling an interplanetary civilization. Musk sees the colonization of Mars not as a luxury but as a necessity. He argues that to survive in the long term, humanity must expand its existence to multiple planets. This belief drives SpaceX.

The first years of SpaceX were marked by setbacks. The company's first three rocket launches failed, bringing both Musk and the company to the brink of ruin. But the fourth attempt was successful and marked the turning point. With the "Falcon I", SpaceX made history as the first private company to put a rocket into orbit.

...

The End of Western Dominance – The Restructuring of the Multipolar World

The Western order, once a symbol of stability, progress and the triumph of democracy, is now facing a multitude of challenges that are shaking its foundations. These challenges arise not only from external factors such as the rise of new global powers or the technological revolution, but also from internal tensions that are testing the social and political cohesion of Western societies.

This book addresses the question of how and why the Western order has faltered. But instead of providing hasty answers or falling into alarmism, the text takes a balanced and analytical approach. The aim is not only to describe the symptoms of the upheaval, but also to shed light on the causes and dynamics behind it. Historical perspectives meet contemporary developments, and scientific findings are linked to concrete examples from politics, business and society.

Over the centuries, the Western world has developed its identity in a field of tension between ideals and realities. Freedom, equality, human rights and democracy formed the basis of a narrative that not only provided orientation within the Western states themselves, but also had an international appeal. But this narrative is increasingly coming under pressure. The polarization of societies, the resurgence of authoritarian forces and growing skepticism towards established institutions and values raise the question of whether the Western order in its current form is still viable.

A central concern of this book is to look beyond the immediate crises and to make visible the deeper structures that are driving the change. It becomes clear that this is not a sudden collapse, but a gradual process in which new actors, ideas and power relations enter the stage. This process is neither linear nor irreversible. Rather, it is characterized by contradictions, conflicts and the possibility of a new beginning.

Readers are taken on a journey that begins in the centers of power in the West and from there traces the diverse connections to other regions of the world. How have globalization, digitalization and climate change changed the rules of the game? What role do social movements that campaign for justice and participation play? And how are Western democracies responding to the increasing pressure to defend their values and institutions?

It is the art of storytelling that distinguishes this book. Every crisis, every problem is not only analyzed soberly, but embedded in a context that brings the connections to life. Personal observations, historical events and the voices of experts are used to paint a multi-layered picture. This approach is intended to help readers not only understand what is happening, but also grasp the social and individual dimension of the change.

At the same time, the book maintains a critical distance and leaves it up to the reader to draw their own conclusions. It does not propagate an ideological program, but rather an invitation to think through and question the complexity of current developments. Because only through a deeper understanding of the causes and consequences of the upheaval can we succeed in finding constructive paths into the future.

We live in an era of transition. What was taken for granted yesterday is being questioned today. But in every crisis there is also the opportunity for renewal. This book is not just intended to be a wake-up call, but also to inspire hope. Hope that the West, despite all the challenges, can develop its values and principles and adapt them to the realities of the 21st century.

May this book help enrich the discussion about the future of the West and provide food for thought for a way forward. Because ultimately it is up to all of us whether we see the challenges of change as a threat or as an opportunity.

...

Is man still relevant? A provocation - Technological evolution and human existence

The question of whether humans are still relevant to the times may seem provocative. It touches on our self-image as a species, our relationship to progress, technology and the challenges that a rapidly changing world brings with it. But especially in the present, when technological evolution is advancing at an exponential rate, it is worth reflecting fundamentally: Do the biological, psychological and social characteristics of humans still fit the world they have created? Or is man, as we know him, a relic from another era that is finding it difficult to find his place in a reality dominated by algorithms, automation and artificial intelligence?

This book is not intended to be a simple treatise or a resigned cultural critique, but rather an analytical examination of the status quo of human existence. Popular scientific explanations are combined with factual presentations to offer readers a well-founded yet exciting approach to one of the most pressing questions of our time.

The technological developments of the last few decades have fundamentally changed our understanding of ourselves. We live in a world in which artificial intelligence already works faster, more efficiently and sometimes more accurately than we do in many areas. Even cognitive processes that were long considered the domain of the human mind - creativity, emotions, decision-making - are increasingly being simulated by machines. What does this mean for our self-image? Are humans losing relevance or are they being transformed into a new form of existence?

At the same time, advances in biotechnology and neuroscience are raising questions that go far beyond technological feasibility. Transhumanist concepts advocate an optimization of humans, a fusion with technology to compensate for their supposed weaknesses. But who decides what needs to be improved? Is the natural human an intermediate stage on the way to a new type of being? And can we do justice to the ethical implications of these developments?

There are no easy answers to these questions, and yet it is essential to address them. This book is aimed at all those who are not just witnesses but active participants in this change - people who think about the future, who question things critically, who are prepared to deal with the possibilities and risks. The following pages offer no dystopian doomsday scenarios or blind enthusiasm for technology, but a reflective and multidimensional analysis that puts people at the center: their strengths, their limitations and their future.

People are creatures of change. Since the beginning, they have shaped their environment, adapted and developed further. But perhaps we are now at a point where people are no longer shaping the world, but the world they have created is redefining them. So are people still relevant? The answer lies not only in science, but also in our willingness to question ourselves and our role in the future.

The real provocation lies in naming things ruthlessly. But it is necessary. Because only those who have the courage to ask uncomfortable and future-oriented questions can find answers that will decide tomorrow.

The question of whether humans are still contemporary is intentional and urgent. It arises not only in view of the rapidly advancing technological development, but also in the context of the fundamental changes that are permeating our social, cultural and ecological lives. It is not just about humans' ability to adapt to these changes, but also about their role as beings who both develop the tools that shape their environment and have the ability to think and reflect on their own existence. The tension between technological evolution and human existence could hardly be more topical.

Over the last few centuries, humans have undergone unprecedented development. What was considered science fiction just a few generations ago is now reality: artificial intelligence, genome research, autonomous driving, digital networking and many other innovations shape our everyday lives. But in the midst of this rapid development, the central question arises: are humans still able to keep up with this technology? Or is it on a path where it is increasingly being overtaken by its own creations?

It is easy to see technology as progress, as a constant improvement in human life. But the downside of this progress is often overlooked: The ethical, social and environmental consequences associated with the spread of new technologies. Technological change is occurring at a pace that is overwhelming humans in many ways – not only on a practical level, but also on an existential level. How do we react when machines begin to independently take on tasks that previously could only be performed by humans? What happens when machines surpass us not only in the production of goods, but also in the creation of art, in research and even in decision-making?

Technology is not just a tool that we hold in our hands – it has become an active agent in the design of our world. This fact leads to a fundamental reassessment of what it means to be human. Are we still the primary actors in the world, or are we increasingly becoming witnesses and perhaps even objects of a technological process that no longer fully belongs to us?

This analysis examines how humans can deal with the challenges of technological evolution in the 21st century. The line between what we consider human and what is considered technologically advanced is becoming increasingly permeable. Humans as biological beings have evolved over millions of years - a process characterized by slow and steady adaptation to environmental conditions. But today, in a world where technology determines the speed of change, we must ask ourselves whether this biological evolution can still keep pace with technological development.

This book combines popular scientific observations with a factual presentation of technological advances to shed light on the question of human relevance in an increasingly digital world. It is a mix of facts and stories that not only aims to inform the reader, but above all to encourage them to think about the fundamental questions that are coming our way in the midst of the technological revolution: What does it mean to be human when machines begin to not only replace us, but also surpass us in areas that were once considered purely human? How can we as a society deal with the unstoppable changes triggered by technology? And what remains of humanity when our creations overtake us in more and more areas?

This is not intended to be a book that provides ready-made answers that are easy to consume. Rather, it is an invitation to lose yourself in the complexity of the topics in order to gain new perspectives through thought and reflection. In a world in which technological change seems to affect every facet of our lives, it is essential that we as humans not only recognize the advantages of new technologies, but also deal with the challenges and questions associated with their introduction.

This text is a deliberate provocation. It calls on us not only to accept the advances and challenges of technological evolution, but to actively enter into the discourse about the future of humanity. Because the question of whether humans are still contemporary does not only concern technology - it particularly concerns us humans, our interactions and our future. It challenges us to redefine ourselves and recognize our responsibility as designers of our coexistence.

Technological progress is unstoppable - but it is up to us how we shape it and deal with it. Will we see ourselves as mere spectators of our own development or as active players who help shape it and act responsibly? This question will accompany us not only in the coming years, but in the coming decades. And only if we consciously face this challenge can we shape the future in a way that both promotes progress and preserves the value and meaning of being human.

In my extended version, I interviewed two different AIs to find out how they "see" humans and how they "define" their future as individuals and as a society.

...